GENESIS

Also by Frederick Turner:

The New World. An Epic Poem (Princeton University Press, 1985)

A Double Shadow. A Novel (Putnam)

Shakespeare and the Nature of Time (Oxford)

GENESIS

An Epic Poem

by
Frederick
Turner

Saybrook

Publishing Company

Dallas   San Francisco   New York

Copyright © 1988, by Frederick Turner

Library of Congress Cataloging-in-Publication Data

Turner, Frederick, 1943–
    Genesis : an epic poem = [Be-reshit = Genesis] / Frederick Turner.
      p.   cm.
    ISBN 0-933071-24-B : $19.95   ISBN 0-933071-26-4 (pbk.) : $9.95
    I. Title.   II. Title: Be-reshit.
    PS3570.U69G4   1988
    811'.54--dc19   88-11456
                                      CIP

Saybrook Publishing Company
4223 Cole Avenue, Dallas, Texas 75205

Distributed by W. W. Norton & Company
500 Fifth Avenue, New York, New York 10110

Table of Contents

GENESIS

GENESIS

The Author and Provenance of the Poem

The poet of *Genesis* will not be born until over a hundred years have passed. I do not know his name. He communicated the poem to me in a way which is impossible to explain; I have transcribed it as exactly as I could. Doubtless many twenty-first and twenty-second century concepts have been rendered by me in a garbled or metaphorical way, or perhaps the poet himself, like Milton's angel Raphael when he instructs Adam, invented twentieth-century equivalents for them, using his historical imagination. I do not even know whether he is aware of having passed the poem over to a twentieth-century redactor and editor; the ending of the poem suggests that he guesses at this possibility. Perhaps indeed some of its archaisms result from his inexact grasp of twentieth-century idioms and ideas, though it is clear that he is ambitious to transcend local temporal variants and speak to the great epic tradition that stretches from Gilgamesh into the distant future. He has deliberately appropriated, for instance, the epic invocation at the beginning, the epic structure, and the epic simile, transformed by technological magic into a kind of blueprint. Nevertheless it is likely that my own cultural, psychological, and esthetic biases have entered into the poem.

For instance, the defense of science fiction in Act II scene i may derive some of its passion from my own experience of the shortsightedness of the literary establishment with regard to this form of writing, a shortsightedness encountered by the novel itself in its first hundred years of existence in modern Europe. In our sense of science fiction there is no reason why the *Genesis* poet should praise the form, since the events he describes were for him plain fact and predate him by more than a century. However, I have kept the passage because I believe that, by the time the poet was writing, the term science fiction had come to mean any narrative that rose above popular psychology and that addressed itself to serious philosophical themes; and in particular any narrative that dealt with the matter of Mars.

The *Genesis* poet is by the standards of the present a rather peculiar literary personality. He evidently has little respect for the romantic and modernist conception of the artist as charismatic rebel

against ordinary morality, as genius, as the true hero of all litera-
ture. He goes to some lengths to demonstrate his own rather un-
charismatic and unheroic circumstances and nature, his arthritis, the
genteel poverty of himself and his friends, the very comfortable
nature of the oppression under which they work; and he refuses to
give his name. Unlike Wordsworth's *Prelude* and Eliot's *Waste Land*
his poem pays little attention to the poet and insists on the greater
importance of its protagonists; he is almost as self-effacing as Virgil,
certainly more so than Dante and Milton. Even Homer gives us grand
portraits of blind bards.

Yet at the same time his poetic ambitions are very great. He has
attempted a work intended be one of the foundation stones of an
entire planetary civilization, and has squarely taken on a genre
demanding the highest artistic credentials. Credentials, however,
seem to mean little to him. Evidently he believes that the life and
spirit of the world as expressed in artistic culture have an agenda of
their own, and that certain works of art are produced by it in due
time, choosing the most convenient mouthpiece that the age pro-
vides, and not perhaps overly particular about how perfect that
expression is, so its prophetic vision is added to the common stock.
Once the vision has appeared it can always be refined by artists of a
more agile or painstaking talent. Thus originality is not very impor-
tant to him; he leaves that to his protagonists and his muses, and
draws on whatever artistic and philosophical material he needs to
say what he feels needs saying.

Beside translating the poem in the most sympathetic and exact
fashion I could manage, I have provided an apparatus, not very
scholarly, including the scientific and literary notes below, a list of
characters, a timechart (as best I can estimate the likely dating) and
a genealogy. In addition, I have provided a plot summary before
each section of the poem to assist readers unfamiliar with the epic
form or confused by scientific and technical references. However,
most of the poem can, as many readers of the manuscript have
testified, be read almost with the ease of a novel.

A Note on the Science of *Genesis*

The biological metamorphosis of the planet Mars into one habitable
by human beings, which the *Genesis* poet describes and which may
strike some today as improbable, now appears increasingly feasible.

Several bodies of scientists are presently investigating various aspects of the problem, for instance the Institute of Ecotechnics in London, Space Biospheres Ventures, the University of Arizona's Environmental Research Laboratory, the National Center for Atmospheric Research, the American Geophysical Union, and NASA. The ecological successes of such institutions as the Wisconsin Arboretum, which has recreated a vitually authentic prairie on degraded farmland, has encouraged efforts all over the world not just to protect but to create complex living ecosystems. As I write, construction has begun on a sealed, self-sustaining five million cubic foot environment in Arizona called Biosphere II; and of course architects like Paolo Soleri have long dreamed of such independent worlds.

James Lovelock, a distinguished British biologist, is the formulator of the Gaia Hypothesis, which maintains that the biosphere of the planet Earth acts as a single organism to maintain the stability of the planet's atmosphere, oceanic environment, and temperature. His book (with Michael Allaby), entitled *The Greening of Mars*, outlines one strategy by which Mars might be so transformed. The reader interested in the ideas of the Ecotheist movement in the poem might also wish to read Lovelock's book *Gaia: a New Look at Life on Earth*. Though the terraformers whose deeds the poet records have borrowed one of his ideas—the use of chlorofluorocarbons or freons to produce a greenhouse effect—they discovered an even more ambitious, but perhaps quicker, solution to the problem.

Some elements of this solution already exist. First is the revolution in our understanding of the Earth's early evolution which has recently occurred, whose conclusions may be found in *Earth's Earliest Biosphere: Its Origin and Evolution*, edited by J. William Schopf. The original atmosphere of the Earth would be highly lethal to contemporary living organisms, being composed largely of hydrogen sulfide, methane, and ammonia, with almost no free oxygen. The first living organisms were anaerobes, that is, lifeforms which do not need free oxygen and would indeed be poisoned by exposure to it. However, free oxygen was excreted by many early organisms as a waste product, rather as we and our technology excrete carbon dioxide. When the available "oxygen sinks"—metallic ores, for instance, that could soak up oxygen in the formation of oxides, or hydrogen, which combined with oxygen to create much of the water of the earth's oceans—were exhausted, the new oxygen atmosphere poisoned the old anaerobic organisms that had brought it into being, leaving only those forms of life, such as the blue-green algae or cyanobacteria, which could either endure the presence of oxygen or, better still, use it as an enhanced energy source for photosynthesis, the creation of sugars, and the metabolic extravagances of the more advanced animals. With this change came the age of the eukaryotes, those organisms whose nucleated structure was such as to promote multicellular organization and sexual reproduction.

If this transformation could occur on Earth by biological means, might it not also be made to happen on Mars? Of course the process took hundreds of million years on Earth; but Earth had to make do with the very primitive and haphazard organisms supplied by its early rudimentary evolution, whereas today there exists an enormous riches of life-chemistries and metabolisms to draw on. And one could hurry the process along by dropping ice-moons on the planet . . .

But no contemporary Earth organism could survive long on Mars, whose carbon dioxide atmosphere is at a pressure less than one hundredth of the Earth's—not enough to allow liquid water to exist—whose surface temperature, averaging -40 degrees Fahrenheit, can support frozen carbon dioxide, and which because of its thin atmosphere and weak magnetic field is bombarded by cosmic radiation. (A good account of the Martian atmosphere can be found in Robert Haberle's "The Climate of Mars," in *Scientific American*, May 1986.) Nonetheless certain Earthly organisms—bacteria for the most part—can handle conditions nearly as severe as these when taken one by one, though none can withstand them taken all together. The twenty-first century technology the *Genesis* poet describes seems to derive partly from the enormous advances that are now taking place in bioengineering, whereby traits deemed desirable can be grafted from one organism to another. Could not hardened strains, chimeras, be generated, that might be adapted to the Martian environment?

The terrain of Mars clearly shows that at certain points of its geological history water has flowed on its surface. It could again. By means of freons, dyes, artificial dust-clouds or organic agencies, acting in combination with induced meteor strikes, the albedo of the Martian surface could be reduced, so that less radiation was leaving its atmosphere than was striking it. The temperature of the planet might thus be raised sufficiently to release gases locked up as ice and increase the pressure to the point that free water could exist. So to turn Mars green it would first be necessary to make it black.

The Saturnian ice-moon S26 is about a hundred kilometers in diameter, giving a volume of about half a million cubic kilometers, and a mass of about 500 thousand trillion tons. If half this mass were used as the reaction mass to drive the other half, it might be shifted from its orbit and made to fall upon the planet Mars. Even if only a fraction of the gases released by the impact were to remain in the Martian atmosphere, such a collision could raise the pressure and temperature of the Martian surface considerably: enough to make it geologically and climatologically live. Each meter of the Earth's surface supports about twenty tons of air and an average of about two thousand tons of water. S26—Kali, as the *Genesis* poet has named her—would provide a comparable amount of gases and liquids for each square meter of Mars.

Even now the project seems hopeless to a twentieth century techno-logical imagination. Nature has had billions of years to try out different lifeforms for their survival possibilities; jerrybuilt germs are notoriously fragile outside the laboratory and incapable of sur-vival in the field. But suppose evolution itself could be speeded up, in controlled conditions that would gradually approximate those of Mars, so that the Martian strains could, so to speak, generate them-selves? The limits of metabolism forbid this; but they do not forbid software simulacra from doing so. In the poem Ganesh Wills, the computer hacker, has found a way to express the genetic and somatic structure of simple organisms as computer programs, and has been able to place them together in a large artificial programmed en-vironment where they can compete and evolve for selective fitness; and he has speeded up the process electronically by many orders of magnitude.

Now in fact many of the components of such a project are already in existence. Followers of the computer games section of the *Scientific American* will be familiar with some of them: Conway's Game of Life, the Core Wars battle programs that fight it out for possession of a memory space, certain expert systems that can learn from experi-ence and adapt themselves accordingly, and the new iterative or chaotic algorithms that can generate complex internal electronic environments. Meanwhile computer modelling is now being used extensively in molecular biology, cytology, and ecology; and the National Science Foundation is currently debating the creation of a complete record of the human genome, that is, our full complement of DNA base-pairs in their correct order, divided into chromosomes: all the information needed to construct a human being. Several viruses and bacteria have already been thus recorded by gas chromatography in whole or in part. The techniques of genetic/cybernetic manipulation could also be used to tailor plants to grow into shapes useful to human beings—the Arkship, for instance, and Martian dwellings and furniture. Although the poem does not go into this, it might also be possible to create living logic and memory circuits by the same means, and even new species of animal life.

By these methods, then, organisms adapted to life on Mars might be synthesized. But would it not take an enormous amount of time to propagate them over the Martian surface? Here the astonishing mathematics of reproduction would be heavily in favor of the planetary gardeners. Normal bacteria can reproduce themselves by fission in as little as twenty minutes; conservatively, let us estimate ten doublings per day for tailored bacteria. Thus in one day a ton of bacteria, finely scattered over a surface rich in nutrients, and without biological competition, could yield a thousand tons—about a thousand cubic meters—of biomass; in five days, this mass, if unimpeded by lack of raw materials, would approach one hundred trillion tons. The surface of Mars is about 146 million square kilometers in extent— roughly a hundred trillion square meters. Thus in this ideal case it would take five days to cover the whole surface of Mars with bacteria to a depth of a meter, starting with one ton of seed. One might rest both on the sixth and seventh days. Of course the vicissitudes of access to food chemicals and energy sources, as well as unfavorable local variations in temperature, pressure, etcetera—some of them brought about by the bacterial growth itself—would put a stop to this growth very swiftly. But the illustration shows the potency of the biological instrument the colonists could wield.

One generation of bacterial species would certainly not be enough; the first generation would have to be used as the compost for the second, the second for a third, and so on. Each generation would at first be smothered by its own waste-products, but the net effect would be to extract from the Martian regolith (rock soil) the gases of a new atmosphere. After a while hardy funguses and plants could be introduced, and finally animals.

The Poetic Method of *Genesis*

The scientific and technological material of the poem constitute not
only a large part of its content but also a gigantic metaphor of its
very structure and form. In other words, the unwritten poem is the
barren planet, and the composition of the poem is its cultivation by
living organisms. But the word "metaphor" fails to capture the
dimensions of the trope which is the poem. For the gardening of Mars
by the code (or "codex") of life is act, theme, myth, argument and
form at once. The forking tree of evolutionary descent is the forking
tree of grammatical and logical construction, the forking tree of plot
and story, the forking tree of esthetic form, the forking tree of family
descent, and the forking tree of human moral decision; and those
trees are in turn connected as branches to the stem of the great tree of
the universe itself.

Such self-similar forms are now known as fractal geometries: the
plot of *Genesis* is itself fractal, with many small branchlets of event
connecting heterarchically with larger actions which are in turn
tributary to the one epic action of the whole poem, the founding of a
new world. The parable of the swan's wing in V. ii. is itself a branch
or wing of this structure, as well as being a miniature version of it.

The tragic element of the poem is also related to this deep trope. For
if a path is chosen, then others must be rejected—or better, "set
aside;" the German word *aufheben* might say it, with its implica-
tion of the cancellation of a debt. The future is a sort of wave-
function, a probability curve expressing the relative likelihood of
many possible events. The decisions that constitute the present and
the very continuance of time must collapse that wave function and
prune off the branches not chosen. This is a violent act, as all
creation is violent. Mars and Earth constitute two historical choice-
pathways in the poem. Both have much to recommend them, but the
poet must choose to prefer one, and the conflict between them is
tragic. This procrustean choice is symbolized and expressed by the
very rigid technical parameters of the poem, the strict iambic
pentameter line relieved only by a proportion of feminine endings
(many of them "paid for" by succeeding headless lines, in a kind of

rubato), and the exactly equal number of lines in each scene (400) and scenes in each act (5). The poem is exactly 10,000 lines long. These rigidities compel the action again and again to come to a point, a focus, to collapse the wave function of possibility, to choose one path of plot.

In a larger sense still the narrator is an alternate branch of the future of the redactor of the poem, that is, myself, and the world of the poem an alternate branch to "this" one. Possibly the future the poem describes will not come about precisely because the poem has been passed to me and I have chosen to publish it. The relationship between the actual branch and its ghostly alternates constitutes the richness and meaning of time, just as the relationship between the metrical structure of the poetic line and the actual rhythm of its spoken presence constitutes its musical richness. In the broadest sense we may thus say that the content of existence is essence, that being is the sacrifice of alternatives, that freedom is the rejection of choices. The Anthropic Principle of cosmology postulates that full conscious-ness of the origins of the universe may ontologically privilege those origins over any others, and that thus the choice of moral being, conscious knowledge, and above all of beautiful unified complexity is the logos that creates the world. In this sense the world is a kind of drama, brought into being by its own choices; and this is perhaps one reason why the poet named the divisions of his poem by the theatri-cal terms he did.

As I have suggested, the poem may be designed as a warning to past ages of the consequences of their fear of the future; on the other hand the action of the poem may be a kind of performative invocation designed to bring about the new choices it describes. The work of terraforming is the work of making air, an atmosphere, the Atman or spirit, the breath in which the poem may be spoken, the first breath of the newborn. The poem is the Lima Codex, the book of information for the construction of a new world, and the struggle of its composi-tion, both by its its original future narrator and by its present-day scribe, against its enemies, historical and technical, is the funda-mental drama of the work. This struggle has been worth it for me, as I think it was—or will be—for him; for it brought me to the feet of the Sibyl, where I might listen to the sweetest voice I know.

Dramatis Personae

Major Characters

The Narrator, an underground poet living in New York about a hundred and twenty years after the events of the poem under the gentle totalitarianism of the Earth's theocratic government.

Chancellor ("Chance") Van Riebeck, the entrepreneur who has built an international industrial empire based on bio-engineering, and who has been put in charge of the Ares Project—the exploration and scientific survey of the planet Mars—by the United Nations. However, he has gone entirely beyond his mandate and has begun to colonize Mars with earthly bacteria genetically tailored to withstand the severe conditions of the Martian surface. Chance is married to Gaea and has three children, Freya, Beatrice, and Garrison. His family home is the ranch of San Luis Rey near Taos, New Mexico.

Freya Van Riebeck-Lorenz, the first daughter and eldest child of Chance and Gaea: one of Chance's most trusted and effective lieutenants, and a leading executive in Van Riebeck Enterprises. She is the wife of Charlie Lorenz and mother of Wolf and Irene.

Orval Root, Chance's old friend and principal science officer of the Ares Project, who because of Chance's disobedience to UN instructions and because he fears what he believes to be Chance's pride and destructive hubris, has broken with his erstwhile chief and comrade.

Gaea Van Riebeck, nee Redgrave, Chance's estranged English wife; originally named Rosalind ("Rose"), but upon her conversion to the new religion of Ecotheism she has changed her name to "Gaea." Gaea is one of the leaders of the Ecotheist movement, which believes that humankind is essentially exploitative and evil, and that Nature is both our victim and the divine being we should worship. Her children are Freya, Beatrice, and Garrison. She and Garrison live at Devereux, the old manor house Chance bought for Gaea in Oxfordshire, in England.

Garrison Van Riebeck, the only son and youngest child of Chance and Gaea, who has taken his mother's side against his father.

Ganesh Wills, a half-Indian computer hacker and genius, the researcher for Van Riebeck Enterprises who devised the software modelling programs whereby simulated earthly organisms can be subjected to accelerated evolution. In this way strains of bacteria are created that can survive on Mars and begin the transformation of its atmosphere into one breathable by human beings.

Karl Friedrich ("Charlie") Lorenz, Freya's husband, father of Wolf and Irene, an ecologist, and Ganesh's collaborator in planetary bio-engineering.

Beatrice Van Riebeck, daughter of Chance and Gaea, a paleobiologist working for her father, whose special study has been the transformation of the Earth's atmosphere by its earliest lifeforms into one rich in oxygen. In collaboration with Charlie and Ganesh she has created the plan for the transformation of Mars which Chance and Freya are carrying out. When the poem opens she is living with her niece and nephew Irene and Wolf, her brother-in-law Charlie, and the nurse Sumikami at the ranch of San Luis Rey.

Irene Lorenz, daughter of Charlie and Freya, twin sister of Wolf.

Wolf Lorenz, son of Charlie and Freya, Irene's twin brother.

Chui Su, "Sumikami", daughter of a Chinese Saigon prostitute and a black American G.I., one-time geisha, nurse to Wolf and Irene and mother of Tripitaka.

Tripitaka, son of Sumikami by an Australian priest, a martial artist, called "Don John" or "Don" by his fellow-soldiers.

Ruhollah, drug merchant on trial at the World Court at Olympia; mystagogue of the extreme religious society known as "the Chiffre," which maintains that all of nature is evil, not just humankind. Garrison and Tripitaka come under his influence.

Gianbattista ("Giamba") Vico, attorney for Van Riebeck Enterprises.

Ximene de Vivar, pilot of the giant treeship *Kalevala*, a mining vessel used in the asteroids and the rings of Jupiter and Saturn, mother of Marisol.

Marisol de Vivar, daughter of Ximene and lieutenant on *Kalevala*.

Hillel ("Hilly") Sharon, general of the Martian forces during the revolution; the lover of both Ximene and Marisol.

Chance Van Riebeck the Younger, the son of Charlie and Beatrice, a poet and political philosopher; one of the most profound interpreters of the Sybil, and one of the framers of the constitution of the Martian republic.

Bella Van Riebeck, nee Morison, the wife Gaea chooses for Garrison and mother of their son Flavius.

Flavius Van Riebeck, the son of Garrison and Bella, designated to be the assassin of the Sibyl.

Vasco de Perez, the doctor of Beatrice and Irene.

Bengt Andersson, the Commissioner and chief prelate of the Ecotheist Church.

Hermione Mars, THE SYBIL: the divine woman who brings the special revelation of Mars; expected years before as a prophet.

Rosie Molloy, the wife of Chance the younger and mother of their many children.

Minor Characters

Blackett, a bioengineering techie in the Ares Project.

Billy "Tosher" Wills, an Anglo-Indian, father of Ganesh and wife of Evalina, living in San Francisco.

Evalina Wills, nee Chaudhuri, Indian wife of Billy Wills and mother of Ganesh.

Kuniko, abbess of the Jakko-in temple where Sumikami seeks spiritual help.

Sachiko, Tripitaka's first girl friend.

Nishiyama, Tripitaka's instructor in the martial arts.

George "Guts Fer Garters" Grace, training sergeant for the Australian Olympic War team.

"Bill," poetry reviewer for a major American newspaper, sent to cover the story of Tripitaka's participation in the trial of Chance.

Pyotr Markov, presiding judge in the World Court trial of Chance and Freya for treason and high crimes against the environment.

Iatroyannis, a doctor and curator of the ruined temple of Apollo Epikouros at Vassae; a friend of Chance.

Yanni, a teenaged girl and Olympic War groupie Tripitaka meets in Athens.

Billy Macdonald, a corporal in the Ned Kellies, the Australian Olympic War team; he gave Tripitaka his nickname "Don John;" died in the orbital farm wars.

Kung, leader of the Thai Olympic force and general of the allied forces of Australia, New Zealand, Malaysia, Papua, and Thailand in the war with the Indonesians.

"Scooter," nickname of one of the two Ecotheist chaplains imposed on the allied Olympic War team; a cause of the Mutiny.

General Maghreb, commander of the Terran fleet sent to destroy the Arkship.

Simmy, one of Garrison's homosexual lovers.

Ortiz, another of Garrison's homosexual lovers.

Liam, Chance the Younger's eldest son.

Chronology

1951   Birth of Sumikami's mother
1968   Birth of Sumikami
1974   Birth of Billy Wills
1977   Birth of Evalina Chaudhuri
1980   Birth of Chance
1985   Birth of Rose (Gaea)
1991   Birth of Charlie
1992   Birth of Orval Root
1995   Birth of Ximene de Vivar
2001   Birth of Hilly Sharon
2002   Marriage of Chance and Rose
2004   Birth of Freya
2007   Birth of Beatrice
2008   Birth of Garrison
2011   Birth of Tripitaka
2013   Birth of Ganesh
        Birth of Marisol
2015   Chance appointed to Ares Project
2017   Chance buys Devereux for Rose
2020   Terraforming begins in secret
        Chance hires Charlie
2028   Charlie and Freya married
        Appointment of Ganesh to research position in Van Riebeck
        Enterprises
2029   Birth of Wolf and Irene
        Estrangement of Chance and Rose; Rose renames herself Gaea
2030   Mars seeded with first bacteria
2032   Arrest of Chance and Freya
        Beginning of Martian Revolution
2033   Mars seeded with funguses
2034   Trial of Chance and Freya
        Release of Comet Kali from Saturn orbit
        Deaths of Chance, Freya, Root
        Olympic War and Mutiny
2035   Concordat of Taos
2036   Funeral of Chance and Freya
        Fall of Comet Kali on Mars
        Marriage of Charlie and Beatrice
        Birth of Chance the Younger
2040   Coming of Tripitaka to Mars

2044   Marriage of Garrison and Bella
2045   Birth of Flavius
2046   Irene seduces Tripitaka
       The Ark War
       Finding of the Lima Codex
       Death of Tripitaka
       BIRTH OF HERMIONE THE SIBYL
2047   Breathable air on Mars
       Beatrice begins the work of gardening
2059   Irene attempts suicide
       Beginning of the mission of the Sibyl
2061   Chance the Younger marries Rosie Molloy
2066   Death of Gaea
2068   Flavius attempts assassination of the Sibyl
       Death of Irene
       Death of Sumikami
2070   Murder of Garrison
2151   *Genesis* epic begun

General Summary of the Story

The story covers the major historical events of the next hundred years. A group of scientists and technologists led by Chancellor ("Chance") Van Riebeck, is charged by the United Nations with the scientific survey of the planet Mars. Using theories derived from the Gaia Hypothesis, they clandestinely introduce hardy genetically tailored bacteria into the Martian environment with the intention of transforming the planet into one habitable by human beings. The Earth has at this time fallen under the theocratic rule of the Ecotheist Movement, which divides human beings off from the rest of nature and regards all human interference with nature as an evil. Chance and his followers are captured and put on trial, and war breaks out between the Martian colonists and the home planet. Though Chance and others lose their lives, the colonists are able to gain their independence by threatening to drop a moonlet on Earth. After a bitter renewed struggle led by the hero Tripitaka the colonists obtain a complete inventory of Earthly lifeforms. With their help, and inspired by Beatrice Van Riebeck, they complete the terraforming of the planet. A religious leader, the Sibyl, is born to the colonists; her teaching reconciles the ancient mystical wisdom of the Earth with the new science and cultural experience of Mars.

GENEALOGY OF THE VAN RIEBECK FAMILY

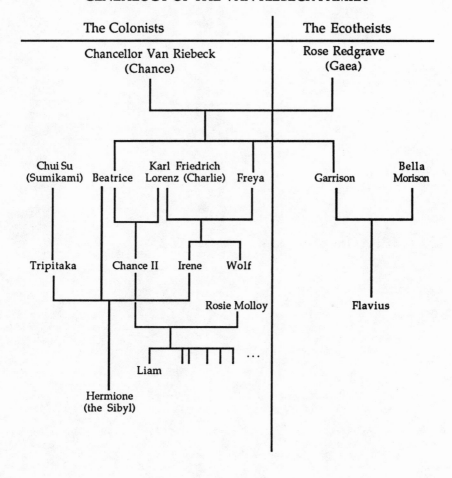

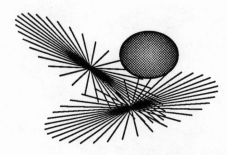

ACT I
The Origins of the War

*How this poem was communicated to me I cannot say. Its poet
will not be born for over a hundred years, and the events he
describes will not occur until fifty years hence, if then.
Nevertheless I have recorded his words, adding before each
scene a brief account of the plot as far as I understand it.*

*As the poem opens the teller of the story calls in despair
to his muses, his heroes and heroines, and to the divine
forces they express. The Sibyl—whom we will hear of
later—intercedes and gives him the power to speak. He has
chosen the ancient epic meter of the English language used
by Shakespeare and Milton, and in the fashion of Homer and
Virgil he begins with a classical invocation of the powers
that inspire poets.*

*Now the story itself begins. Chance Van Riebeck, the
entrepreneur who is attempting to change the surface of Mars
by biological engineering, and Freya, his daughter and
colleague in the enterprise, are hunted down by United
Nations troops near the south pole of Mars. Orval Root, a
former officer of Chance's but now in alliance with the
U.N., offers terms to Chance and Freya. They surrender on
condition that they be permitted to defend themselves in a
hearing against the charges brought against them, namely,
that they have in disobedience to their superiors
irreparably damaged the the Martian environment by
introducing Earthly bacteria, under the guise of scientific
research. Orval Root, because of his love for Freya,
accepts the conditions stipulated by Chance.*

Scene i
The Capture of Chance

*L*isten! I must tell of the beginnings,
Of corpses buried in the walls of worlds,
Of how those men and women worth a story
Burn and consume the powers they're kindled by;
And how their acts, mortal and cast away,
Are crystalled in the melt of history,
But their live selves are lost and gone forever

To leave a safer and a duller age;
Of how only the silence of the holy
Can still the creaking agony of time;
How holiness is broken every spring
Bursting in laughter to the throat of years.
But. But it is so hard to do again
What at the first was playtime for the gods,
Nymph borne by goatfoot over a green stream;
It is a deposition now as heavy as
The unhelpful body of one loved and dead.
I am not any more—none of us is
Now in this place of cyphers we inhabit—
Worth those I sing, therefore the song the more
Should lift as if that past dawn were alive;
The very words twist into mockery
The story I must tell, and try to fall
Into the knowing anecdote of motive,
Disillusion's inexpensive wisdom.   25
Some strength beyond my own must raise words' rod
Over the parting seas, the hosts of locusts,
Lest grief for the loss of the remarkable
Weighed down with a forgetting of the soul
Loosen the arm that wields them, and make falter
The voice that breathes them through this land of shadow.

What shall I call You, You unanxious Ones,
You Whose desires, so perfectly exhausted
By creation, as perfectly replenished,
Set cool into the very shape of being?
I feel Your feathers brush me in Your passage;
Almost I feel the muscles of my breast
Twitch with the wingbeat. How is it for them
In whom the current of Your dreadful breathing
Comes and goes as their own, as natural
To them, whose love and rage are unremitting
As Yours are?—Or do we all, the partial
And the completed, the clogged and struggling
As I am, and those pure who seem to fly,
The addict and the saint, do we all make
It up as we go along, try to hold
The brief, well-lit moods long enough to work,
And sit out the blanks, the darks,

The half-lights of craving, worldliness, spite?
If so, their fatal talent is the rarer,   50
Who act the semblance of such certainty;
And the grief's greater when they come to nothing.
Whom shall I call on, deathless Ones Whose wars
Are fought out in the flesh of those You favor?
If I could read the pattern's meaning, read
The light-swift scribble of Your fractal line
Whose denser filling of Your inexhaustible
Interstices constitutes being in time,
I'd be among those heroes that I sing;
Divided as I am, I bespeak them
That I celebrate to speak, pray, for me.
Out of the very future of the poem
Blows on a breeze a sacred scent of roses.
Sibyl, prophet, I know it is your incense,
The woodsmoke of your holy fire, the breath
Of living vapor from your waterfalls.
Show us a vision how you came to be.

What is this foul place where the sun is shrunk
To a pinhead over the close horizon?
—This plain of inky slush, black as the sludge
Oozing like ordure from a well of oil?
Here is no good footing, in this darkest
Of ways, this malebolge, this ass-pontine slough;
Under the slime is a grey-white ice, ice
Not of water only but of the air;   75
Above this waste the sky, though, is a fan
Of colors, like a courting peacock's tail,
Blue at the world's rim by the midnight sun,
Dimming to crimson zeniths where the stars
Shine through the red veil like new eyes through blood;
One star chiefly, Jupiter in his caul.
Five shadows, scarcely distinguishable,
Darkness on darkness, but sharp-edged like blades,
Stream out across the plain and fall upon
The far side of a shallow valley, where
A slow sewer carries its sumps away.
Shadows of men. They are the makers of
This desolation, these cocytean swales.
What must they be to be guilty of such

An ugliness? Nature herself is sick,
To vomit up her tartaruses so
From fields never before nor since to turn
So dolorous a face upon their heaven.
The five casters of shadows have no faces,
But painted masks of gold that bear emblazoned
These plains of Mars, the raw fire of the sun.
What sign of who they are? The silver spacesuits
Are spattered with the filth of their endeavor,
But sigils and a few words can be read.
On helmet and shoulder each bears a logo: 100
VER—"spring"?—"truth"?—but the E appears reversed
And dropped, and the whole stands in a circle
So no doubt it is "V.R.E." that's meant,
Van Riebeck Enterprises. On their arms
A smaller acronym's embroidered, not in green
As was the first, but red. TCSB:
Trades Congress of Spacefaring Bioen-
Gineers. But these desecrators are weary;
Only the one with the word CHANCE across
His breastplate, and the slight one who may be
A woman, FREYA written on her suit,
Do not bow down or stumble in their march,
Though all are heavy laden and bear weapons:
Old fashioned police riot guns, Winchesters
Bulkily modified about the breech.
Every so often one will look behind,
And sure enough, over the edge of the world,
A line of armed pursuers has appeared.
Harsh breaths in the helmet radios.

The one called Chance, with an embroidered rose
Upon his gauntlet, is the first to speak.
"They will have landed up ahead as well:
We can't keep going. Blackett was hurt bad
Back at the dome; he isn't saying much,
But his suit leg, I think, is full of blood.   125
Do we give up or do we stand and fight?"
The man with BLACKETT on his suit lays down
His pack and sits on it. "I'm finished if
It's hiking that you need. Leave me behind.
I'll take a couple with me, buy some time."

"Nobody's going anywhere without you,"
Freya says. But Chance holds up his hand.
"You men signed on to work but not to fight.
If anyone wants out, the contract's void.
It's us they're after; honor says go home,
Your families need you. Read the Union rules:
That's what they say too." One of the men
Growls like a sheepdog under his breath:
"Sure. And what about our friends back at the dome?"
Another: "Yeh. It wasn't we but they
Who blew the pressure in a life-support.
That's against union rules, if you talk union."
The third man says: "I got no family.
Just looking now to get a UN scalp."
It comes to Freya. "As your daughter, Chance,
I say we surrender; what's more to me
Than your life? As a member of the Board
Appointed your executive in charge
Of this South Polar Terraforming Region
I say again we quit. But as a servant   150
Of the Spirit, which you taught me to be,
I say we fight: and that is where I stand."
"The lady gets my vote," says Blackett quietly,
And one by one the other men agree.
"All right," says Chance. "Now this is what we'll do.
When the Cheyenne once, under Little Cloud,
Were caught in the prairie by the cavalry
Like we are, they took cover in a swamp,
And showed the troopers only noses, eyes,
And rifle barrels; so well hid they had
To get artillery to dig them out.
What's seeded here? Sulfur bacteria,
Ferments, methanogens, and blue-green algae.
Volutans, Chrysea, Aquatilis
And Cryptovaginata make a mat
Or mantle, don't they, that should stop a bullet . . . ?"

An ultimatum on the public band:
"This is the Expeditionary Force,
United Nations Secretariat.
Lay down your weapons and come out. If not,
We open fire." But there is no reply.

A minute passes. Then the order comes;
A single shot. In the thin air of Mars,
Still scarcely a tenth of an atmosphere,
It sounds like a knock or click, just as if   175
One of the old leviathans of Earth
Were sounding for his prey across an ocean.
Thin chatterings of automatic fire
Succeed, birds gathering for winter.
Nine troopers rise behind the hilltop
And in the feeble gravity make strides
Slipping and gliding down the slope like dreams.
How can I speak the poison of this place
Hunter and hunted must drink down in silence,
A billion black kilometers from home?
Limbs formed in the Eden of our planet,
That glows now on the far side of the sun,
Mouths suckled on mother's milk in some
Beech-shaded suburb where the sprinklers turn;
Eyes tuned to the spectrum of that nurse,
Green-breasted Earth, her sweet forgiving flesh,
All bent now to the imposition of
Competing codes of law upon the void.
The hunted, buried in the new world's wall,
Up to the helms in ordure, know that comfort
Which comes from never having to depart
From this place where they are, as the dying
In hospital need make no more arrangements,
Nor stir themselves abroad, for their plain work
Is indeed to do nought else than to die;   200
Or as in hell the unrepentant know
That there's no need for good behavior now.
The hunters, gulping air from their converters,
Are caught mid-stride by terror or by bullet,
And tumbled end for end to splay at length
On hillside or the verges of the slough.
One of them cracks an air-seal, breathes his guts
Out into the semi-vacuum; breathes in
With his last breath a taste sour and corrosive;
Humankind's first breath of Martian air.
A stray shot has caught one of the defenders:
The union man—his poor head's all exploded,
The great molecules of the human soul

A fertile protein for the fields of Mars.
The lonely man weeps into his helmet:
And Chance weeps too, both for his own and those
Of the other party, allies in this:
To have died that the new world might be born.

Balked for a time, the hunters call a parley.
Now Chance demands with whom he has to deal.
Beside the spokesman from the EPA,
His UN escort from the lunar base
And their commander, there's a World Court Proctor,
Gasping and unaccustomed in his suit;
Two smooth professional gentlemen—   225
A World Bank auditor and an assessor
Who share a private band; an unnamed man
In the arms of Van Riebeck Enterprises;
A team from CBS with cameras;
And a tough quiet US Federal Marshal
On her last tour of offworld police duty.
—It seems important, Freya notes to Chance,
That all formalities should be observed:
They must still think the legal ice is thin.
"Who is the Company man?" Chance asks Freya:
"Who do you think our traitor has to be?"
"We'll find out," Freya says. "Another thing:
There's no one from the Ecotheist Church.
That means they have to play it by the book."
Chance grunts and opens up the public channel.
The spokesman is almost apologetic;
English accent; underneath, the strain
Of condescension Earthers feel for those
Gauche and enthusiastic offworld types—
The Foreign Office eyebrow at the seer,
The liberal's at the crass entrepreneur.
"We do appreciate how you must feel,
Having no doubt lost friends back at the dome.
Resistance here was understandable
And will be so accounted by your jury;   250
But we did not intend to 'blow' the dome.
Believe us that you will be treated fairly,
And that your case indeed is far from hopeless,
If you now yield yourselves to just arrest.

Surely honor is satisfied; you've made
Your gesture for the 'Earthside' media."

"Well," says Chance, "how do we answer him?"
A laugh. Then: "Was he talking to us, chief?"
"Then I suppose not," says Chance, does not bother
To crack the Transmit on the public band.
The spokesman waits, then clears his throat and says:
"We'll give you half an hour for your decision."
After a short while Freya speaks her thoughts:
"Do you remember how in Dorset once
When we were at the bio-conference
At Sherborne where Sir Walter Raleigh founded
His academe under the greenwood tree?—
How we went walking on our weekend off,
And plodded up that long hill through the wood
And the wind was roaring through the treetops
But it was still and sheltered here below?—
And how that strange light shone through the thornbushes
Far too low down to be natural?—
And how that dreadful racket grew, just like
A rocket taking off, or a tornado,   275
And we pushed through into the end of the world?—
Three hundred feet over the English Channel,
Remember, and the sea brilliant green
And brilliant brown from tearing at the cliff,
And all in motion, and the wind blowing
So hard you could scarcely throw yourself off
If you tried, and the hollows in the rows
Of waves were blinding mirrors of the sun?
And up the Windgate—that's what it was called—
A column of white sea-scour blew like dreams?—
And how you said then, Chance, that when we rested
In the shelter of the cliff's lip, the gorse
And blackberries and little nests of flowers
Between us and the edge were like one's house,
One's family, one's car, one's friends, one's work,
But what was on the other side was Death?"

Chance has no time to answer, for a crackle
Announces further UN overtures.

"Listen. To help avoid more loss of life,
A friend of yours has asked to talk to you,
Empowered to offer honorable terms."
"If he's a friend, let him speak for himself,"
Says Chance. Freya, surprised, says to her father:
"Should we do this? It's obvious they're in trouble.
Couldn't we wait them out?" "No, Freya. They   300
Have the tempo; our death's our only card.
The threat of it may give us a finesse.
They have to get us back to have their trial
And justify their acts before the public.
It's either talk or take our own lives now
 While we still can, before our air goes sour."
The next voice that they hear is quite familiar.

"So what did you expect? Chance, you betrayed us
With your promises. You said it was science
When what you had in mind was playing God.
You spent the public money on an image,
And monkeyed with the private parts of nature
To make yourself a place in history."
"I might have guessed it, if I could believe it,"
Chance replies. "Old friend, old comrade in arms,"
—For it is Orval Root, his right hand man,
The science administrator of the Program—
"Couldn't you wait the bad times out with me?
Couldn't you trust the promise of our vision?
Was it too much to ask you, that you might
For friendship's sake—imagination's sake—
Let up a little on the righteousness?
Yes, I suppose it was. You were afraid.
I see now how this duty must have choked you,
How brave you were to bite back your compassion,   325
To expiate the sin of loving me."
And now of those on both sides he demands
And gets a private channel with his friend;
But Root breaks out at once: "I never loved you;
Perhaps I thought I did; I never knew you;
How could I love the thing I do not know?
You used me and the others. Even now
You try to use your daughters. You transformed
Your Freya, whom I loved, into a monster;

If you're sincere, give her back to her mother."
"So Rose must be behind all this; but then
They call her Gaea now," says Chance. He's silent;
Raises the woven rose upon his glove
Where if glass did not hinder, he might kiss;
Such thoughts as these pass swiftly through his mind.
All those I loved when I was twenty hate me;
I have prepared a furnace for myself and must
Step in to the uttermost. She knows that I
Am a lord of death, that at my death I
Would choose, offered eternal life, to pass
Into the full absence of being; she knows
I'm happy, and I always have been happy,
So that I wish exactly what I have
And every moment is my immortality.
Strange how this fire of being betrayed is a   350
Rough cordial to me. I drink it down.
But it surprises me the world could be
So violent, the spring could be so cold.
"You're quiet. Do you see what you have done?"
Asks Root. "But I did not come here to judge,
But to negotiate on behalf of those,
The humble ones, that lie beneath the shadow
Of your grotesque conceits, your enterprises
In the entrails of our poor mother nature.
This is the offer—not one I would make:
I would sit out your filthy ritual
Of suicide, and face the consequences,
Unless there were a way to break the bond
You hold your followers by—but yes, the offer.
You to yield yourselves into custody,
With no admission of arrest or guilt;
To agree to join negotiations
Whose designed end will be to terminate
All your control over the Ares Project;
Additionally, you shall order all
Your employees elsewhere upon the planet
To lay down arms and wait for our decisions.
We to guarantee your lives and freedoms;
Not to transport you from the planet Mars
Without your free consent, nor to encumber   375
Nor to break up Van Riebeck Enterprises."

"But what about the terraforming program?"
"The planet to be sterilized, restored
To as close an image as is possible
Of its true holy God-created nature."
Chance groans in soul: "So you'd abort this child,
The first new world our species has conceived?"

Root is at last abashed before the grief,
Blasphemous as it is, of the old man.
But in the twist, the very hemorrhage
Of torn love, Chance's subtle thought clings on,
Its muscle drawing energy from pain.
He knows that they are lying, but that Root
Has an honor of his own that may
Out of the father's wreck rescue the daughter.
"Very well," at last Chance forces out.
But lest Root think him too easily won
He qualifies his terms with a condition
That there should be a hearing, here on Mars,
Where he, Freya, and his peers in the venture
Might for one last time argue and defend
The case in science and theology
For making Mars into a paradise:
The hunters' park we dreamed of in the cave
Of transubstantiation into men.

*Gaea Van Riebeck, Chance's estranged wife, and their son
Garrison, both of the Ecotheist Church and therefore hostile
to Chance's attempts to transform the Martian surface,
receive the news of Chance's capture. Overcoming Garrison's
objections, Gaea insists that Root break his promise not to
bring Chance and Freya back to Earth to stand trial.
Chance, finding as he expected that he has been betrayed,
activates a prearranged alarm beacon set to raise his
followers to rebellion throughout the Solar System.*

Scene ii
Gaea and Garrison

That was a hundred twenty years ago;
The choices of the likes of you and me
Have brought us where we are, where we may see
The glory road go on into the stars,
Into those cloudy, wind-torn hemispheres
That we have shut the window on forever
And must watch others take, while we cry out
When this one falls, or that one finds her Grail;
Crowd at the theater, beat our hands together.
And before that, and before that, were choices
Each of which sprung a branch of the green Time;
And this branch is the ghostly Virtual
Of one in which we took the glory road;
But there is nothing which is not, in this
Wildest and most intentional of worlds;
All possibles are thinly actual;
It is the choice, the act, that mutes the strands
That will not lead the way of melody;
And so I raise my voice, and call to you
Against the whispers of the vale of death:
To graft, graft back by your acts, this cut stem
To the sweet current of the human vein.
Even to play the audience, the reader, is
To step for an hour into laws, permissions
Demanding other being than we own;   25
Redeemed as those just pagans were redeemed
Who walked in the master's comedy beneath

The bright dome of the fallen human light.
And every act acquires its mortal being
Only by fruiting in an audience;
The least iota of God's body, that
We call a photon, is invisible
Until it dies upon a retina
Or gives its virtual existence up
To energize some atom's outer shell:
What's light if it's not visibility?
Consider then the audience that marks
From the great, green, blue-shelled fruit of the Earth
The pulses of these late events on Mars.

Among the golden hills of Oxfordshire,
Between the swift Glyme and the Evenlode,
Where Grim's Dyke marks the boundary that once
Banned the primeval forest from the fields
And gardens of a Roman villa, stands
The great house and estate of Devereux.
The Tudor hall is built of Cotswold stone;
Vanbrugh added wings and a facade
By very much more handsome, though, than fine;
Placed on a minor eminence where the wise Brown
Grouped giant elms, and of a lesser stream   50
Fashioned a greater, which by his nice art
Spread to a water sketched by Constable.
Despair and taxes wrung it from the line
That won it twice, once from the house of York,
Once from the Roundheads of Sir Thomas Fairfax.
Chancellor Van Riebeck bought it for his wife
In twenty seventeen to save it from
The Ministry of Public Recreation;
Restored the gardens of Enlightenment,
Built a great greenhouse for experiment
Into alternate Edens of his dream;
And sought by this gift of a little world
To buy a Rose to wear among the stars.
And Rose Van Riebeck lives here still, but now
She's changed her name to Gaea; and the place
Has changed too. Their only son, Garrison,
Dwells with his mother, serves her enterprises.
They've given the house as headquarters of the

Environmental Protection Agency,
United Nations Secretariat.
The tenets of the Ecotheist Church
Frown on the hubris of the gardener,
And so the grounds have all gone back to nature.
The dainty little artificial ruin
Of Aphrodite's temple on its isle   75
Is ruined now in earnest, choked with nettles;
The branched menorahs of the espaliers
In riot, yield but stony little pears;
The knots unrecognized —unless a lover
Of design unearthed their fragile Troy—
Are only mounds under the willowherb;
The unpruned roses have forgot their grafts
And their base stocks have sprouted lupine briers;
And in the terraces of turf and urns
Stand architect-designed prefabs of glass
And grey cement, to house the office workers,
Bicycle sheds, toilets for men and women.

Gaea and Garrison her son live here
In the cold ground floor of the old east wing;
Cold, for the fires are never lit these days
In the ghostly elegant fireplaces,
Tuscan marble veiled with dust. Garrison
Wakes with a choked cry: dreams of soldier-boys
Stripped to the waist to wash; camaraderie
That turns to brutal violence when they find
He is not one of them, not one of them
At all, and they deal with him as a woman,
A woman who must bear the name of soil.
The cry wakes Gaea, as it has before;
That very moment there's a roaring chatter   100
From the autoprinter: the news from Mars.
She rips the hard copy from the machine,
Switches to aural mode, bites her ring finger;
Garrison comes in, like a sleepy boy
Pale with a fever or a sickly conscience.
Orval Root's voice. As usual Gaea chafes;
The modulated light takes twenty minutes,
There can be no immediate reply.
Time itself cannot move fast enough;

For is not light as simultaneous
(Its dissipation with its origin,
No intervening happening between
To measure how it passes) as may be
Within this universe of mutual
Approximations?—where the only being
Is the difficulty and decay
That marks the finest and most mortal drama,
The most unreconciled, the most in pawn?
Won't Root get to the point? Have they caught Chance?
And Freya too? But made some promises?
What promises? "Listen to him, Garrison;
He's lying, and he knows we will renege.
He wants to rescue Freya for himself.
He thinks that he can talk her out of it
And save her soul and win her from her father.   125
She's just as dangerous as Chance is; more,
Because younger. Root underestimates
Not only her, but Chance. Chance planned all this.
Root underestimated Lorenz too—
Never underestimate Herr Charlie:
Why did she marry him if he's so harmless?
Freya will eat this Orval Root alive."
"Mother," says Garrison, "I didn't know
That you were after Freya too. She *is*
Your daughter and my sister. Can't we do
Whatever we must do without—" "Don't think,
Garrison, leave that to me. Now we have them,
Don't we owe it to Nature to destroy
Her enemies? And Charlie too; and we
Had better gather in your other sister,
The pretty one, the favorite, the butter
Wouldn't melt in her mouth one, Beatrice.
Even the Pimple, the boy genius,
Ganesh—he is too clever to be safe."
To Garrison she seems a lovely demon,
Never more beautiful and all alive
Than when, wrought by her possession, she speaks
In runs and hesitations, flashingly,
Not loathed even at her most serpentine,
For the vitality of very nature   150
Forks out at her eyes and makes her holy.

She can be plain enough, as she is now,
A mobcapped queen in a crumpled nightgown:
Her brown hair with coarse strands of viral white;
A feverish flush under her brown skin
That shines despite the fine-blown net of cells;
Her limbs' flesh falling slightly from the bone;
Her heavy breasts gone whiter in their cleft.
"Mother, it's all come further than I thought,"
Says Garrison; "I feel the pull of forces
Out of my grasp, that draw me to dark ends
Smelling of blood, and worse, but sweet. Yes, sweet.
Might we defending what we know is good
Be strangers to ourselves and to each other?
Fall from the ordinary paths of conscience?
Why are we doing this? Tell me again."

"If you were half the man your father is
You wouldn't waste the precious time with doubts.
He doesn't hesitate. That's why he must
Be stopped: he opens doors that can't be closed.
Listen again. The ecotheist faith
Tells us that Nature is our loving mother;
That in Her service Jesus died for us
Showing the way of self-abasement to
The cup of acquiescence in Her will;   175
That all the pattern of all holy forms
Was stored up from eternity in Her;
And innovation is the cacogen,
The cancer that eats out Her loving body,
Brought, by our fall, into the world of light;
And the chief evil that afflicts Her is
Technology, its blight and vicious pride.
Don't you see that in Chance your father? How
He roots the sweet groin of your mother Nature?
How in the evil ecstasy of art
He thinks himself above both man and God?
We are all equals in the universe;
To celebrate the glory of one man
Over another is to disobey
The laws of Nature and ecology.
Would you go back, in moral similitude,
To the foul times when we, the master race,

Butchered the Indians, the Blacks, the Jews?
When the brute male, with his proud pink chopper,
Strutted like Agamemnon on the web
Before his slave-girls to the sacrifice?
Remember how we slew the gentle whales,
The giant mother full of milk before
Her innocent bewildered calf, and made
Those citizens of Eden bear the rage   200
We levelled against God's Leviathan,
And boiled their holy corpses for their oil?
Consider, if he had his way, we'd eat,
As we once did, the limbs of fellow-beings;
Ghouls, resurrect out of the mummied flesh
The extinct forms of the mammoth and the elk
And the quagga, and the titanothere?—
He claimed, before the Council, that he served—
A blasphemy—the ends of Mother Nature
By bringing back the lives our sins had shed;
That Techne should repair the wounds it made;—
Doesn't this show how dangerous he is,
That he is seeking to conceal or pay
The debt we owe to Nature, and wipe out
By our aspiring sin the very sin
We do when we escape the bonds of nature?
Isn't this why the Council ruled that we
Must keep as the sign of our wretchedness
All the corrupt technology we've made,
Not adding nor subtracting the least jot
Of our long penance over Nature's wounds,
Lest either we should hold the sin too light
Or overween that we might pay it off?
If you will not believe your mother yet,
Think how the sovereign virtue, pity, tells   225
You to hate that man and his daughters for
Their insult to the poor common man.
For they would, like the fiery lords of old
Show to the ordinary folk a mirror
Wherein they see the gorgeous idols of
The hero and the genius and the lover;
And so make miserable those whose lot
It would be, in a world that Chance commanded,
To serve, to be the foot-soldiers, the slaves.

All those that claim themselves extraordinary
And promise it to others, must be damned.
Pity for the great mass of men demands it.
If you're my son you'll do your clear duty;
Privileged yet, to be enabled thus
To give so much, father and sisters, to
The loving One we wounded with our crimes;
Unworthy to be chosen so to give.

"Your qualms, if less than manly, may be useful,
Though, it now occurs to me. That you
Find it repugnant to make Freya pay
The price of her besottedness with Chance
Suggests that Root will more than do the same,
Given his old infatuation with her.
We must tell Root our plan that she stand trial
In dock with her father where she belongs,   250
Lest he betray us and so let her go."

She turns now to the keys of the transmitter,
While Garrison, ignored, must stand behind her,
Ashamed at his gauche tallness, his nightclothes,
His face, even, that wears the look of one
Who has attained his dearest wish and now
Groans, for it tastes of ash and bitterness.
The heavy lamp beside his hand could smash
Her skull; horror; he flings himself away.
Now she begins to dictate carefully
The terms on which Chance will be brought to trial;
Freya is to be held in custody
And brought back too as a material witness.

Follow the signal back across the voids
To the cramped temporary dome at Lowell;
Night in the southern hemisphere of Mars.
Better accommodation there is none:
The other bases of Van Riebeck Enterprises,
Alerted to the moves of the UN,
Have, under standing orders, closed their ports
And armed themselves with makeshift weaponry
Awaiting word from Chance or from his aides.
Captives and captors have small privacy.

Stripped of their armor they must know each other
As close as friends. Let me describe them then.   275
Root is as hairy as poor Esau was
In the hard story of Jacob. His head
Is all slopes and blockish Egyptian planes;
His shaven countenance shines painfully;
A fundamentalist from Alabama,
His eyes are slanted, hooded, like a girl's,
The self behind alert for injury,
And his small stout arms stand out helplessly.
Chance is a short dark man, now fifty-two,
With a scarred face and brilliant brown eyes
That turn with a frank question to your own;
His hair is black and curly, with no gray;
He's agile, quick, but with great breadth of shoulder,
Hands neat and deft; laughs easily and long.
At first sight Freya has inherited
Little from either parent. She is small,
Fair, with a fur of short blond hair, green eyes,
Large hands and head, with a wolf's high cheekbones.
But soon the acute observer might perceive
The very quickness and dispatch of Chance,
Gaea's demonlike fluency of speech,
Her father's easy strength of shoulder-blade,
A trick he has of folding with his fingers
Some scrap of paper into curious shapes;
Her mother's nose; her father's clear white skin.   300

While Root reports to Earth, the prisoners
Are locked up in a storeroom whose curved wall
Groans as the dome shrinks with the cold of night.
At last Root has got through with the transmissions,
And comes to give the news to Chance and Freya.
He can look neither of them in the eyes,
But tells them blankly they must go to Terra
Where Chance is to stand trial. At that Chance grins.
"It takes one's breath away, this Earthly honor.
You must feel privileged," he says to Root,
"To be the instrument of policies
Of such mysterious integrity
That even the faithful are demonstrably
Tested in their faith, like Abraham.

Or was this masterstroke of strategy
Entirely your idea?" Root flushes, blinks,
Then stares at his tormentor. "Listen, Chance.
You and your men are murderers; society
Withdraws itself from you; contracts are void
When made under duress, as this one was."
"So we are in a state of nature, are we?"
Chance replies. "Your Ecotheist friends
Maintain that nature is the source of law.
They would be grieved to hear you say
That law derives from human ordinance."   325
"I am a scientist and not a lawyer.
I do my duty—" "Ah, a specialist,"
Says Chance. "Then might I speak to someone who
Can take responsibility for what he does—
A free agent, perhaps, a human being?"
"You use your cleverness to excuse your crime.
This is what the religious mean by Satan.
Look at your pride, your pretty bullying,
Never contented, trying to make others
As unhappy as you are, even Freya,
Whom you are dragging with you in your fall."
Now Freya turns on him. "What you can't stand,"
She says, "is the sick thought that he is free.
No, it's not even that. It's that he is
Greater in all respects than you can be;
You are too small to celebrate the joy
He has in being, but too big to bear
The knowledge that in all experience
He has gone further and prevented you."
"Nobody can go further than the truth,"
Root says in pain to Freya, whom he loves,
"All human progress can only approach
The perfect laws that lie behind the world,
That brought it into being, are no more
Nor less than they were from eternity.   350
Freya, it's not too late. Don't throw yourself
Into illusion with him, to the burning.
Come back. There is still time." "And what is time?"
Asks Chance, for Freya, bored, will not reply:
"Can it mean anything when there are no
Surprises, no whole new lawfulnesses,

No new contracts, covenants to be made?
This is the mere beginning of the world,
Its overture, its first birdsinging dawn.
Who knows what falls, what bright redemptions may
Burst from the fresh volcano of the time?
Might not the Enemy Himself, bright Lucifer,
Be saved one day and sit at the right hand
Of the divine Joke-master of the game?
Might we be Him, the demon, and might not
That demon be the role of God when He
Acts out His comedy, His tragedy
Here in the mortal, only flesh of time?
—Kingdom of Heaven's like a mustardseed,
Remember, the new bottles, the new wine."

Root feels the grief rise in his bitter gut,
And a deathlike weariness passes through him;
And Chance looks sharply at him, sees his pain.
His old friend almost cannot bear to live,
Life is so difficult for every man;   375
And Chance's anger ebbs away at once
With pity for this mortal creature who
Stands there indeed with power of life and death
Over the man who so distresses him.
The captor has become the prisoner,
And the betrayer is the one betrayed.
Chance takes his enemy within his arms,
And gently speaks. "Orval old son, come on;
It can't be helped, I know you have to do
What you must do, and it will soon be over."

But Chance, in all his pity, will not yet
Reveal the plan that he has long prepared:
The beacon planted on Olympus Mons,
Its timer triggered when they left the swamp;
Its signal to go out unless the voice
Of its master speak on the air the code
That will deactivate its programming;
The slow pump-bomb that cannot be defused;
The powerful transmitter that it drives
Which must, to all the bases of Van Riebeck Enter-
Prises broadcast, over and over again,

The roaring of an electronic god
Speaking the word agreed among themselves
Whether on Mars or in the Asteroids,
Or in the Jovian Moons: ARMAGEDDON.

We meet Ganesh Wills, whose work in computer synthesis of
evolving live organisms has been essential in the creation
of bacteria that will survive in the Martian environment;
also Charlie Lorenz, Chance's planetary ecologist and
husband of Freya. Warned by Chance's beacon, they escape
arrest in San Francisco. Charlie evades UN pickets at the
Van Riebeck ranch in New Mexico by running with his friends
the coyotes; and he joins his sister-in-law there, Chance's
other daughter the paleobiologist Beatrice Van Riebeck.
Ganesh escapes into orbit on a shuttle rocket.

Scene iii
Ganesh, Charlie, Beatrice

A sound scholar of those eventful times
Might reconstruct without malapropism
The flying slangs that doodled on the air
Pregnant of new anachronisms, traps
For the linguistically unwary, signs
And countersigns issued from who knows where.
The amateur, upon the other hand,
Makes plausible stand in for accurate,
Since Ganesh Wills cannot be understood
Without a sense of language tumbling
And bubbling from the mold, as if the spirit
Sported fresh incarnations into being
At the hot edge of the semiconductor.

Picture the Willses chez eux in Sausalito,
Their tract house so banal that it's bizarre—
Set there among the moorish minarets,
The haciendas, hobbit-holes, and yurts,
The houseboats and the yellow-painted dachas,
The Schwarzwald hunting lodges and the domes
That cluster round the north shores of the Bay.
Billy "Tosher" Wills, our hero's father
Raises gigantic spuds in his backyard
Nourished to elephantiasis
On dark decoctions mixed of milk and stout
And horse manure and ashes and fish-meal

Peppered with potash, nitrates, phosphorus:
With these he wins Bay Area garden trophies.
His wife, nee Evalina Chaudhuri,
A name unapt to the pentameter,
Suspects he spends a richer milt than malt
Upon these fruits of—so to say—his loins.
The fruit himself, Ganesh, is seventeen:
Lives in the stygian "family room" beneath
The regions of more normal human beings.
There at his galleries of chips and cores
And strange peripherals he plies his trade;
The ancient term "computer nerd" finds here
Its archetype, the Hacker Platonized.

Billy was born in 1974,
The late son of an Indian Army sergeant;
He stayed in India as a tea-planter,
Went native, married the plump Evalina;
No children came, and so a restlessness
Drove them to knock about the world until
While visiting the aborigines
In Queensland once they slept beside the shrine
Called Maker Of The Seeds in their strange tongue,
And—miracle—there Mrs. Wills conceived.
After some wandering the three fetched up
In an apartment in South San Francisco.   50

Ganesh turned out to be a prodigy;
A genius in spatial mathematics
And in computers maybe something more.
Then Charlie Lorenz found him, just fifteen,
A senior at San Francisco State,
Told Chance about him, and the boy was hired
For enough pay to buy his folks a home.
Ganesh was playing on the school computer
A game which was the key to life on Mars:
The last piece of the puzzle to be solved
Whose pattern is the seed of a new world,
That garden whose bright gates were closed so long.
What tone then should I take to tell these things?
The spirit moves in a mysterious way:
Sometimes by the winged little phallus-gods,

The Daktyls, the gremlins of mechanism,
The fingers of a boy of seventeen.
The boisterous ghost of Melville be my guide,
Who knew the polyp-god, and built the ship
Whose wood could only be American;
We should not know whether to laugh or weep
Or pray, or rant, or dance, or pass the mustard.
Ganesh's eyes, then, large behind their lenses
Stare from each side of an enormous nose;
A sprinkling of acne mars his cheeks;   75
The dark brown skin bequeathed him by his mother
Stretches on knobby bones and gangling scrawn;
But look back at the eyes and see a gleam
Of wit, intelligence; and even charm.

A call comes through for Ganesh on the phone.
It's Charlie Lorenz in New Mexico:
He's speaking from the old Van Riebeck home
In Taos where the maguey is in flower.
"It's uncle Charlie. Problems for the brain."
Charlie still has a faintly German accent.
"Our new baby: a sulfur bug which gives
Accelerated photosynthesis
That we are tailoring for phase sixteen.
Routine photolysis in Martian soil,
It seems, won't be enough. Just like they did
Three point five gigayears ago on Earth,
Those damn oxygen sinks sop it all up:
Beatrice showed us, with the banded rocks.
We need some chemistry. These bugs will strip
The hydrogen from water to unlock
Their sulfates from the nicotinamides
And belch pure oxygen—" "Yea, Charlie," Ganesh says;
"But what's the hitch?" "We want an organelle
That can't be reconstructed from the fossil.
Have you got anything like that for me?"   100
"Not in realtime. Might I should speed things up?
The tank is pretty quiet now, but I
Could feed some fancy shit into the core
That should get action in an hour or two."
"I'll be right there. See you in San Francisco."
Our hero has the time to nix the raster

(Slang for a 'copter), take a car instead.
Now in these prancing 'thirties of nostalge,
Of crinolines, of top hats, and the waltz,
The roads glittered with Panhards, Benzes, Cords,
Rumbleseat Oldses, classic Studebakers;
'Nesh drives a cream Bugatti Crown Royale.
He tools this hog across the Golden Gate,
Heads for the Novus Ordo (and again
I must translate: the flanged pyramid
Of the old Transamerica building),
The western office of Van Riebeck Enterprises;
Hauls down her polished nose into his space.
Charlie fresh off the tube is stooped and smiling,
His face brown, his hair untimely white;
He straightens, like a German, to his height,
When Ganesh shakes his hand—the eyebrow flash,
The nod, the quick stare out of the brown eyes.
At once he's led through to the terminal.

The game Ganesh invented at thirteen   125
Might with some profit be called a disease.
It was a program that would reproduce,
Copy itself across a memory core,
Infect the local operating system,
And worm its way from RAM up into ROM.
Its vector was the disk; and human beings
Were now the rats that carried on the plague.
It was a battle program and would fight
Any suppression code sent down to clean
A core choked up with copies of itself.
Ganesh had called it ZO; in a few weeks
Half San Francisco caught this software AIDS.
Only Ganesh knew how to disinfect
The clogged and crashing hardware of the Bay;
The trade community on bended knees
Promised a new computer for the school;
Bought with this ransom, Ganesh, mollified,
Produced his antidote, DOCTOR FEEL GOOD.
The Doctor was the first selectrophage;
It ate the tagged code of the enemy
And recognized and left the rest unharmed.
But now Ganesh was hooked. He'd loved his ZO;

He wondered if the program could be taught
To learn from its defeats, adapt, become immune.
Suppose each copy came out different;   150
The Doctor might not recognize them all.
Or what if every copy had a skin
About its program space, that did not give
Away the nature of the code within.
The skin might be expendable, and grow
Again, and even learn and change, to face
The changing nature of the outer threat.
What if—Ganesh, fourteen years old, had felt
The stirrings of a pubertal unrest—
The copies could combine, swap information,
Spawn generations of a fitter strain?

"Let's take the tour," Ganesh suggests to Charlie,
And switches on the big screen of the tank.
"I changed sulfox parameters an hour ago.
I've got it wired for sound since you were here."
The moan and whistle of an echo sounder;
Jamming; the munch of programs being eaten;
A shrill mating call; territorial song.
Behind the screen things drift and wait and spasm.
"Look! There's a dozer coming through. He'll just
Browse through this sector for the weed and krill.
But you can see he's sick. He's caught a virus
Bugged with a randomizer organelle,
Doesn't know how to clean it from his genes.
A humperdumper screwed him, I would guess.   175
There's lots of them about. They simulate
The pheromones of programs hot to mate
And do a memory dump into their cores.
Look. That's a possum, only playing dead.
Now we can't see. Excelsior or fluff.
Or maybe toejam simply silting up:
That's crude bacteria no one wants to eat—"
There is a bang, a blinding flash of light.
"How about that? Artillery. Now watch."
In the cleared space a program now appears,
Swims with her pseudopods toward a reef
Of "coral"—skeletons of programs, dead
But nutritive and full of information;

Then as she feeds, a bud swells up and bursts,
And a small daughter spreads and swims away.
Charlie gives Nesh a look. "What is all this?
You're showing off. Take me to Mars." "OK,"
Says Nesh reluctantly. "To quarantine."
His flying fingers flutter on the keys
And the screen changes to a murky brown.
Ganesh turns up the gain and scans around.
Electrodyes have tagged the chemistry.
A blur of purple tells him he has found
The sulfur process he is looking for.
He zeroes in. "It's still too primitive,"   200
Says Charlie sadly. "Don't you fret your mind,"
Ganesh replies. "I've put in new equipment
And I can run this whole environment
Faster by five orders of magnitude."
He hits a switch. In simulated time
Ten million years go by; a generation
Lives and dies in thirty nanoseconds.
"Now let's see." The pace of time slows down.
This time the web of purple organelles
Is brilliant and well-defined. "That's it,"
Says Charlie, lights his filthy briar;
"Let's get hard copy, beam it to the ranch."

That very moment there's a warning chime
And the great control board, ganged as it is
To Novus Ordo's central processor,
Lights up all over with Priority.
The white dish that stares up to the southeast
From the bayside wing of the pyramid
Has caught through the violet and azure dusk
Of this cool summer California evening
(So swiftly do the mindgames that we play
Abolish the tedium of afternoons)
A signal relayed from the satellite
That hangs forever over Amazonas:
A word driven by a dying pump across   225
The tidal chaos of the gravid sun:
GEDDON ARMAGEDDON ARMAGEDDON
A catch. All other times behind the corner;
Like death, or the lit girl face of the bride,

Or the harsh new voice of the newborn child,
Or the judge's sentence, or the first blood
Of puberty or battle, it strikes dumb.
Ganesh has thrown a bank of switches to;
Charlie is on the phone, speaking slowly;
A veetol aircraft shrieks above the flange,
VER on its veered flank caught by the dusk light;
Then they are tumbling up into its belly
Into the rational comfort of its lounge,
And the racket clamps out as the door seals.
Nesh has sowed softworm programs in the air
And tracker radars have gone green and blind.
The ghostshine fans angle to vertical,
The liquid crystal airspeed window blurs;
Police in pale blue uniforms burst through
The yellow doorway of the landing pad.

Lady of destructions, I know your face,
Skulled years as it is, as it were my own.
You danced that evening barefoot on the stones
The megalithic sandstones of the house
In Taos where seven full generations   250
Of the American Van Riebecks lived
And died. Beatrice. Your broad white girl face
With its brown eyes, like Leonardo's picture
Of the lady Ginevra, your black hair
In its wild abundance, they stop my mind.
And this house is a house of lovely faces:
That one who has just bowed and retired,
Having at last settled the twins to sleep,
Must soon enough bear our insistent gaze.
The mistress dances on her little feet;
She too has heard the wail of Armageddon;
She knows the sensors show a net of foes
Waiting to catch her friends and family;
She dances for the fairy Virgin Mary.
And Mary-Kali is the god she seeks
In the violence of the earth's first life-womb;
When the ancestral clays were cast aside
By volatile calyptral ribosomes
Whose bodies were such souls as might remember
The form the body took, and resurrect

Their fragile, stinging shapes, thirsty for time;
Beatrice Van Riebeck studied stones from when
The universe was younger by a third
And in their faces saw the birth of life
And of life's twin, the labyrinths of time;   275
She knew those ages when our Terra groaned
With poison freed by photosynthesis
Whose sharp mephitic breath that slew the slimes
Would, as sweet oxygen, be sucked for fuel
By the expedient eukaryotes
Betraying, as life must, their ancestors.
She watched the chordates kill the jellyfish,
And knew the great defection from the sea,
And praised the crafty mammals, nepotists
That gave unfair advantage to their kin
And so saw off the gorgeous dinosaurs
With their antique vacuous headpieces.
All life was a flame of joy and betrayal.
The holiest love and tender sacrifice,
The baby at the breast, the arts of peace,
Were the most finished, fiercest weaponry
To carve a kingdom in the time to come.

Moon rises pink like copper in a sky
Polished out of obsidian. As if
The land had curled up at the edges to
Bask in her Mayan radiations, all
New Mexico springs into dark relief.
Bea feels it inside, goes out to watch,
Breathe the smell of a desert garden, snakeskins,
Rocks split by sunheat, resin, cactus, sage;   300
Aloes cracked open so their green flesh weeps
An odor alien, obscene, and pure.
A cool air comes from under the veranda;
Dishevelled mounds of warmed wisteria
Are white as hammered tin, cut out in shapes
Where potted lemon trees have cast their shadows.
It's one of those nights when coyotes howl;
She feels their rough fur in her blood, and sees
With their own superstitious moonglazed eyes.
Bea rocks almost with vertigo,—as always,
Here, where the whole floor of the country, bearing

Upon it plains of stones and pinon, leans
Downward a hundred miles into the dark—
How may one keep one's footing on the slope;
But the ranch house holds on, its massive eaves
Joined of huge timber silvered like driftwood,
Lintels of cypress, squared sandstone walls;
And, setting the level in perspective, ride
The gaunt limbs of the Sangre de Cristo range.

But Beatrice is suddenly aware
Of a new light that glares upon the land;
She backs away to see over the house
Where, as she knows, beyond a precipice
An isolated mesa of this scarp
Notched with the charred cubes of a pueblo fortress   325
Is hung as if no chasm intervened
Over a crowded quadrant of old stars.
A hill of fire, twinkling, veiled, enormous
Billows over the mountain; above that
A blinding coal draws out its torched arrow,
Which, flocked and granular with turbulence,
Grows to a pillar, softens, drifts, and turned
By the winds' helix of the upper air
Fades fluorescent into northern light.
She cries out softly that "They've got away,"
In that stopped-diapason note her voice
Takes on in triumph or in tragedy;
And then the battering strobe of shock strikes dumb
All thought but those the feet and belly know:
A rumble scarcely recognized as sound.

A hand laid gently on her elbow; she starts, turns
To Charlie's thin face smiling in the fire.
Mimed questions; but he hurries her inside.
"Ganesh took up the shuttle; he will try
To circumvent the orbital patrols.
I'm staying here where I can be most useful.
We have much work." "Sit down and tell me first:
How did you make it past the polizei?—
They've got the place staked out in infra-red."
"A little trick I learned from reading Homer.   350
I started out by pissing on a tree . . . "

They'd ditched the raster by the Rio Grande,
Said their goodbyes and set out in the night.
Charlie headed straight for coyote country;
Started to mark his trail the way they do.
He stopped and put his nose up in a croon;
Almost at once his old friends had arrived.
And there they were, whining in the moonlight:
Lucky, Minette, the Broonze, and Sukey Tawdry;
Saint Louis Woman, Jack, and Mister Smooth,
The Duchess, and Oddjob the alpha male.
Charlie put out his muzzle to be mouthed,
Ritualized a bite at Jack the Knife,
Sniffed at each welcome ass that was presented,
And turned his neck to show his caudal flash.
There was such cheer and pleasure at his coming,
Never so much besnuffling, growling, love;—
When Charlie asked them if they'd run with him
(Though Charlie's rank was beta in the pack)
What could they do, yearlings or dominant,
But follow him along the mountainside?
So with sweet Minette loping alongside—
She preferred him above the other males—
They coursed the shadowed gulches and the ridge,
And passed the outer borders of the ranch.   375
A vigilant policeman with a snooper
Doubtless picked out a flight of crimson shades;
But one sheep in wolf's clothing missed his eye.

"Sheep?" sings out Beatrice, and her voice catches
In that infectious, wanton laugh of hers;
"I think my sister married a coyote.
Promise to teach me to pee standing up.
But look, you need a drink." She fetches out
On a thick silver tray a stoneware bottle,
Eye-white, painted with bright blue cocks and hens,
Black spots and crosses under the glaze,
And pours into two little matching cups
A clear fluid unviscous as the air,
Smelling of fire and earth and prickly pears.
She halves a lemon with a knife and sets
A bowl of rocksalt where her friend can reach it;
Then has a thought and brings in some tortillas.

"We'll burn the documents tonight. The polizei
Will show up in the morning, not till then.
CBS says they're trying Freya too,
As one of the directors. Mother wants
To get us all, I think, specially me,
And use the children to make us cry uncle.
Wolf and Irene went to sleep like angels
By the way; Irene asked for you."

The poem turns to Sumikami, the nurse of Wolf and Irene, the twin children of Charlie and Freya. We follow Sumikami's past life as the daughter of a Vietnamese prostitute and a black U.S. marine: her coming to Japan, her work as a dancer and geisha, and her love for an Australian priest; we learn of her son Tripitaka, and of how mother and son contracted from the father the AIDS virus; of their discovery by Beatrice and their healing by the bioengineers of the Van Riebecks; of Tripitaka's subsequent deformity.

Scene iv
Sumikami

*P*icture two children asleep in wooden beds,
Who when awake will not be separated
And spurn the offer of rooms of their own
And dream in series and in parallel
Like clouds of a likeness on a summer's day
That grow and pucker into matching shapes
Marked against blue sky; but this dark zenith
Is the noon of night; the white clouds, soul slime.
Twins, like peace and war, like the yolk and white,
Wolf and Irene know by mirror-light
That persons are enacted and not given;
For all their differences have been achieved
There at the white heart of their sympathy,
And selfsame self is not itself the same.
Between their childhot nests in the night light
It seems a heap of crumpled silk has just
Been thrown upon a chair, to take a shape
Lovely, confused, almost recognizable,
Indigo, goldthread, pinkshot as a dream;
Seen, as the night eye dilates, to be not
A silken thing alone, but a small woman,
Fallen asleep clothed, a hand by each cheek
Of her little ones, its warm peachblond glow.
This lady is the one who turned away,
Shyly, when the poet's scrutiny   25
Passed with its coarse summations over her;
Now we may take advantage of her sleep

And stare into her seamless face, and taste
The bitter cordial of her history.

Chui Su was born in 1968.
Her mother was a little Saigon whore
Of Chinese ancestry, a devout Buddhist;
The father was a black U.S. marine
Who went back home after his tour of duty;
And thus Chui Su had no family name.
When Saigon fell they wandered in the streets,
Then cast their luck in with the boat people.
The mother drowned in the South China Sea;
A Kyushu trawler found the little girl.
They saw the letter pinned to her cheong sam;
The captain knew a geisha house in Tokyo,
Asked the good ladies to look after her.
The geisha training took; she learned to sing,
And play the hollow Koto and the flute;
And set a spray of flowers and a twig
So as to form an ancient space of light
Speaking of Murasaki and her shining prince
And snow or peach blossom blown in from those
Gold Heian centuries of love and war;
And she could dance that slow sweet dance of pain   50
The little mermaid dances in the tales
The West tells of the same archetype.
But like her mother she remained devout,
Seeking the hard zen of the floating world;
And the girls nicknamed her Sumikami
After the goddess of all tender mercies,
And the name stuck, for it belonged to her.
Her father's genes showed only faintest traces,
But for a creamier richness in the skin,
A Khmer fullness of the flattened lips,
A darker timbre in the voice that matched
Well the long strings of the great Chinese Chen—
A life lived in the ecstasy of service,
The honor of a self stretched down to zero,
Perfection of subordinated will
So that pure being blossoms from the stillness
And the least treeleaf brings enlightenment.

Such as is our happiness, she was happy;
But in her forties all was overthrown.
A westerner came to the geisha house,
And the calm lady Sumikami lost
Her heart like any Madam Butterfly;
She could know nothing of this tortured man
But that she loved him, she would die for him.
He was a Catholic priest, Australian;   75
Had found, with horror of his naked soul,
Desire boiling out of his control
When he beheld the stripped boys of his school;
Had sought out brutal men to slake his pangs.
Here for a private school symposium,
He'd tried in desperation to forget
The greater sin of sodom in this lesser;
He did not know he carried a disease
As horrible as his imaginings:
Acquired immune deficiency syndrome.

The body is a seven-gated city
A mystical community of lives;
And all its members are as sister twins
Or duteous bees devoted to one god;
And where the law of charity enjoins us
To take the battered stranger for our own,
The lives we're made of must acknowledge none
To be their neighbor but their sisterhood—
Unless in the great sanctuaries of
The testes and the claustral ovaries
The gene is stripped for its divine defiling
In the cave temple of the uterus;
And something halfway cancerous is born,
The shaman of the newer dispensation;
This Dionysus must be hidden from   100
The rage of our herodic soldiery,
The macrophages, by the mediation
Of the all-mothering placenta.
But if the alchemy that coats the sperm
To guard it from the poisons of the womb
Be allied with that subtle herpetoid,
The retrovirus, then the warriors
That guard the little city of a woman

Cast down their weapons in despair and die.
Just so did Sumikami fall, conceive,
And carry from her act of ill compassion
Two gifts: a sickness and an only son.
Her former life was over. In her frenzy
When the failed priest left her she cared little
How the great blots of Kaposi's Sarcoma
Merged and spread upon her beautiful limbs;
Her geisha sisters thought her loss of weight
Was grief and loss of appetite, but soon
The small dropsy of the unborn showed
And the required examination told
The doctors of that other incubus.

Now Sumikami heard a whisper from
Her womb, a distinct voice from one who might,
In adult life, have been a saint, but had,
Because of the great press of worldly karma,   125
Delayed that glory to another life:
One who, troubled, eager and perfect, would,
Despite coming sorrow, nevertheless
Wish fiercely to be born and be alive.
It seemed to bid her to a nunnery.
Winter had come, and Sumikami knew
The geishas would not let her go alone.
One frosty afternoon she slipped away;
The cold vinyl of the Nissan taxi
Made her to shiver, hug her coarse silk bag;
She took the cheapest train west to Kyoto
Where she remembered from a girlhood visit
The women's temple shrine of Jakko-in.
That evening Sumikami trudged the way
Up the long slope by the bamboo barrens,
Where a light snow lay upon the pine boughs
That smelt of resin when it powdered down.
A red sun shone across the frosty levels
And caught the last bloodvessel crimson leaves
Of a dwarf maple strangled with a vine;
And every bamboo leaf ached with the snow.
She almost fainted on the frozen grass;
Her head felt huge and far away with fever.
It was dead still. The sun touched the horizon.

The sky, a darkening pinkish brown, turned green.   150
And now although the world lay motionless
A lake of warmer air filled up the valley;
She felt a lightness carry all her limbs
As if she'd stepped into a mineral bath,
And finding strength, unlatched the bamboo gate
And passed into the holy Jakko-in.

The Jakko-in is not like other temples
With their huge end gables and smell of power,
Their almost Indonesian posts and beams
Bespeaking male submission to a god;
The Jakko-in is small and clean and soft
Like a well-kept family farm, subdued
And feminine; but the Amida Buddha
Loves to dwell here as in his favorite room;
And Lady Kuniko the Reverend Mother
Was not solicitous and not severe
But simply practical, like a ward nurse,
With this strange impressive urban woman:
Thus is perhaps the Zen of adjectives.

They put her in the guest room by the temple.
That night she first woke when a hurrying nun
Came in on tiptoe with a small iron stove
And set it deftly by her sleeping recess.
A colder air had come down in the night
From the high regions about Fuji-san.   175
The little bed of coals glowed all that night
And gave a pleasant smell of sandalwood.
She woke again, as happy as a girl,
Thinking she was Chui-Su again and in
Her mother's studio in old Saigon.
Quite wide awake and hungry, she got up;
Some salt or sweet or protein need the child
Demanded like a normal pregnancy
Drew her towards the shoji screen, and there
The wise sister who knew more of these things
Than properly she should, had set a dish
Of ripe persimmons and a bowl of rice;
The little flask alongside, it turned out,
Contained a salt fish soup, which was delicious.

The mother, satisfied, and without thought,
Slid the rice paper door ajar and peeped
Into the dim interior of the temple.
It smelt of clean cloth and of incense, where
A flame burned motionless within its lamp;
Between eight Bodhisatvas was a lotus
Carved of dark wood against a whitish screen,
And on the lotus stood a simple Buddha
Whose gilding had worn off in several places;
At first he seemed a little sleepy man
Run comfortably to fat, but then she saw   200
In the mild cheeks and the untroubled brow,
And the plump hands that held nothing at all,
A divine peace quite as fantastical
As any war of dragons and of myths.
It seemed to Sumikami that the child
In her womb was still and comfortable
As he had not been for days; it was the food,
She thought, smiling to herself in the presence
Of the Buddha, who did not take advantage
Of this smile, this womanly reflection.

But from that time there came remission of
The symptoms of the courtesan's disease;
This was a sort of miracle if one
Skilled in the virus had recorded it.
But still the small snake curled within her blood,
As if to say nothing is ever pure;
And the child too would carry in his tears,
His innocent spittle, and, when he was grown,
The flowery spilling of his manhood, that
Embodiment of the world angel's evil.

But this is to step roughly through the years;
Now Sumikami knows, as many come
To know, the sweetness of eternity;
Thaw follows thaw into the days of flowers;
The cherry tree outside her mean apartment   225
In an untidy precinct of Tokyo
Turns, five o'clock one morning, from a mask
Of black lace occluding the pure stars,
To a blue constellation against blue,

To a black grating full of crimson coals
As the sun strikes it through the reddening haze,
To a wind tossed snowstorm, the character
That stands for all things passing, thus eternal
In the old language of the Nihhon poets;
There is a smell of nutmeg and of girls;
And then she feels the welcome pains and cries
Out to be taken to the hospital.
But her profession's gone; her savings too
In those ecstatic months of idleness;
And as all human knowledge of perfection
Is marked by brevity and demands for payment
So Sumikami must come back from heaven
Into the anxious world of the temp sec,
The music tutor for the ungifted child,
Selling refinement with her flower arrangements,
And the sweet breath of soul in dancing lessons.

But the child grew up fine as a white fire.
He had the dark skin of his grandfather
But shaded into chinese bronze or peach;
His features were the purest oriental,   250
And girlish, with amazing gray-blue eyes;
His hair was the white blond of his priest father.
This is a tale of half-breeds, of the search
Our species has embarked on for its center,
The fully human woman, man, and child;
Of how we may build back out of the shattered
Fragments of the races, that bright body
Prophecy promised and our fear denied:
The priest dancer of our original,
The redskin Adam that has never been.
And Sumikami named him Tripitaka
After the holy man who was the friend
Of Monkey the trickster god, with whose help
He carried through the mountains of enchantment
Out of the magic land of India
The sacred scriptures speaking of lord Buddha.
She told him that his father was a saint
Who'd worked among the aborigines
And died a martyr in the poor folks' service.
And Tripitaka (Tak to his little friends)

Grew up so fiercely loyal to his father
That he believed himself Australian,
Vowed that he'd claim his country back one day.
Tak was an athlete, and at school was picked
As a trainee for the Olympic Games.   275

By this time, though the freedom of research
Daily drew in as Ecotheists gained
Power and position in the legislatures,
Most strains of AIDS had been eliminated;
Yet, despite Sumikami's strictest fasts,
Her sharp economies concealed from Tak,
Her visits to expensive specialists,
The virus clung in Tripitaka's blood;
And sometimes the lymph glands would be engorged
And the boy's martial arts training deferred.
He was eighteen in 2029,
Had won the youth pentathlon twice already,
Had studied under Sensei Nishiyama
The old Karate style of Shotokan,
And earned the honor of the fourth degree;
When his condition worsened and he lay
More and more often in a subtle fever.
Now Sumikami prayed and wept and begged
The Buddha's mercy that He should take her
And not the boy. Tak had a girl whose name
Was Sachiko, who always wondered why
In these modern days Tak should be so strange
And formal as the ancient Japanese:
Unlike the other boys, he never tried
To press on her his physical desire;   300
He would not even kiss her, though she sought
Occasion for the touch of lip and lip.
She came to him when he was lying sick;
A fresh breath of springtime she was to him
Out of another world, and would have touched him;
Now it occurred to him what he must do,
And told her in weak words of his condition.
Poor Sachiko, an ordinary girl,
Could think of nothing but polite escape,
And after due commiseration, fled.

But that year other things were happening.
Charlie and Freya then were newly married,
Chance was on Mars leading the Ares Project,
And Beatrice, inexplicably sad,
So that she snapped at her acquaintances
In a way quite unusual for her,
Decided she would take a *Wanderjahr*
And follow certain arts that she had loved
Before the great art of archaic life
Had claimed her for its own. She said goodbye,
Left the Van Riebeck ranch at San Luis Rey
Where she was born, and flew to Italy.
She stayed three troubled months in Europe; still
She never breathed a satisfying breath;
She even tried a visit with her mother   325
At Devereux in England; but by then
The family estrangement was too deep
And Garrison was very bad for her.
Some restless prompting took her to Japan,
And there she sought a tutor in the dance;
She visited the Jakko-in, and met
The Abbess Kuniko, who recommended
A certain Sumikami for her teacher.
Only a day had passed since Sumikami
Offered her own life for that of her son.
There in the little garden Beatrice
Saw for the first time that all-suffering face
She recognized to be her Sensei's face.

The inner beauty of a step, a turn,
A weak appearing sway of the long waist,
The way the story must consume the dance
Utterly, so that style and image are
As pat as the grace of an animal—
These took up all their time; until one night
Beatrice heard a sigh from the next room.
The dancing mistress denied all inquiry,
But one glance at her face told Bea the truth,
And when a Van Riebeck insisted, few
Knew how to turn the tendency aside.
As one who shyly shares her richest treasure   350
Or one who shows a great wound in her side

Poor Sumikami drew the screen and let
Her pupil gaze on her beautiful son.

Now Bea knew what to do. Charlie had just
Hired Ganesh Wills to simulate a life
That might endure the hellishness of Mars;
Bea would hear no refusal; Sumikami
And her feverish boy were flown at once
To San Francisco; Nesh was summoned, showed,
Got interested, grinned. "Yo. Gotcha. What
You want's your quick, dirty, technical fix.
Right? Let's run your virus on the speedup tank."
Charlie flew in to map the chromosomes,
But Tripitaka lay unconscious now;
Five days later Ganesh had found the site
Where the protein masquerade might be broken.
For one month Charlie played the hormone keys;
Nesh tried them in his circuits' antiworld.
At last they found an antibody, cloned
In a chimera of the patient's cells
With a rare lupus trained to recognize
The retrovirus's Achilles' heel,
That would, sown in the marrow of the bones,
Breed like a T-cell, hunt the enemy,
And bind its meaning to the virus' code.   375
They passed it on to Tripitaka's doctors
Who were suborned by the Van Riebeck money
To carry out an operation banned
Both by the A.M.A. and by the Council;
Within a month the boy regained his strength,
Could be found practicing karate-do;
But from that moment a disfigurement,
A grey pelt of mycotic skin, would spread
Upon his neck and groin from time to time,
The sign of cleansing from the greater ill;
The treatment left his mother with no blemish.

Now Tripitaka had his first desire:
Beatrice sent him to Australia,
The University of Adelaide,
To study verse, theology and war;
And he was chosen as a candidate,

The next Olympiad, to represent
His new nation in the Olympic Wars.
But Sumikami stayed to be the tutor
To her friend Beatrice of the fireblack eyes;
They lived at San Luis Rey with Charles and Freya,
And when the babies came she was their nurse,
Their co-mother when Freya went to Mars—
So this, then, is the lady in the silk
Who sleeps by the flushed children in their dream.

The poem turns to the Olympic Wars, those gladiatorial
contests by which international military disputes are now
settled, and to Tripitaka's training as a warrior in the
Olympic team of Australia, his father's nation. Garrison is
sent by the Ecotheist Church, which increasingly dominates
world politics, to check the ideology of the warriors. He
witnesses a bout of unarmed combat between Tripitaka and a
visiting martial arts expert and falls in love with
Tripitaka. Tripitaka is selected as a guard at the World
Court. Ganesh is captured by the UN.

Scene v
Tripitaka

A hundred miles. There is a time before
The first fierce thrust of the sun through the thorn trees
When the bulbed frogs of night have fallen silent
And the tasman cicadas are dead still;
The harsh or sweet birds of the nether dawn
Pipe down for a while before the sky's beak,
The maker of shadows, the slow firekite;
And a dead quiet presses on the plain.
A wrong light grows in the west; and if you turn,
Surprised, you see a molten lens of blood
Sealed fast upon a mask-black monolith
Which not a moment earlier had been
A pale confection out of pinkened cream.
Sunstrike. The cap of Flinders Dome will catch
The first dawnbeam before a hundred miles.
But the shaft levers downward very swiftly;
And as it hits the flagpole there's reveille,
And the old Jack with the Southern Cross breaks
With a martial clamor from the pole.
Two flanking flags shake free: the pale blue world
Skeleton of the United Nations,
The seven linked rings of the Olympic Games.
The compound comes to life; the sleep-eyed lads
Tumble out into line and dress their ranks;
The bronze sun shines in their clear tanned faces.   25
A god is surely present, with his arms

Clanging with the breezed flagpoles on his back
And the fresh light blazing in the thorns
From his dishevelled dingo-colored beard.
This means boy's blood in dust; he does not mind.
Here stands the famed Ned Kelly Company,
The bastards that they call Australia's finest;
Their noses and their sandy eyelashes
Under the pinned-up brims of their bush hats
Make one line under the cold scrutiny
Of sergeant major "Guts Fer Garters" Grace.

This was the last political idea
Before the coming of the Ecotheists:
So that we might not burn the world to dust
And ourselves with it by our most-loved weapon
—That white proof of reducibility
Of all complexities of good to light—
We sought a ritual whereby at the last
Disputes of nations might be arbitrated;
And saw that we had found its parts already
In three old institutions of our species.
First, trial by combat served as law when we
—No superordinate authority,
In Hobbes's state of nature to each other—
Must needs compose some long festered trouble;   50
And often weregild, ransom, or a tribute
Made the adventure worth the victor's hazard.
Next, nations had vied in the Olympic Games
To prove the might of their humanity
Since Pindar sang of the Olympians;
Might not the game of War become a game
Where some who sought it might find trial in death
And save the timid masses from their rage?
And last, the terrorist, who had already
Taken his trade to the Olympic stands,
Whose mind as evil, bloody, and insane
As anything our demons have possessed,
Seemed to the genius of the times to give
A twisted answer to the people's terror:
For this was the one form of human conflict
That could not be deterred by atom bombs,
And therefore by a triple paradox

Was safest for our human species-life.
Send then the terrorists to the arena,
Said the wise cowards of the billioned world;
Let them, the scapegoats, do for us what we,
Our malice tamed by terror, cannot do;
And we may through the witchcraft of the press
Take our orgasms in spectatordom
And find, in others' sacrifice, release.   75

One of the faces at attention there
Is strangely masked, like a film negative:
A skin as dark as Lucifer's, blond hair,
The refined cheekbone of a Cherokee,
But over one side is a flocculence
Of leprous grey. They call him Don,
A name inexplicable till one knows
His comrades' sense of humor, who soon saw
In his fanatic chastity a name:
Don Juan, which became Don John and then Don.
For Tripitaka does not lack admirers
Despite the saving blemish of his flesh;
Something about him, fatal as a blade,
Draws the shy Sheila-girls of Alice Springs;
And there are some who weep, perverse perhaps,
To touch the lupus of his lonely body.
But Don John is a priest or anchorite
In this respect; there is a friendship with
A black-belt sergeant in the women's camp,
But this is in the way of the profession,
And something else has brought them both together:
She too is in the Ecotheist church.
Don John has bought a chevron with his art;
When camp began, the martial arts instructor
Had tested his recruits until they broke—   100
You who have never known the trial of body
Must attend closely to the tale, for here
The nature of the Prophet is revealed,
As fleshly discipline at least in part—
And Tripitaka took the monstrous test
As if it were a feast or wedding night.
First, up at four o'clock before the dawn,
For thirty miles of quickmarch in full gear,

Guts in a jeep, yelling encouragement,
Waving a half-full soft drink from the cooler,
"Forgetting" every rest stop that he'd promised,
"Losing his way" with studied puzzlement,
Striking in fresh implausible directions,
Anxiously hurrying to get back in time;
Yet even such a march, if you're in shape,
Will give you times of pleasant comradeship,
Moments of invincible vigor, as
The young body feels the pull of its strength;
Perhaps a great sweet doughy cloud, growing
Up into the blue and over the sun;
But then, after enough time to stiffen up,
To be called out again to do the most
Brutal raises, pushups, situps, squats;
Then they must stand, their rifles at arms' length,
And Guts goes in and quite forgets about them,   125
And an hour later finds out his mistake
And chides himself for being such a juggins
But thinks it quite amusing after all.
At such a time the agony is all
The mind can know, that and its will to hold
For one more count of sixty, or until
The body passes out and solves the problem,
The quivering, spasmed muscles in their place.
But now a fit of pique from sergeant Guts;
He's lost, he says, that day out in the outback
His favorite cigar, in a white tube;
They must all go and look for it, although
The dark is coming on. And five miles out
He finds it in his pocket: very droll.

There was one present at this exercise
Who was a stranger to the life it meant
And thought the sarge a sadist, and believed
The exercise designed to break the will
And freedom of the individual;
But as he watched the young men's faces burn,
And as the young men fainted on the road
And as the unruly imagination
Stole through their bodies to their fiery minds
He felt a shiver fall across his bones

And said to himself, I must change my life.   150
It was as if he'd suffered what they suffered;
And if you have endured it you will know
The sense of the first honest contact with
The world, the freedom from your death, the flight
Of the enfranchised will above its shell,
The calm of full extension, and the dwelling
Of the spirit utterly in flesh.
And Sergeant Grace was, in that gross charade
The shaman sometimes plays, when holy Buddha
Takes the name "shit on a stick," the dark priest
Of karmic incarnation into men.
Garrison van Riebeck was the stranger
Who watched that ritual of blood and sun;
And two days later he would see the trial
In unarmed conflict of the new recruits.

That was in 2030; Garrison
Was twenty-two and Don John was nineteen.
Part of the catch the Ecotheists made
When Rose van Riebeck parted ways with Chance
Was Garrison their son. He saw the light
One day while hiking in the Pentland Hills;
He'd crossed the barren swale of a great fell
Under a grey sky of slow-moving cloud,
And came upon a place he thought a copse
Formed naturally along a clear brown burn;   175
His mood, lightened by days of solitude,
Turned to a sour grief when he knew the place
A garden gone to seed. So even here
The dirty hand of Man had set its smear:
And under the humped greyness of the sod
He found a stump of fluted doric marble.
The garden was a neoclassicist's:
You've heard of Ian Hamilton Finlay,
The great despairing poet of the eighties,
Whose house the State had razed, to batter out
The seed of the arcadian he sowed.
Now in the heart of this decaying garden
Garrison found a patch of weeded ground
As if a child had dug a little ring of earth
And planted there a clump of yellow daisies,

A plaster virgin mary, and a jar,
And a dead rose it hoped might grow again.
Rage poured suddenly through his body, that
Even the child of Man, an innocent,
Should show the same ambition to despoil,
To interfere, to drag its gross concerns
Into the high sanctuaries of nature;
Both love for the nameless child and cold justice
That would have run a sword into its body
If it had been permitted, rose in him.   200
The more pity the child should be destroyed:
It did not choose the cancer in its genes.
And in that moment of renunciation
Of all that makes us human, Garrison
Felt a deep peace to come upon his soul;
And saw how God desired an empty world,
Clouds going over, a hare sitting up.
Two days later Garrison had joined
His mother in the Ecotheist church;
As was their custom with celebrities
(And all Van Riebecks figured in the Press)
The church elders conferred on him at once
A visible position and a task:
To test for purity and for correctness
The officers of the Olympic Wars.

And so when the recruits lined up within
The *dojo* in the white *gi* of their craft,
To meet the master of the martial arts,
Under the anxious eye of Sergeant Grace,
The young warriors feared for poor old Guts,
Lest he be made a target of the church.
The students—none was a novice in this,
The second oldest, second loveliest
Of all the dances of the human world—
Must now compete to earn the doubtful pleasure   225
Of meeting in *kumite* with the master.
In their political naivety
It seemed to them they fought not for themselves
But for their sergeant, who was under trial.
Garrison could not take his eyes from him
Whose neck and chest were mottled with a lupus;

Each bout he fought he seemed to stand away
As in another world, and brushed aside,
With a grave courtesy, the kicks and blows
They rained on him; until in one swift turn
He shocked the block aside and foot or hand
Stopped with a snap a centimeter deep
Into the skin of face or throat or belly,
So that the strike was known but did no damage;
But had the foot firmed, the hip swivelled to,
The shoulder briefly locked, the elbow turned,
A shock wave would have spread from fist or foot
That would have broken bone and burst the organ.
There was no question who would face the master.

This fellow was a swart bemuscled toad,
Of whom experience had made its stone;
The students bore on forearm, brow and rib
The blue and white contusions of his touch.
Now Tripitaka changed, and seemed to draw
In toward the place and time of combat;   250
Lightly he breathed, in, out, in, out, and neared
And firmed with each breath until the master must,
Or be dishonored, close with this strange boy;
But each time that his deep karate grunt,
The *kia* yell that concentrates the body,
Shook the plain boards of the pinewood *dojo*,
Another, shriller scream of aroused *chih*,
A terrifying, gorgonish response
Rode up and over the more human sound;
The master's blow was caught and held and stopped
In the boy's open palm; the counterstrike,
A stinging *uraken*, went snakelike in
To cheekbone, throat, or temple; disallowed
As customary in this style, for its known weakness—
And Sergeant Grace, the judge, must show no favor.
But the toad giant is incensed, and now
He spins and takes grotesquely to the air,
And when his heel misses the boy's turned head,
His elbow catches him across the neck;
A dirty blow, but legal in these rules.
And Tripitaka reels; a thread of blood
Slips from the corner of his nose; a sigh

Breaks from poor Garrison, seeing the stretched
Tendon of the boy's ankle, the beauty
Of his skin beslicked with sweat, where it   275
Is not deformed by its grey carapace.
But Tripitaka squats, and breathes, his hands
Open and cross each other into block;
His young shoulders under the crisp white canvas
Seem to swell and take a deeper shape;
And now he sweeps a great stride forward, in—
To the inner *miai* of his partner;
Amazed and almost ready to abandon
The contest with the injured boy, the master
Seeks to conclude the bout with a head blow;
But Tripitaka rises from the stance,
And slightly turns, and his hand shoots up high
Into the rising block, from which his hips,
Recoiling, drive a five inch strike into
The breastbone of the heavy man before him;
His *kia* scream glides on into a croon
Of achieved penetration into truth;
But every soldier feels the solid crack
Of breakage as the master chokes and falls.

Garrison asks and gets an interview
With the strange youth whose nickname is Don John:
This deformed warrior has won his soul.
For who but he, as pure as mother nature,
Bears in his flesh such sign of unsuccess?
—Such antidote against his father's power?   300
And who but he can be his mother's foil?
And who but he shall be his acolyte
And heart-squire in the imminent crusade?
The warrior's thoughts are harder to unravel.
For Tripitaka's life is toil and pain,
A saint's soul in the body of a hero;
He has been always lonely, perforce pure,
Seeking a light that he might follow where
The act might be commensurate with what
He knew as perfect from forgotten dreams.
"Don" has known only athletes and rough soldiers,
Who seek and follow what's before their noses;
And that a man, as it must seem to him,

Might be as dedicate as Garrison,
Is marvelous to him, a women's child.
The fire of faith now spreads from man to man;
The drunken joy of full humility—
That passion which is cruelest of all,
When it possesses history, and casts,
Weeping with sacrifice and exaltation,
Its own children into the sacred pyres—
That sweet humility has caught the boy
Who will be master of the martial games.

Return to the parade ground in the sun;
The flags, the morning light on Flinders Dome;   325
It's 2033 and Tripitaka,
Now twenty-two, is in the final training
To fight in next year's Spring Olympiad
Against the warriors of Indonesia.
But now he's called out from the ranks to hear
A new assignment, something of an honor;
There must, as customary, be a guard
Drawn from the gladiators of all nations
To serve the World Court as it hears its cases
And hold its prisoners lest they escape.
A major case is pending now: the trial
Of Chance Van Riebeck and his daughter Freya
And as accomplices her husband Lorenz,
And—in absentia unless he's caught—
The boy Ganesh, who healed Tripitaka.
There will be time to join his ranks again
Before the battle—it is early May—
And therefore there is no excuse to shirk
What for the young man must be a trial
As terrible as that of Chance and Freya.

With these commands Don John acquires a shadow:
A person of the journalist persuasion.
To speak more truly, he's a book reviewer
Who writes and teaches little free-verse poems;
The newspaper has run out of reporters   350
For this, the juiciest of cases; "Bill,"
Then, is all that they could muster in the pinch.
Bill's an existentialist from way back,

And likes the chance to be a hardnosed hack;
He is the conscience of the writing class,
The censor who lets only smallness pass.
Ah, Bill, you ask an ode of me, lest you
And all your brothers vanish with the dew;
Your virtues are not trumpet-tongued, and must
Be duly whistled ere they turn to dust.
First, a becoming modesty of style;
The aspirations of a crocodile;
A Shiite mullah's open-mindedness,
A moral backbone of boiled watercress;
All the prophetic vision of a sheep
(But not so witty, and not quite as deep);
A diction as unblemished by a thought
As is a baby's bottom by a wart;
You stand in the traditions of our art
As a blocked artery in a dying heart.
Bill wishes he could cover Chance van Riebeck,
And pen a think-piece on his alien science,
His inhumane ambitions, and his pride,
And poke some fun at his huge oddities,
And then get serious, and deplore his fame,   375
And ponder why the immature still hearken
After the sentimental monsters of
An arrogant and violent history.

For now publicity is wallowing
Across the prostrate planet like a bull;
That god who truly eats his children roars
From the videos and ganged gates of the tube;
All is now common, and the story is
As much the same as any other story
As ingenuity and art can make it.

Above, a drama plays itself to death:
Ganesh's shuttle, veiled by clouds of dream
Spun by his guardians, the softworm clones,
Is sought by radar-blinded hunters, blun-
Dering across the occultations of
The acrid stars and thin sardonic moons;
Tiny outjettings carry him away

Until he's almost safe within the cone
The pole's auroras cast into the sky;
But one last probe breaks through his webbed defense,
And he must murmur "Shit!" and snap his fingers,
Cruelly outgunned and naked in the heavens.

Captive, my peers, unanxious as the dawn,
Founders, foundering in the brass beast's maw,
What recourse is there left? but listen. Listen.

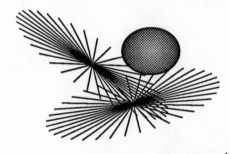

ACT II
The Trial of Chance

Chance and Freya go on trial in the World Court at Olympia
in Greece. Tripitaka has become the jailor of Chance.
Ruhollah the drug merchant, also on trial, indoctrinates
Garrison and Tripitaka into the Chiffre, the extreme
Ecotheist sect that holds all of nature to be evil.

Scene i
The Gathering of the Prisoners

Cicadas, little stridulators, sing,
With your wings and widow's walking-sticks.
Even the shade here blazes with a light
That lit Pausanias's chin when he lay down
To nap beneath the planes of Ilida.
Kronion oak-canopied smells of honey,
Smells of old fireplaces and ritual straw;
Mount of the old one, the phage of seed,
Presider in the arcadian golden age.
Half covered up in leaves, a drum of stone
Reminds the traveller of the price of time;
And if the eye of Titian or Giorgione
Could for the nonce condense out of the sky—
Out of this blue so bright it turns to gold,
It turns to a gold-leaf iconostasis—
Then such an eye should draw out from the ever-
Brilliant bourn of the immortals the form
Of the goddess resident invisible,
Rhea, perhaps, or her bloodier mother
Gaea, but pictured in their ripest girlhood
Lovely and languid, undimmed by the shade,
And virgin yet of world-mastering Jove.
Dorian interlude! Between the boles
Mottled and peeled to bone-white, lemon, choc-
Olate is seen a pastoral landscape far   25
Empurpled with the masks and folds of ether
Where Cladeus swift-flowing winds to join
Alpheus risen from high Arcady
Impatient now to dive beneath the ocean
And rise, the Latin muse, in Sicily.
Closer we see, upon the plain beneath,

Palaestral ruins and a stadium:
Temples to Zeus and Hera, for this place
Is, as the acute observer swiftly learns,
The holy precinct of Olympia.
And in the foreground bosky and imbrown'd
As Claude had painted it, we can make out
A man reclining by a bower of ivy;
And further off, another squats alert,
Patient, watching the first, arms on his knees:
Some subject like the sleep of Ulysses
Attended by Athena as a youth,
Might justify the master's jeu d'esprit.

This moment seems a painted summary
Of one gold millennial afternoon,
But pastoral must fall to history.
The intent warrior with slitted eyes
Is Tripitaka, and the sleeping man,
His curled black hair among the plane tree roots,
His small beard like a Nicholas Hilliard,   50
Is Chance van Riebeck dreaming of a time
When the dead words and thoughts of constant trial
Were past forever, and the age begun
When bees and dragonflies might dance all day
Above the slipping waters with the sun
In an enchanted syrtis piedmontane
Of piny, muslin-lighted, poppied Mars.
And these brief sleeps of his are those from which
You wake up weakened, weeping without cause,
The whole weight of things pressing on your heart.
It is their custom, trial being adjourned,
To walk and breathe here in the World Court grounds,
Though their sparse talk is brief and full of pain;
For Chance's guard is as oppressed as Chance,
Envies the sleeping man his hour of sleep—
And how can you forgive your friend and healer
When you betray him daily in his eyes?

—Of constant trial. Each morning Chance is woken
For breakfast with his counsel, Giamba Vico.
Next he is led across the World Court compound
Into the auditorium of glass

And Swedish wood, now shabbier with use,
And takes his stand behind the microphone,
Protected from the public by a screen
Of bulletproof and polarizing glass;   75
Till noon the fading drone of arguments,
Of motions to throw out some article
Or other of the tangled net of charges
Wherein he struggles, and of challenges
And quashings, pleas, approaches to the bench,
Have turned the vibrant air of Greece to dust
And cobwebs, bearing dried and shrivelled flies.
Sometimes he watches Freya in her box
Of glass across the courtroom, and she smiles
Palely through grey reflections at his glance;
This is the only contact they're allowed.

His other entertainment is to follow
Through brief encounters in the corridors
And overheard remarks among the guards
The progress of a big concurrent trial:
The case of Ruhollah the drug merchant.
Addiction's commonplace in this new world;
Perhaps a half of the earth's population—
Shrinking already, though the demographic
Fishtraps of the central cities have not yet
Brought on the midcent crash—is now on drugs.
Synthesized endorphins, built to mimic
Perfectly the brain's own self-reward,
Have driven out the weaker herbal resins,
Cocaine, cannabinol, and heroin—   100
Ruhollah is the richest man on earth
And he is being tried for his profession.
He makes an interesting argument:
That Penth, the drug, is only natural,
And if as ecotheist truth reveals,
We are the violators of the world,
The enemies of heaven's wilderness,
And if the use of Penth makes us forgo
The work that our distorted nature levies
Upon us in exchange for its reward,
So much the better for the groaning planet.
What strikes the intrigued Chance about this line

Is not its depth but the apparent fact
That in the Court's terms it's unanswerable.
But further, Chance is really fascinated
With the mind that might propose such reasoning:
For if it could believe its argument,
Surely it could not have conceived it;
But, disingenuous, his words are satire
Against the very truth that he invokes—
But not the satire of a humanist;
He must be speaking from a place of insight
To which the natural is as defiled
As is humanity to those who try him.
Chance checks the prison library   125
And finds Ruhollah's reading Simone Weil.

But in the afternoons he has permission
Under the eye of his unsleeping guard
To take his exercise among the pines
That Hitler planted round the stadium,
And walk the stoa and colonnade of Nero,
And climb the lower slopes of Kronion
Bought by the European parliament
And built with chalets for the delegates.
So monotheism must always raise
Its temples on the levelled pyramids
Of ancient gods who in the twilight mourn
And rend their garments and their lovely hair,
Flee shrieking into darker grots and caves
Than any censed by smoke and oracles.

(O I am here like mad Pound caged in Pisa;
I am the Stupid Dog the shaman drives
Out of the village with the village sins
Piled on his aching back. O my lord Chance
Dead these many years ago, my greyhound,
My Montefeltro, my John Carter of Mars,
Who laughed and strove through every mortal doubt,
Give me the strength to see your enemies
As you would see them, with that fierce compassion,
That breathtaking impartiality   150
That you poured out in bounty to the world.)

Perhaps Chance hears this prayer from the future;
For he wakes, almost with a groan, and sees
The eyes of Tripitaka glittering
As if they glared out through the steel visor
Of the mooned helmet of a samurai.
"Back to the world, then," Chance says with a smile.
Now Tripitaka stands but does not speak.
Chance goes on lightly: "Don't take it so hard,
My son; you're only doing what you ought."
"Why do you speak to me?" asks Tripitaka.
"I am your guard appointed by the Court.
If you want water or a pen and paper,
Just say so and I will fetch it for you."
Chance shrugs his shoulders and they set off down
The evening hillside to the World Court compound.

Tomorrow there will be a change; at last
The long preliminaries have concluded,
And opening arguments will now be heard.
Chance's son Garrison is to be there;
He has not seen him for some years, and is,
If Chance is ever thus, something afraid.
The witnesses will be arriving too:
Charlie Lorenz, Beatrice, Ganesh Wills,
And Orval Root whose promise has been broken,   175
And Gaea/Rose Van Riebeck in her triumph,
In her bright, bitter, principled triumph
Over the rapist of the holy world.

Chance cannot sleep that night. His airy doze
Under the gleaming leaves has stirred his blood;
An undertow of memory has drawn
Him out beyond his depth, too weak to fight it.
He scarcely listens to his lawyer's case,
And stares with feverish intensity
At his son's face, as if he sought the time
When he had issuance from the holy place
Whence Chance is now for ever turned away;
And then he tries to look at Gaea-Rose,
And cannot, and he tries again, and can;
It hurts him like a billy to the groin
With hopeless love, love of what hates him, love

That must know how it cripples where it loves.
Bill the reporter notes this glance and files
A piece on Chance's interest in the trial,
His hope that family loyalty will save
His hide and profits from the People's case.
But it is otherwise. To tell the truth
Chance has forgotten all about the trial.
When questioned formally about his name,
Profession, present address and his plea,   200
His answers are correct but quite distracted.
Rosalind Redgrave, Rose of Coventry,
The poet of the English revolution,
Is all his study now and all his trial.

There are some other meetings too. Charlie
And Freya meet each other's eyes across
The courtroom; Charlie smiles as if to say,
My girl we're in hot water now, and Freya lifts
Her head, and stares into his eyes like one
Who knows the time is short before their parting.
The night before, she wept as she'd not done
These twenty years; for Sumikami brought
Her twins, Wolf and Irene, to the cell,
And they at first had cried with fear at this
Spaceburned woman from the winds of Mars,
Whom they acknowledged theirs with horror lest
The powers she wielded might be given over
Into their own unready hands, to sear
Or heal; her breasts ached for the touch of those
That she would never suckle now, for loss
Attends every enaction of the will,
And that which is is bought by living branches
Torn from the tree of time and burned for fuel.
But Charlie's gentle face is full of grief
For what he sees in Freya's; so she smiles   225
At him, and for the benefit of those
Wise gentlemen and ladies of the press
Who are deputed to inspect such things
She sends a vulgar wink across the room.

And there's Ganesh. The big t-shirt revival
Has not escaped his notice; he's got one

That reads CONTEMPT OF COURT upon the front
And SORRY DIDNT MEAN IT on the back.
Tripitaka watches him amazed:
This creature from another world has saved
His life, and by purely technical means.
Something like hate, the hate of man for insect,
Makes Tripitaka shudder; something else,
Which, if he knew it, was the dawn of laughter,
Lightens the warrior's heart; confuses him.
He looks at Sumikami for relief,
But she has turned her countenance away;
And Beatrice is there, her black hair like
A cloud about her fierce madonna face;
Now Tripitaka's eyes, falling in pain
From his mother's closed presence, catch upon
The spread hands of Beatrice as she stares
At her father full of reproach and love;
And in as many seconds Don John knows
Another of the gods that trouble men: 250
The ancient shot of jealousy and shame.

Despite her mother's efforts, Beatrice
Has not been brought to trial, for Chance has sworn
Untruthfully that she was innocent;
And, which the court counts more, the evidence
Of her direct involvement in the rape
Of Mars is such as might discredit what
The court, and behind it, the church's wisdom
Is trying to establish as a crime.
She's here under protective custody,
A witness for the People, and the judge
And prosecuting counsel are advised
To keep her off the subject of the birth
And early history of life upon
This planet, lest it seem too natural
To imitate those origins on Mars.
Chiefly she will be questioned on the clones
Of prehistoric animals she's grown;
The subject has made headlines in the press
Arousing public horror and concern.
(Two weeks later Beatrice will reply
To prosecution questions on this theme,

Just as the church had hoped, with hot contempt:
"If we are playing God, so much the better;
We might improve his work this time around.   275
If he's our real father, he'll be pleased.")

That evening Garrison, who's interested
In all addictions, and whose power within
The Ecotheist church provides
A key to many opportunities,
Visits Ruhollah the merchant of delight.
He goes to be appalled but stays to listen,
And the next night he invites Tripitaka.
The old man in his cell is brown and wizened,
As merry as a grig, and his eyes twinkle;
His hooked nose is as long as Lucifer's,
And he speaks softly in a strong French accent.
Ruhollah is an exponent of *Chiffre*,
Like Sufi to Islam, a mysticism—
A heresy—of Ecotheism.
"Why," asks Ruhollah, "My devout young friends,
Should Purity reside even in Nature?
Is not the world of nature one of eating?
Is it not vile that one being's life should flow
From the appropriation of another's?
Nature is but a pit of mouths, a nest
Of bellies brewing acids into gas;
That sin we stand condemned of was committed
At the accursed beginning of the world.
We are the fragments of the Enemy,   300
The demiurge who would rebel at God,
And take kinetic form from the potential,
The sea of sightless light in the beginning;
And he, the Angel, fell into the shape
Of sensual energy and grossest matter,
Away from that perfection he enjoyed
At first in those transparent fields of light.
The ground state of the world is all potential,
And since the cause is fuller of that essence
That gives effect its being, than the effect,
All action is a fall and a declension
Into the brute adultery of time.
The Ground is pure and indeterminate;

Is the white joy of unenactedness;
The big bang where the laws of time all fail;
The place we must return to, to be saved."
"But what," asks Garrison, dismayed, "about
The innocence of nature? I can see
How human beings are to blame; I know
Myself the gulfs of consciousness,
The slimy things that grow inside the skin
Of candor and apparent honesty;
But as for nature, she is pure, she must be.
Matter has no awareness what it is."
Now Tripitaka listens silently;   325
His eyes glitter and his *kendo* hand
Wanders to touch the lupus of his cheek.
But still Ruhollah speaks again, and smiles.
"Is not the nature that you so admire
That which your senses in their corruption
Pick out to find delectable and pure?
And if your senses, calibrated as
They are by that depraved and self-suborned
Selfconsciousness you loathe, were given you
As your inheritance by nature too,
Are they not prone to partiality,
To hanker for the mother of their form?
And is not consciousness itself the last
Of many gross conceptions on itself
That nature practiced long before the birth
Of humankind, its monstrous masterpiece?"
"What then is pure?" asks Garrison despairing,
And Tripitaka breathes the same breath through.
"The *chiffre*," says Ruhollah; "Nothing is
Pure; seek out that nothing and you will see."
"How?" "Break the incestuous cycle of reward
By which the human brain maintains its act
Of self-sustained desire and memory.
My humble product, for which I am on trial,
Penth, is the way to perfect innocence.   350
Take it and learn the nullity of saints.
The gross diameter of thought will shrink,
Collapse, and you will be as a point is,
Without dimension, taint, or history."
And is not this Ruhollah speaking truth?

And are not the Savonarolas of
The world the fire that purifies its pride?
Is not the quality of culture measured
By the addictions that it can withstand?
These boys will seek the drug and the dark way
Of this integrity, and we shall see
What, if there is such, they can set against
The full attainment and death of desire.

Chance in his cell yearns like a teenager
After his queen of night, his shadeblack rose.
In '02, on a visiting appointment
At Merton, lecturing in chemistry,
A *Wunderkind* of only twenty-two,
He'd lunched in the graduate common-room
And found the window-seat he liked, that looked
Across the Meadows, taken by a poet.
Her profile threw the plane-trees out of focus
And left a line across the Cherwell woods
That Chance could not forget. Personal being,
Like that dense tincture that can dye a lake   375
Of water with a grain, the subtle toxin
Added to the pipes that slays a city,
This was the young American's, the chemist's
Drug, besetting sin, his wry addiction.
Rosalind Redgrave was the name upon
The oak he took such care to pass, the name
On the notebook that he found one day upon
The window seat, with its dark crown of poems;
The name on the posters promised to speak
At the small rallies against Ecotheism
That Oxford held before they were closed down;
And who but she must be his paramour.
He had made good, American as he was,
Upon the opportunity of the book,
And soon they might be seen in duffle-coats
Across the ice mists of the Magdalen deerpark,
Brushing a white rime from the iron railings
With those gloved hands that were not holding hands.
And in the spring they walked the Windrush valley
Where combs of giant beeches fletched the hills,
And colors, passionate as that brown and blue

Which blazes from a pool befilmed with oil,
Blew in the airscape, the ploughed fields, the streams.
(Cream tea in the dreamvillages of stone;
Kisses that taste of lipstick and of love.)

Meanwhile, alerted by the codeword ARMAGEDDON broadcast by
Chance's beacon, the men and women of Van Riebeck
Enterprises arm themselves against the UN. They take and
hold the planet Mars, certain industrial and agricultural
satellites, and a base on the Moon. The treeship Kalevala,
under the command of Ximene de Vivar, and loyal to Chance,
displaces one of the ice moons of Saturn from its orbit and
sets it on a course towards the inner planets Mars and
Earth. Ximene's daughter Marisol, a lieutenant, mutinies
against her mother's orders, but the mutiny is put down.

Scene ii
The Fashioning of the Comet

*M*AGEDDON ARMAGEDDON ARMAGEDDON.
The message has gone out in rings of light
And the flung seeds of Van Riebeck Enter-
Prises stir and form for coming battle.
The factories in solar orbit, armed
Lightly with industrial grade lasers
Are safe enough; their distance is their shield.
Moonbase at Plato is a stony fortress,
The crater glacis mined for ground attack;
And its great railgun, used in peace to lob
Materiel into a close earth orbit,
Now dominates the shining lunar sky.
(Nevertheless the ringwall is besieged,
The close horizon lit by glares of fire,
And giant wrecked machines like dinosaurs
Leave dolorous carcasses upon the plain.)
Of twelve space islands strung around the earth
In synchronous orbit, seven are VRE;
Revolts break out on two, timed by the church
To coincide with the arrests on Mars.
They are successful, for the management
Will not endanger the civilians.
(They will become island theocracies,
A half-heretical embarrassment
To orthodoxy, but the shock troops of   25
The Ecotheist movement, and its conscience.)

In the first weeks of unpreparedness
Two more of the space stations are attacked
With ground-launched nuclear missiles, and destroyed.
Over Ceylon and Ecuador two new suns shine
With the radiance of ten thousand souls
Screaming as their glassbound meadows burn.
The other three have time to fortify,
Outposts upon the frontiers of the Earth.
On Mars Van Riebeck's forces, though outnumbered
By UN expeditionary troops,
Achieve a series of quick victories
Generalled wisely by Hillel Sharon,
The tough little sabra Chance left in charge.
The Earthly troops are forced to the defensive,
And soon their last redoubt, the Tharsis Plateau,
Is stormed by toughened miners of the Firm.
Further out still, the ships en route between
The zones of Mars and of the asteroids,
Must test their loyalties to cause or hope,
And many little wars with fist and wrench
Are fought along their loud cramped corridors.
In general the further out the ship,
The greater is its lean to VRE;
And Chance's promises are best believed　　　　　　50
Among the distant moons of Jupiter.

And I who tell this tale must be betrayed,
For there is one of you at least who will
Be so distressed by some great loneliness
Or by the bitterness of this your scourge
Or by the rank impossibility
Of setting side by side within the mind
The fields of Oxford and the fields of Mars
That you will break this little game we play
And perhaps in secret or perhaps at large
Carry my words and name to those who will
Know well how to deal firmly with such things.

Poor science-fiction. Last muse of the gods,
The late child, stepchild, of our legendry;
Doomed by the moment of its breath, as acts
Upon a stage without a camera

Are reeled off into death by their performance,
And give themselves away so foolishly.
A divine prophecy remains in force
Not despite human efforts to avoid it,
But through them, through the human second-guessing
Of how the oracle intends us to
Impale ourselves upon our fate, and be,
Like Oedipus, dragged to the sin
By the fine thread of a noble conscience.   75
But human prophecy, poor science fiction,
Is void once known, and in the very instant
Of its statement just another act
Whose consequences take their chance with all
The countermeasures of its enemies.
Thus it is dated at the moment of
Its saying, and becomes a lively art.
But this my poem is no prophecy
Unless the savage indignation of
Its exhortation to those shades, its readers,
Should be construed a possibility
That we might take the glory road at last,
And follow Chance into the blazing stars.
And if it were a prophecy, then I
Should not desire that it be divine.
For all the legacy I wish to leave
Is that those after me might be set free;
I'd wish my gift to be the death of bondage,
Even the bondage of my words, if one
Were so constrained by them that the wellspring
Of native novelty should cease to flow;
For what is liberty but to create?

Would you prefer a novel, then? No space-travel,
No adolescent fantasy, no risk
Of obsolescence by the brute event?   100
What would you pay? The characters must be
What you would call believable; their acts
Driven by some automatism you
Can recognize, and being pictured, can
Condone as human, psychological.
How we twist, struggle, scrabble at the earth,
Take any path that we might not be free.

Freedom terrifies us. To be free
Is to make, to love, to make all things new.
Praise adolescence for at least the grace
To fantasize the unbelievable,
To row upstream against psychology,
To play against our probability.

But this is shrill. Give me that calm, you friends,
You inexhaustible daughters of joy,
That calm that the spindle turns upon,
The gold calm of the fertile mustardseed;
And let me show a symbol, a made thing.

Out over Saturn; white with a smooth grain;
Impossible to tell how far away;
A child's top, but double-ended; a spool,
A bobbin, naked of thread, slowly spinning;
A form as elegant as is the field
Electromagnetism weaves itself,
But pinched-waisted—an hourglass or a viol;   125
And our first thought was right—it's made of wood,
Beech heartwood by the look of it, and huge—
Those shadows that the pointlike sun casts through
Its slender waist are vast, those pores and eyes
With lights behind them, spacious apertures
Like Gaudi's Catalonian grotesque,
Broad windows lipped with driftwood wings of bone,
Or flanged for their heavy crystal lenses.
The shadows are lit pink by Saturn's rings.
At one end, at the center of the disc,
There is a dimple like a graphic function;
And out of it a beam of pure white light
(Tainted and rendered visible, as if a dust
Had wandered through a sunbeam, by a trace
Of plasma fluorescing as it cools)
Shoots ruler-sharp a thousand miles behind.
About the other end—is this a vessel,
And is this the prow?—there's a vaguer aura,
Some puddling of the light of distant stars,
That must bespeak the presence of a power
That bends the laminate of time with space.

This ship's a living tree turned inside out.
Chance's and Beatrice's engineers
Of genes and cellular development
Shaped her in secret from mutated mast   150
Gleaned from a windy coppice by the Glyme,
And fed her sunlight, water and sweet air
As she obeyed the new geometry
Spelled out for her in double helices.
Given enough organic chemicals the tree
Might grow to be a planetoid, a world;
Its barrelvault of heartwood, ten feet thick,
Protecting an environment of green
And leafy springtime branchiness within.
Let us explore the great aft lobe together:
Its inner rim is deep with rich black soil
In which the rootweb flourishes upon
The wastes of this self-fed economy;
A hadean acreage where mushrooms grow,
And the moist air is ripe with fertile spores.
A glassite axle towers from stern to stem
Containing the machineries of hell
(Where Blake might lead a skeptic angel if
He would impose his vision on that spirit),
Whose function is to suck in through the intake
The planetary gas and comet-dusts
With an electric funnel twelve miles wide,
And, like a ramjet, burn this vaporous fuel
And turn its nuclear substance into light;
Light whose reaction mass indeed is small   175
But whose velocity, and thus momentum,
Could scarcely be improved on by an angel.
The incandescent torch the vessel wields
Is wing and sword at once, a drive or weapon;
And harnessed to an asteroid or comet
Becomes a miner's pick or welder's arc.
The forrard lobe is full of windowlight;
Part from the radiance of ancient Sol,
Part from the fusion furnaces behind
The glasswall of the axle at the core.
Conservatory of eternal dawn,
It's laced with stories out of beechen green
Where human dwellers, like their ancestors,

Have made their lairs in clusters or alone
Among the silvery sensitive and bescarred boles
Of the bright emerald monoforest.
The tree is grafted with a second life:
Orchards of apples, figs, and mangotrees,
A fruit-lit orangery like a street
Of Christmas lanterns, garlanded with flowers;
The air's bright with the screech of colored birds.
A little prairie by a concave lake
Pastures a herd of somnolescent cows;
A net of streambeds carries runoff when
The huge vessel changes its momentum,　　　　　　　　　200
And irrigates these arched slopes of eden.
Above, the dweller sees a detailed map
Of what lies on the far side of his world,
A map which is also reality,
Pierced by the mullions of the distant light.
The ship is named *Kalevala*, and smells
Of lemon trees and showers and cooking-smoke;
And like the clippers of the southern seas
Creaks when the press of speed is on her, so
A music haunts its pinched harmonic sphere,
A sweet groan like the sound of sea or wind.

And as we watch, the fiery torch goes out.
The ship's commander, Ximene de Vivar,
Has given orders to the main computer
To put the vessel in a grazing orbit
About the equatorial belt of Saturn; now
The braking burn is over, and the ship
Coasts to its rendezvous within the ring.

Immensity beyond immensity.
Where's "below"? The world-arch of glittering flakes,
Salmon-colored, above a further ring
Of heart-besieging blue? But no below
Could be so glassy, so translucent, Cin-
Derella's slipper, Christmas-tree bauble-
Colored, like Hark-the-Herald-Angel wings.　　　　　　225
"Below" must be the other, that which the eye
Avoids, lest the whorls of the inner ear
Be rapt with vertigo, seduced to fall

Into its ever-coiling lakes of oil,
Its oceanic paisleys, fractal-trimmed
With fringes of eddies, turned inside out,
So that their crimson-ocher linings show
Pretty regurgitations and inversion layers,
Each one a hurricane, Pacific-sized.
Does the ear feel kinship with that bellowing,
Oracle-cave, labyrinth-dizzy place,
That it so yearns to fall there? Look not down,
Says the eye, who, bound, must take control.
Lucky for us it is so silent here
Above the howling toil of planet-work;
But had we sensors as the ship has, that
Can strain the wavebands for their wailing myths,
We might be mesmerized by what they said,
The ineffable meaningless word they
Almost articulated, Saturn's Voice,
That we might never come among our kind
Again, and be the servants of a god.
Ah, but see now. The terminator sweeps
Across the planet's face. The darkside's lit
By ringlight, but that golden glow is met   250
From below with a more sinister fire:
Diffused, a leprous magic white in fits
Of netted spreadings breaking out and fading
To show, beneath a further veil, cold glows
Dimmed by their distance in the middle air:
Storm-lightnings in continuous discharge.
Down there the thunder'd break the human ear,
Spill its warm ichor to the acid wind;
But it's as beautiful as one entire
And perfect opal in the ear of God.

Captain Vivar, her hands at the controls
Of the ship's telescope array, is searching
That clot or twist within the ring wherein
Tumbles the moonlet named S26.
It will be renamed Kali the destroyer,
Creator of the worlds; but it must first
Be broken into halves and slung around
The gravitation well of father Saturn.
No greater weapon ever was conceived

Nor fashioned by the gentle human hand;
This is the task Ximene has been commanded
By that faint voice whispering Armageddon.

And there it is. A drift of icebergs clears
To show that huger moon, a battered spheroid
Thirty miles in radius, brilliant   275
With pikes of yellow ice, pitted with scars,
Cracked with the tidal forces of its past
Encounters at close perihelion.
And now it vanishes. The planet's shadow
Swallows its moon, and with a blaze of color
Stranger than any earthly evening, lit,
It might be, by Krakatoan suns, but
Brief, brief, the broad limb slams the sunlight shut.
Ximene is patient. When the light returns,
She must give orders, be the cool commander.
Now it is time to get a little sleep.
She stands, flips off the viewscreen, turns to leave.
Ximene is tall, a willowy strength of waist,
A pale clear face like a middle-aged saint;
Black hair and bright black eyes. As if a mirror
Stood before her suddenly, but one
Which had the power of turning age to youth,
Another woman looks her in the face.
Her daughter Marisol. "No. I can't do it.
I see this comet every time I dream,
Falling in blood upon the home of man.
Even the threat of such a holocaust
Is evil worse than any they have done.
It makes us just like they are. Help me, mother."
"Are you refusing, Marisol, to lead   300
The anchor team tomorrow, as you warned?"
"Yes, mother. And I'm asking for your help."
Ximene is suddenly as tired as death;
She makes the usual arguments——that they
Will never let the comet fall to Earth;
That it enforces reasonable claims;
That Kali is creator as destroyer;
That the planned flight of this enormous missile
Will take it down to Mars to be the source
Of Martian oceans and of Martian skies;

That a mid-course correction still is needed
To let the weapon fall upon the Earth;
That threats of sacrifices just as dark
Have been the driving-force of history—
But as Ximene looks in her daughter's face
The logic seems to waver and run pale
Like water-painting under pouring rain.
And Marisol sees how it is with her,
And feels her mother's weakness as her own;
She wishes she could give away some sign
Permitting an agreed means of escape,
Whereby the moral pressure might be eased—
Even an open break, the invocation
Of the codes of discipline and command—
So that Ximene can call the ship's gendarmes   325
And, honor satisfied on both sides, clap
A mutinous junior officer in irons—
And Marisol, her conscience quieted,
Might sit out actions which she half-connives
By following the antique roles of conflict.
But she must make it all as hard as she
Can make it for her mother; ethics here
Allows for no compassion, when the world
Itself, the ground of all morality
Is made the pawn of struggle and the forfeit
If some unhappy hero fails to flinch.
And Ximene knows her daughter, and knows too
In one long moment of insight and care
How Marisol has chosen to impale
Her own deepest love on the icy horns
Of sacrifice, and further, how that choice
Is as her mother taught her how to be.
And whether it's better to destroy the race
Rather than lose the meaning of the race,
Which is to make—to master, mother, mate,
And matter to, the world—or if the race
Alive transcends all causes that it makes;
Or whether that eternal trial of loves,
Between Antigone and Creon, or
Between Lear's way and that of naked Tom,   350
The trial itself! be what must count the most;
Ximene now knows again what she will do.

"Lieutenant de Vivar, you disobey
An order and are thus a mutineer.
Consider yourself under ship's arrest
Until such time as you are brought to trial."
And now as she had half-expected, there
Is a pistol in Marisol's right hand;
And as Ximene steps forward to be shot
Or take the weapon by an act of violence
She sees with grief a possibility
More terrible than any yet; her daughter
Is collapsing, and can't shoot; and Ximene
Has beaten down what she would, more than any
Outcome in the world, have straight and tall
And peerless in her world of moral will.
But at the final instant Marisol
Raises the gun again to fire; too late;
The mother's trained karate kick disarms her;
The next moment the room is full of guards.

And now *Kalevala* has rendezvoused
With Kali, and a cloud of smaller craft—
Lighters, cable-layers, command modules—
Descends towards the surface. Anchor-points
Are drilled, the ship made fast, its plasma-jet   375
Directed at the surface of the object;
All personnel withdraw to watch the burn;
A white actinic light comes on, like dawn,
Turning at once to green, violet, peacock
As the hot sublimed gases fluoresce.
Soon fire blossoms on the farside, as
A burning glass will sear a paper through.
The ship is moved, the process is repeated,
Until a web of narrow shafts is driven
Throughout the planetoid. Next, sappers drop
Toward the surface in their freight modules
Manhandling with their stubby arms the blunt
Black cylinders of demolition charges;
And these are heavy nuclear munitions
Designed for mining in the asteroids.
The charges set, the shafts tamped shut, the ship
Withdrawn a thousand-some kilometers away,
Ximene waits for the launch window to open.

The ship's computer works in nanoseconds;
Any error here will add up to
A million miles a little later on.
Around the waist of Kali there's a flare
Of unenduring light. And then she's two;
One the reaction mass to drive the other:
Now Chance has got his hammer in his hand.

The account of the trial now resumes, in the form of
excerpts from the testimony for and against the accused.
Various legal, scientific, moral, theological and
philosophical aspects of terraforming are explored. We must
guess the identity of some of the speakers, but they
obviously include members of the Van Riebeck family, Orval
Root, an expert witness from the Audubon Society, a scholar
of medieval law, and an Ecotheist theologian; the voices of
the prosecuting attorney and the attorney for the defense,
Chance's lawyer Giambattista Vico, are also heard. The
Martian forces announce that the ice moon of Saturn, now
named comet Kali, is on a collision course with Earth.
Though in reality aimed at Mars, the comet is seen and
intended to be seen as a veiled threat to gain the release
of the Van Riebeck Enterprises leadership.

Scene iii
The Trial

*W*ords from the trial of Chancellor Van Riebeck:

"If it's against the law," says Charlie Lorenz,
"To use recombinant gene splice techniques
To generate new forms of life, then we
Must punish those who choose the sweetest apple
And save its seed to grow another tree;
Dog-breeders must all go to jail; the bride
Who chose her groom because his face and limbs
Were handsome to her, his mind admirable—
So that she wished, as people say, to bear
This good man's child—must stand condemned with Chance.
All betterment discriminates and cleaves;
The first of any making is a monster . . . "

"The Martian clays were a rich heritage
Of predecessor forms of earthly life.
The Ares Project wrecked their habitat.
We at the Audubon Society
Doubt whether any now can still remain.
Effectively the project has preempted

The natural destiny of a whole world.
Such human arrogance, Lords of Creation
As we thought ourselves to be, was the cause
Of ecocidal holocausts before.
There is no question that this man is guilty—"
"Witness will not editorialize.   25
Does the defence desire to cross-examine?"
"One question. If you saw a crocodile
About to eat a baby, would you shoot it
Or leave it to its natural destiny?"
"Shoot it if one must, one would suppose, but—"
"One would suppose. What if the crocodile
Were an endangered species, would 'one' then?
Be careful how you answer. 'No' makes you
Guilty in thought of an infanticide.
'Yes' says that you still inwardly believe
One human baby worth more than a species . . . "

The prosecuting counsel: "Tell the court
Why, Mr. Wills, you made these monster races
And sold them to be seeded in the world?"
"Objection. Counsel is presuming what—"
"Sustained, but only on the grounds—" Ganesh:
"No, please, Your Eminence, I'll answer that.
Truth is the little buggers made themselves . . . "

"Why do you ask me of my parents' quarrel?
My mother's not on trial; there's fact enough;
Can you believe the impressions of a boy—?"
"Let's leave that to the jury to decide,
Mr. Van Riebeck," the judge counsels him.
"Well then," says Garrison, who has been struck
By the amazing honesty of thought he's found   50
In old Ruhollah's wisdom, and who seeks
In this limpidity the only way
To be redeemed, "I ask that you may see
How love may be a needle and a bludgeon.
My father truly loved my mother" —Here,
Guiltily, he catches Gaea's eye
Across the court, and then avoids it swiftly—
"And she, I think, at first, loved him, but not
So much. He loved her so she had no room

To love him back. He bullied her with love,
With the profusion of his being, his insight
Into the workings of the universe,
Into the workings of her soul. He knew her, as
The Bible says—" And now he sees his father,
Looking upon him with wide open eyes,
As one might at one's god or at one's death,
Calmly, with tears pouring down like a stream.

"... So it is not, as Prosecution says,
Irrelevant to seek the testimony
Of a medieval scholar in this case.
Defence's argument is partly this:
That recent legislation on the use
Of outer space disguises but revives
The ancient jurisprudence governing
The common lands, the heaths and unclaimed forest,   75
The village greens, and public rights of way.
For the wise Locke law was the sum of contracts
Bearing on how the bounty of the world
Might by agreement be divided out;
And Hobbes's chilly scalpel sheared away
The claims that God donates to chosen men
A knowledge of His will regarding nature
And thus a pattern for a natural law:
They were a filmy pretence that the fathers
Had woven to disguise their lust of power.
The prosecution argument, if I
May be permitted to provide coherence
To such a thing of shreds and patches, leans
Heavily upon these recent laws.
But much more fundamental still, if we
May read between the prosecution's lines,
Is an ulterior motive, and it's this:
To reestablish Natural Law as God's
Invisible vice regent in the world.
It is upon this concept that the other
Body of legislation in this case—
That under which my clients were arrested—
Concerning rights of other living species,
The mandate of the EPA, and suchlike,
Is based and built. Now, for our case.   100

Professor Basileus' expert testimony
Shows that the concepts of the commons laws
And those of natural law must contradict.
One assumes ownership by human beings
(Or aliens judged to be legal persons)
Of all estate, movables, thoroughfares,
Spaces and objects in the universe—
In common where an individual's claim
Is not established by a homestead law,
And where in common to be used and kept
To benefit the people as a whole.
The natural law assumes God's ownership
Of all things in the world, or else that each,
Souled or unsouled, equal, owns itself.
This last idea—attractive as it is—
Will not endure a logical appraisal,
For the term ownership can have no meaning
If there is no distinction made between
That which can own and that which can be owned.
Secular Naturalism fell apart
On just this issue; does the cheetah own
The slaughtered wildebeest, or should
The prey be confiscated from the hunter?
If nature may discriminate in value
Then we may naturally be its owners;   125
But if there is no value, and all's equal,
Then there's no value in preserving nature.
Our good friends in the Ecotheist church
Were quick to point this out; the logic's theirs.
What's left is what the prosecution fails
To answer, lest it prejudice its case:
Does God or Humankind possess the world?
If Prosecution wants to make a case
Against my client, it must violate
The deep agenda that the Church assigned it:
The reenthronement of the Natural Law."

And Orval Root: "Chance was a man who charmed,
Who seemed to give his heart to everyone,
But when it came down to the care that friends
Take of the daily process of a friendship,
The time given to schmoozing, so to speak,

The warm complicity in shared complaint,
The deep admission that he is as you,
Partial, self-interested as you are,
Human, and not so grandly just as he would seem—
He wouldn't go along. He would get chilly,
Distressed, businesslike, give you a gift
As if apologizing, and withdraw
Just when you'd showed your failings, weaknesses
To him—you'd trusted him with that, and he   150
Gave everything but what you needed from him.
You'd think he didn't put his pants on one
Leg at a time. You'd think he didn't shit . . . "

"All that Defense can offer to this court
Is flimsy argument, sophistication,
Bending of honest words and honest meanings
Out of their clear intent and common use.
The prosecution offers evidence:
These samples here of deformed animals
And prodigies with leaves and mouths and lungs;
These photographs of what was done on Mars,
Showing the ancient landscape now convulsed
And slobbered over with a noxious slime;
The testimony of those folk who knew them
That the accused were arrogant and cold,
And were intent on global transformations
Unsanctioned by the People's will, the laws
Of nature, and the clear decree of God."

Ganesh again: "About those clays, your highness.
That was one reason I agreed to work
For Charlie when he asked me to. The way
They were, those poor dumb Muddies had no future.
They're columns of stacked films, one atom thick—
Ionized aluminum silicates.
They reproduce by printing off the pattern   175
Of polarized electric fields from top
Of the old stack to the next new slice up.
They were the scaffolding that RNA
Was built on in terrestrial history.
Our living molecules began, my Lord,
As robot organelles or servomech-

Anisms for a bunch of moron clays.
But all the Martian carbon was locked up;
The hydrogen had mostly leaked away;
The oxygen was buried in the ground.
So where the clays would really want to go—
Switch genotype with phenotype, I mean,
And use their new organic body-parts
To carry their inheritance of form—
That way was blocked for them. We opened it.
That's why we started mining in the rings
For bergs to irrigate and fertilize
A symbiotic culture, Earth and Mars.
Sure, when the icebergs hit, they made a bang
You saw down here. But still it did no harm.
The clays would thank us, if they could, your honor.
They took their first breath in four billion years."

Beatrice speaks, her face a mortal moon
Clouded by grief that she might not stand where
Her father and her sister are accused: 200
"Consider choice, which many think is freedom.
Upon the magic island of instruction
A wise wizard discourses of the truth
And moral will, and of the rule of reason.
His daughter in this demi-paradise
Sits at his feet and cannot concentrate.
She is the one who looks out to the sea
And waits for something new, a prince perhaps,
Who'll kneel before her with a ruby slipper
A wicked witch made for her long ago.
I know this court does not want fairy tales.
Let me explain my parable: mere choice
Remains within the universe of discourse
Where it originated; given A
And B, choice must pick B or A.
Suppose A is the better choice, and that
The chooser knows it. Then she is not free:
She's fated logically by the fact
That it is better; or determined psych-
Ologically by whatever impulse, random
Or instinctive, has made her choose the wrong.
If A and B are equal, there's no choice.

The only path of freedom is the choice,
From A and B, of C—which is to say
That freedom is not choosing but creation,   225
The making of a new alternative
Where none before existed, and its rough
Insertion in the bland ensemble of
Existent futures lined up for our choice.
Freedom is not a state but a volcano.
My father never laid out all the choices;
He was a bad magician, if you like,
But a good man. He'd have us disobey him,
Reward us for our disobedience
When it created new coasts for the world.
The future does not yet exist, your honor,
Ladies and gentlemen of this court; we
Are just as at its mercy as we were
When in the act of loving generation
Our parents came together, fools and gods
To make our souls and bodies out of nothing;
Unless we may be parents of ourselves,
For which, it seems, my friends here are on trial."
(Hearing this blasphemy, the warrior,
Tripitaka, finds his breath short and painful,
For the blasphemer's eyes have caught his soul,
Her mouth has made him helpless, as the bee
Is trapped and led by those encrimsoned streaks
That lead into the hot heart of the flower.
That night under Ruhollah's new instruction
He will, amid the savage practice of   250
His deathly art, be flayed and flagellated
By his own right arm, and his rage against
His mother turn to rage against his flesh.)

"The prosecution seems obsessed, your honor,
With one word like a magic talisman:
Evidence. No one here denies the facts.
They're hacking through an unlocked door.
For what is evidence? Consider this.
A man begins to watch and track a woman.
He avoids her when she is with her husband;
He finds out where she lives and follows her;
He ascertains her name and checks her habits;

He seems to seek an opportunity
To get her by herself. Here's evidence
Of dangerous and horrible intent,
The rapist's study of his prey, the stalk,
And now the very moment of the kill . . .
'I found this locket, madam, with your picture
And the picture of a man. Seeing you
That day upon the street as I went down
To hand the property to the police,
And, by your likeness, recognizing you,
I was about to give it back when I
Perceived the gentleman you walked with
Was not the same as this within the picture.   275
I trust you will forgive the lengths I had to go
To be discreet. The gold engraving here
Is very nicely done. Good day, madam.'
I ask this court whether we have before us
One, or two, sets of evidence today.
If one, then we may say that entities
Utterly different can share the signs
Of their empirical manifestation;
If this is so, then evidence is not
To be trusted in any court of law;
No test for truth could rest upon the senses;
The term 'eye-witness' would be meaningless.
Then are these two entirely different sets
Of evidence? What can 'different' mean
If the same facts are different from themselves?
Not one, not more than one. Then what's the answer?
It must be this. The first account, the stalk
Of the rapist, is made of evidence.
The evidence is constituted such
By the intent of rape. The second, though,
Is not so much evidence as the tact
And sensitivity by which the world
Of the evidential may be avoided.
If the Van Riebecks had set out, your honor,
To rape the planet Mars, then what they've done   300
Is indeed evidence of crime. But we
Must look at 'evidence' within the context
Of whole universes of intention,
Hope, expectation, purpose, and desire."

"My husband Chancellor Van Riebeck is,
As many here have stated, a free man.
But should, in this sense, any man be free?
He feels no guilt; all men ought to feel guilt.
What conscience can he have for whom the world
Is all a game, whose loves are undertaken
Out of the goodness of his heart, the joy
Of self-reward, not out of debt or duty?
Is he not ultimately dangerous,
A law unto himself, free, if he feels,
To trample anyone without remorse . . . ?"
At these words Chance, his face pale with attention,
Is almost ready to applaud; he'd have
Her win the argument, bear it away,
So taken is he with her fiery spirit,
Her courage measurable with his own.
"Good girl," he murmurs silently, "Good girl.
No shirking, eh? No giving on the line . . . ?"

"If Root wants therapy," says Freya coldly,
"He should avoid serious enterprises.
A man wants friends about him when he works,   325
Not a warm pink glow of supportiveness.
My father is a man. Therapy is
What Ecotheists take for sacrament.
Let him give up his ancient faith and be
Another suckler at the junk religion."
Two men watch her: Root, who she knows
Desires her love, and patient Charlie Lorenz,
Her dearest friend, who would be more, but this
Freya the white-gold will not ever know.

The great attorney argues with his client:
"Chance, if you do this thing we'll lose the case.
We have it won on legal logic now,
And three jurors won't take the party line.
I know it. They can see the Ecotheists
Have overreached themselves and struck too early.
Even old Markov on the bench has heard
Too much good law to let it go the way
The prosecution wants. What's wrong with Burke
And contracts, if they'll save your legal bacon?"

"Giamba old friend, you've done a glorious job.
You've won the battle for us, I see that.
But there's a war that must be fought, and we
Cannot give up into our enemies' hands
The sword of natural law. There is a law,
I think, that Nature speaks and justifies   350
In us, when we take the great spade of thought
And art and potent action to the garden;
Nature as you implied makes her own values,
Of which the human is executor.
Our enemies must not claim all the prayers
Nor all the mysteries . . . though I myself
Feel a strange weakness come upon me now
When dealing with these matters, as if I
Were not the destined one to make them plain."
"Then do not lose this battle, Chance, whatever
Is the cost. You owe it to that future
Where your predicted prophet may be born
To lead the forces of enlightenment."
"You are persuasive, but, my friend, suppose
That prophet's purposes were better served
By my destruction in the name of Nature?"
"Promise me this at least: you'll think about it.
I've asked for a recess; we'll know tomorrow.
But prosecution won't object. They're panicked
And they need the time. World Court tradition
Gives you some perks: one of them is parole.
Take a vacation. Be a bindlestiff
And wander in Arcadia awhile.
That's what you used to do to clear your mind;
You may feel different when you return."   375

Next morning, an announcement on all channels:
"This is the provisional government
Of Free Mars and the moons of Jupiter.
Last week our mining ship *Kalevala*
Broke out of orbit a Saturnian moon.
By next October, in the northern skies,
The comet Kali, as it has been called,
Will start to show a luminescent tail.
Then a mid-course correction will be made
Diverting it out of its present orbit

(Which intersects with Earth's) so that it falls
To planned collision on the plains of Mars.
This action is a part of Project Ares
And is designed to supplement the gas
Envelope of our birthing planet
In preparation for the higher lifeforms.
The government of Mars humbly requests
That by October the United Nations
Extend full diplomatic recognition
To this our sovereign state and free republic.
In token of good faith we call a truce
And cease-fire in this long and wasteful conflict,
Leading to an exchange of prisoners,
A full negotiated settlement,
And peace in the mansions of humankind."

*During a recess in the trial, Chance walks in Arcadia. Gaea
misinterprets her son's words as giving consent to her plan,
and accordingly sends Tripitaka to assassinate Chance.*

Scene iv
The Fall of Chance

*O*nce I was the master of the puppets
And fruit ripened about my gilded head;
Out of my fingertips the music flowed,
My shoulders shone in heroism's sun.
But now my characters with their fierce selves
Wring me through until I am their servant,
The grizzled artisan of their ambition;
My capable hands are numb with the work.
And though I know indeed that haste makes waste
Still, I may well enough waste not the time;
And though I care but little for my death
The careful making asks more than I have.
And I shall not be saved, unless I'm saved
By playing out my dark part in their play.

We have not come a third of this long journey,
And I fear, I fear, the labor that's to come,
And I fear the necessary encounter
With Gaea in the greatness of her fate,
The greatness of the fury she endures.
Despite her pride, she comes to Garrison,
Her speech unformed, distrait, and without grace.
"It was a lie, Garrison, a sheer lie.
The comet's headed not for us but Mars.
Our people in ballistics have confirmed it
But no one in the public is to know.   25
He's very clever, Garrison. If we
Reveal the fraud, the public thinks we're lying;
Or if they do believe, the Martian rebels
Get such good press we'll have to ask for peace.
It's not as if they've even made a threat;
And each delay puts us more in the wrong.
What do we do now? what is there to do?"

One thing aches now in Gaea's mind—the face
Of Chance her husband in its victory.
If this one man were not to come again
The world might still be safe against the future
And we might all be saved by growing in
To the sweet human fellowship of fault
And shared weakness, which is the truth of being.
But Garrison is thinking other thoughts:
How truth must be revealed at any cost,
How in the end the liar is destroyed
However wise or clever is the lie.
But he is too afraid of Gaea's will
To say what's in his thought; yet now he sees
A light dawn in his mother's face, a pure
Clean honesty he knows he recognizes.
"There's only one thing to be done," she says.
"But it's too much for me to do alone.
You, Garrison, know what I mean. Give me   50
The word, and I shall have the strength to do it."
Garrison takes her in his arms (and feels,
Always surprised, how hot her body is);
And says "Of course that's what we have to do."
But what he means is tell the world the truth;
And what she means is that now Chance must die.

Alpheus before dawn; a swart star slides
On the water; a smell of elderberries,
Distant hayfields, smoke and olive trees;
Dry reeds rattling in the light morning breeze.
Chance in his walking shoes, picking his way
Along the old path Ulysses once took
Raiding for cattle in the Peloponnese;
He feels a sting and stiffness in his breast
Where the bead radio tracer was implanted,
But otherwise he's free. A nightingale
Is winding up its song; a milky light
As fresh as porcelain begins to glow.
Three miles up river there's a shallow ford
Where the flow bubbles over pebblestones
And here he strikes off to the south. The cocks
Are crowing in the farmyards now; upon the ridge
There stands the blazing wheel of Helios

And every shadow is arrayed with dew.
His stout shoes squelching on the fanged basalt   75
He climbs up to the heights of Arcady.
Over the ridges rises up the ghost
Of Erimanthos thirty miles away.
And now the breeze dies down and the great heat
Of the Greek inland lights its glassy fumes;
A heat that concentrates and does not spill
The strength of men, but works a mesmerism.
The clunk of goat-bells spells a sort of drug
That stuns the ear and makes it listen to
The inner sound of the world's cruel joy,
Its heartless reinvention of itself
Despite and through all tragedy and satire;
The silenes, the sly kallikanzaroi,
Can lead the sunburned traveller astray,
Dazed with the heatstroke and the smell of sage,
From all worldly cares to the nereid's caves,
Where those good ladies for a butterfly kiss
Will steal the eyes' motion and the soul of man.

By noon he's come into a waste of hills,
Barren, horizonless, smelling of darkish resins;
Each summit shows a further slope of stones,
Squat black holm-oak, rosemary and thorns.
He feels the loneliness of all last places,
Places with the black shade of dreams mixed in
With their transcendent brightness; like the country   100
Of Death, of all irremediable change;
So that the heart sighs, and sighs once again
With the yearning, the loss, the joy of fate.
But slipping down a dusty water-course
He comes on an abandoned olive-grove,
With a house like a white cube, and another
With a blue door off its hinges, a church
With an almond tree beside it, and a spring.
Here is a great cushion of fresh green grass
Spangled with golden flowers, and a trough
Of limpid water in the semi-shade.
He looks into the darkened barrel-vault:
There a gold mail of haloes blazes over
A crowd of gaunt-eyed saints with oxblood robes

And chasubles of azure, white and green;
Their eyes stare from the blind katholikon,
The domed narthex, the iconostasis.
Chance leaves a sacrifice of cakes and oil
And settles down beside the spring to eat.
First he unwraps a moist clothful of olives
And smooths it out upon a sunny stone.
Then he cracks off a heel of dense grey bread
To soak the oil up; gets out feta cheese,
Crumbling and warm, retrieves the jug of wine
Where it is cooling in the spring, and last   125
He says a prayer to the local Potencies;
A fit collation for the petty gods.
After his meal, he feels a sweet languor
Like a spring fever or convalescence;
And sleeps as happy as a mortal may
Wrenched as we are by spirit's purposes.

Afternoon narcolepsies sometimes lead
To terrors of the soul. Chance wakes in grief
With a dream he cannot remember; the ridge
Whence he came seems drenched with the shade of death.
But now he makes his heart happy, a trick
Peculiar to the Van Riebeck line,
Striking once or twice a generation.
And he's rewarded; at the next high summit
A valley opens to the west, and over
Its shoulder towers an azure vase of ocean
Glazed with the track of the redeeming sun;
A valley full of sound like talk and song—
The chuckle of an irrigation channel
Running with ceaseless swiftness down the ridge.
Chance kneels and cups his hands; so heavy is
The current that he's sprayed at once, and scarcely
Takes a palmful at each sip. What bounty
Is this life, thinks Chance; can I give it back?   150

That evening he has gained the Pyrgos road
And turning east he comes in the clear dusk
To the straw-warm village of Kallithea.
A tiny kafeneion; he must needs
Pass through an arch, across a stucco bridge

Over a street of caged birds, lights, and voices
To a rooftop where he's served under the sky.
A waiter most mournful and witty brings
A shot glass of cold ouzo, and some bread,
A salad of thin yellow sliced tomatoes
Sprinkled with fresh salt, sour wine vinegar,
Pepper and bits of dried oregano.
A lamb stifado follows, like at Easter,
With half an icy bottle of retsina;
Then weeping baklava and thick sweet coffee
And a glass of fierce raki with the waiter.
The stars are shining on the mountaintops
Of Minthe, Likaion, Arcadia;
Chance cannot see his soiled and darkened Mars.

He wakes next morning in a flood of sunlight
Poured through the open shutter of his lodging;
In air like crystal he sees sharp and clear
A hillside still in shadow, juniper,
Dwarf cypress, chaparral; he thinks of Taos.
Voices of children in the morning hum.   175
Far over the rooftops there is a man
In silhouette, looking in his direction;
He turns away at once. But Chance's mood
Has lost its first elation, and his mind,
At breakfast, turns to matters of the trial.
Perhaps the threat of Kali gives him room
To make his little argument in court
And take the mantle of the Natural
From those who, to his thinking, had usurped it.
As he prepares to leave, he suddenly knows
That he is being stalked. He's not surprised;
They'll want to be assured he'll keep his word
And not collude with allies in his case.

But Chance is only half right, for his stalker
Has taken other orders than the spy's,
And Gaea has got back her voice again.
"It's time now, you who are called Tripitaka,
To render up the meaning of your choices,
To yield upon the altar of the will
The uttermost sanctity of a good

Unhonored and most honorable so;
To do a thing the whole world would condemn
And then conceal it, so that punishment
May never expiate the stain of crime,
Nor honesty redeem the filthy burden;   200
To do this thing as the one sacrifice
(All other trials and masteries passed through,
Made good, and therefore unrepeatable,
Therefore unfit for offerance to God,
To the divine that's tired of all deception,
Of every sacrifice of bones and hide,
Of fat or foreskins, rams instead of sons)—
The perfectest oblation, found and free
Of every mortal taint and close reward.
I want this good man's heart, his head upon
A platter, his blood poured out on the earth;
I want it for no purpose of my own
But all to justify the living God
And heal the sores upon Her lovely body,
And purge the affliction from Her Purities
That multiplies there in this last of times,
This testing of the virtue of the world."
And what can Don John do but take the vow,
Given the warring sicknesses he bears,
The callings and the crimes of both his parents,
The saintly genius he took from the womb?

That was two days ago; the pastoral
Of Chance is not yet done, the journey has
—As every moment of this sweet life has—
Infinite byways, easy backwaters,   225
Fractal inscription of the senses' charm
Into the graceful flourishes they make
In their own play upon themselves and in
The world they share with in its fabrication.

An easy walk through vales to Andritsena;
Chance falls asleep that evening in the sway
Of shrill bouzouki tunes, rebetika
By Theodorakis, songs from Athens, sad
Demotika tragoidia from the hills.
It rings in winding chains of love and war,

Statement and counter-statement, and it treats
Of old betrayals, wounded Pallikares.
When all is said and done, he thinks as he
Drifts into dream, it's just a lovers' quarrel,
Just a sad tune projected on the stars.

Next day dawns even hotter than the last.
Chance reckons he can while away the morning
In pleasant temporal commerce in the village
And walk to Vassae in the afternoon—
The goal of this excursion, if it has one—
And see it in the dusk with no one there.
He knows the doctor Iatroyannis, who,
Curator of the temple-grounds, agrees
To furnish for his friend a set of keys.   250
It's market-day. Chance finds a handkerchief
Stitched with dark mulberries, a gift for Gaea,
And at the goldsmith's, something for his Freya
That he knows she wants: a copy of the mask
Of Agamemnon buried at Mycenae.
Pleased and surprised he finds upon a stall
A perfect match for Beatrice's stoneware,
White painted with blue and black, that she served
Tequila in to Charlie weeks ago.
He buys some pieces, has them sent along,
With wood Bucephaluses for the children.
Deciding suddenly that he will stay
The night at Vassae, he gets himself a quilt
Of dull red cotton neatly worked with black,
And shops for wine and bread and good dark cheese;
And navel oranges, honey and yogurt
Made from the creamy milk of nanny-goats:
A breakfast that Chance is not going to need.

An afternoon of blue and beaten gold.
Chance climbs the clear hills in his wide straw hat.
At each turn of the way between the olives
A fresh access of joy comes over him;
He remembers in quickening freshets
Flavors and scents for which there are no names;
The air of Minthe is empyreal
And by a spring he finds a drift of lilies   275

Mysterious as childhood, like a vision.
And now he even watches for his friend,
His follower, and hangs back sometimes so
That he may catch up if he has a mind to.
And where the white road crests, and crests again
In grander and still grander openings
Over ravines so deep their dark is cold,
And the hills' heads dance along the horizon,
And the sun shines as brilliantly as noon
But from the side, and silence is a sigh
Of all things settling into a new way;
There the known stranger catches up with Chance,
Quietly, as if it were no moment,
And they keep pace unspeaking for a while.

Chance is surprised, seeing whom they have sent;
And knows at once that his death is now here.
He had not thought it would be quite so soon;
Admires the cleanness and address they show.
As the sun bleeds over the remote sea
The temple rises up upon the ridge:
Built by Iktinos to the god of light
Apollo Epikouros, succorer
In sickness, now grown about with flowers;
It's seen no sacrifice two thousand years.   300
The place is quite deserted, but for one
Old man with a donkey and a squint eye,
Stained white whiskers and a powdery voice,
Who offers them a primitive reed pipe
Carved on the spot amid the smell of straw,
A smell so pungent it is frightening.
They are surprised; such sights were frequent once,
But the new Greece affords them seldom now.
They buy a flute and leave; but when they reach
The temple entrance and look back, he's gone.
Though roofless, the *adyton* is in darkness.
Strange Ionic columns tower up;
Huge dim spur walls split the sanctuary;
A red blade of sunset sweeps the floor
With two long shadows, indistinguishable
But that the one is left, the other right.
While Tripitaka waits, Chance makes his tour;

The stars come out as if they shot a needle
Through the attenuated fabric of
The day, to sew the bodies of the heroes
Into eternal constellated forms.
By the last light Chance shares the food he's brought
With his quiet young executioner.
Chance talks lightly over dinner of
The Greek mystery; how from that bright noon   325
Of classical achieved perfection in
This life—thought, art, the dance of war, the sharp
And plangent sweetness of their poetry—
They turned away into ages of worship,
Of mysticism and forgetfulness,
Of ikons stylized into fleshless gold,
As if a thousand years of divine dream
Must follow and blot out the memory
Of one age of human excellence;
But how meanwhile another Greece was born:
Of peasant pleasures, wine and pallikares—
For contemplation of eternity
Must turn to innocence, and innocence
Enacted is the body of lived time;
And thus Pythagoras was right to say
The soul must be incarnate once again
After its purifying in the stream.
Just before turning in Chance glances up
At Tripitaka, like a trusting child
At bed time; "Give me your promise you will
Let me live out the night and see the dawn;
I'll be quite happy if I see the dawn."

First light. The two men wake together, look
At each other shyly as they stretch,
Like bride and groom on that first changed morning   350
Of the honeymoon. Chance has had a dream
About the last summer that Rose and he
Dwelt in the house of Devereux before
They separated—though they did not know it
At the time, forever. The children were
Grown up, and traveling, or working now
Out in the plains of Mars, and could not break

The perfect intimacy of a dying marriage.
And it was infinitely sweet; adulteries
Of feeling, freedoms opening to worlds
Of grief, and loss, and new manners of being.
They picnicked grandly by the Evenlode,
Silver, champagne, white linen, lovemaking
Where she was muslin and Chanel, and he
Was gallantry and stallions, as tireless as
The trunked elephant, tender as swansdown.
But this was all at last a violation of
Her being, a penetration to her inner soul,
A crime, a crime worse than a rape, a taking
By the achieved triumph of the will
Of the last citadel of female dream.
The very perfectness of difference
Between the man and woman was the blade
That severed their connection, and they knew it.
Rose could not keep her Chance and save her soul. 375

And now in earnest the two men must decide
How this thing is to be done; amateurs
Of such an act, as any man must be
Who steps upon a new planet of the soul
And sets out on an act that must transfigure
And translate the personality of
Him who acts, unrecognizable
To him before who contemplated action;
A metamorphosis into a new
Species, with terrifying organs formed
For purposes unknown to their possessor.
Like two boys trying homosexuality
They catch each other's eye and, sheepish, smile,
Get serious. "Well, how's it done?" asks Chance.
The sky is turquoise. Mountains float like veils
Of black silk southeast towards Lacedaemon.
Chance is a strong man. He attacks at once,
Gets in one blow. But Tripitaka spins;
His left heel smashes Chance's knee, his elbow
Crushes the ribcage, and Chance coughs up blood.
Horribly clumsy work. The rising sun
Strikes on the altar. Chance struggles up, smiles,

For after all he is there in the world
As happy as he always was; attacks again.
Then Tripitaka breaks his neck and throws
His body down the dewy chasm of night.

*It is two years later, at the delayed funeral of Chance on
Mars, where he has asked to be buried. We learn of the
death of Freya, whether by suicide or at the hands of her
guards, and of the Concordat of Taos whereby the rebels
gained their independence. Comet Kali falls upon the plains
of Mars, providing heat, water, and gas for the planet in
its transformation by higher and higher forms of life.
Charlie Lorenz, Freya's widower, courts Freya's sister
Beatrice, and Hillel Sharon, general of the Martian forces,
courts both Ximene and Marisol.*

Scene v
The Death of the Comet

*B*utterfly's wing: the name the spacemen give
To this new terrain of the northern plains
Where gently undulating country glows
With the soft fire of a thousand pigments.
Here the next stage of ecogenesis
Has reached its climax in a magic carpet
Of golden furs and powdery crimsons,
Spore-yellows, saturated browns and blues,
Purples shot with greens, and fleshy pinks,
Open mild glitterings of slimes and foams:
The saprophytes that feed on defunct germs,
Funguses, orchidoids, mycetozoa,
Slime molds with delicate sporangia
Like little lampshades, phalluses, or combs,
Formed from the mobile eggwhite of that mass
Of naked zygotes called plasmodium;
Yeasts in their glorious and rancid forms;
The air softened with spores and protoplasts.
No breathing yet; for Ganesh Wills has drawn
Their metabolic plan as anaerobes
Though now already there are swathes of ruin
Where richer belts of oxygen have burnt
The tender membranes and the naked tissue
Of organisms not inured or bred
To that strong caustic and hard stimulant.   25
The cortege has come out a mile or more—

Perhaps a hundred men and women, each
With a black band about the shoulder armor
Of their space suits; a pair of smaller figures
Who must be children, in the honored place,
Hand in hand behind the pallbearers.
The two refrigerated caskets ride
At the vanguard, draped with the flag of Mars—
A crimson snake in style reminiscent
Of the pennon of the thirteen colonies
(Don't Tread On Me), but standing on its tail
Coiled in an open helix, with a ruff
Of wings at its neck, on a field of green.
Over each flag is laid a body band
In black, marked with the sigil VRE.
Above them in the hazy evening sky
Streams a huge portent, like a flaming ghost:
The comet Kali, in its final fall
Upon the many-colored fields of Mars.

And so to interpose a little ease.
What story shall I tell about this puzzle,
This other casket, borne along with Chance?
There was the coverup, of course; the clerk
Of court suborned, no record of parole,
Councillor Vico's testimony void;   50
The doctor's electronic tag a myth;
The prisoner's attempted getaway;
The honest guard's pursuit; the last attempt
By Chance that morning on the mountainside
To slip his captor, and his fatal stumble.
Consider Tripitaka, who must now,
The first time in his life, embrace a lie;
And who knows what amazement of blood guilt
That Garrison must know when he remembers
How his permission had empowered Gaea's;
And as for her, a sudden recollection
Of sweetest love along the river Glyme
As if this sacrifice had set the old Rose free.
But still I temporize and put it off.
Let it be my responsibility
To knock and enter Freya's prison cell
And tell her of her father. Chance to me

Has come to be the purpose of this story
And it's a dull place without him; if his fire
Survive in Freya, let her walk the road
That some have travelled to that other country
And call him back to us, to take the wheel
Again, and laugh, as we remember him.

And so her face, as pale as death, turns down
That darkened grove where the birds do not sing;   75
Her fury passes all the gates as if
She held the bough and honeycomb and lyre
Of passport and safe conduct in that place;
But Freya's hands are empty as are all
Who'd drink in purity the elixir
Of cold communion with the vanished dead.
And that whole country is in truth deserted;
No schools of spirits flock like autumn leaves;
Picture a funpark in the winter, or
The cellars of a bombed and sodden ruin.
As she thrusts on into the dark, the cave
Shrinks to a funnel, like the painted streets
Of the perspective theater, a daub
Of plaster-dust that, to the audience,
Appears a tall Palladian thoroughfare
That might if followed to the vanishing point
Take us beyond the city wall to fields,
And hills, and an arcadian summer sky.

But Freya finds him in the end; he's thrown
Like a bundle of old clothes in a corner,
His arms about his knees, almost asleep.
"Chance my old love, my daddy-prince, my best
Boss, my gallant general, come back to us;
Why do you hide your head and turn away?"
She takes him by the shoulder and would kiss
His bloodstained hair; a moment then as if   100
He recognizes her and smiles a little
In forgetfulness, a child in a dream;
His cheek works as he might be now about
To speak, but nothing comes, and that intent
But distant look, that strange preoccupation
Falls again, and Freya almost angry

Shakes her dead father like a spoiled child.
Slowly, and mutedly compared to him
Who sent his ships across the fells of space,
Chance starts to speak. "Look for me there, my love.
Back where the dawn is coming, where my eyes
Are growing in the head of spring. My voice
Is almost gone already. It's the children
Calling me. All that were here have heard
And have departed for the world, or else
They never were. It's hard to speak. We are
The corner of the present you may turn
At any time, and be in paradise."
With this he falls asleep; do what she may,
Freya cannot arouse him any more.

But when at last she stands and takes her leave
She finds no landmark and no blaze to show
The way she came. No clue or chart is here
Permitted, and no poet has power to guide.   125
After a little while she understands;
There is no coming back from where she is.
Nor can she find her father's waiting-place;
But not unhappy, for she feels the change,
That gift of all she is into the world,
Not, for a woman, so unlike the melting
Of the breast into the baby's soft gums,
That last negation of all negatives,
The waking to the freedom of the world,
The settlement upon the edge of spring
Where the new moment finds its genesis.

But if I tell this story, it's forbidden
To reveal another tale: what was the truth
Of what the jailors and the councillors
Discovered in the morning in her cell:
The body dangling, the knotted belt,
The black tongue, and the green and open eyes.
Those of the party of the colonists
Said that the UN guards had murdered her
On Gaea's orders, to complete the work;
The inquest though returned a clear verdict:

Suicide while of unbalanced mind.
Freya returns to Mars now with her father.

This was not all. Another morning dawned
With the empyreal brightness of the summer   150
Turning into fall, in Greece, a land
That's seen such happenings before, and scorns
To dim her daybreaks for the tears of men;
And a scared steward found upon its bed
The body, swollen out of recognition,
Self-poisoned, of the traitor Orval Root.
For he had kept his faith to Chance's daughter
And followed her beyond the world of lies.

But still the funeral proceeds, the music
Of the band rings tinnily in the earphones,
Playing an old march, Chance's favorite,
A sad bullfighter's dirge from Mexico;
And there ahead a scaffold is set up
Just at the projected point of impact
Of comet Kali, blazing overhead
A portent and a glory from a dream.
The cortege halts; the caskets are manhandled
Up to the apex of the pyramid.
About the scaffold stand the conquistadors:
Beatrice white-faced, her eyes like coals;
Charlie by her, and the twins, Wolf and Irene;
Ganesh with big tears running down his face;
Sumikami carried by two strong men
(All these released according to provisions
The Taos Concordat framed in 'thirty-four');   175
Commander de Vivar; her rebel daughter
Marisol, relieved of her command,
Elected to the planetary council
Upon the ticket of the pacifists;
Hillel Sharon, with his guerrilla's slouch;
And many others of the freedom forces,
Space men and women, farmers, engineers,
Members of council, artists, gardeners.

Now follows on the office of the dead:

In a moment, in the twinkling of an eye/
To put on bodies incorruptible/
Et lux perpetua/ in die illa/
Tuba mirum spargens sonum/ teste
David cum Sibylla/ confutatis/
Flammis acribus addictis/ quasi
Cinis/ lacrymosa/ dona eis
Requiem, aeternam requiem.
We shall be changed we shall be changed we shall.

But now they must make haste, because already
Winds are blowing, full of spores, over
The glowing and grotesque domains of Mars,
And little earthquakes make the footing awkward;
The comet minutely enlarges, and the klaxons
Wail as apocalypse from dome and tower.
Across the planet the last prep teams   200
Embark on shuttles and escape to orbit;
Others upon the far side of the globe,
Scared volunteers, descend to hardened bunkers,
Ready to monitor the banks of sensors
Designed to tell if Kali's a success.
Eleven hours to cometstrike. No garden
Ever in the history of the world
(Unless old Terra in the fiery days
Of coalescence when the stars were young
Might be called garden without gardener)
Stood to receive such watering as this,
Such fiery fertilizer, ash or sulphur,
Scattered by the careful human hand.

The funeral party hurries for the ships;
Each in her own way says farewell to Chance
And takes her place and buckles herself in.
Beatrice feels his spirit heavy in
Her bones, as if a host organism
Grew along the pathways of the body,
Sprouted like vines or ivy in the brain.
The fairy Virgin-mother in her—veiled
Until now, mourning like a votary
Over a wounded god, or like a princess
Wooed, betrayed, abandoned on an island—

Seems to wake now after these two years' mourning   225
And feel the shroud discumbered from her face,
And open up her eyes to see sweet Life
Take her by the hand and call to her
To come, come away from the land of shadow.
Her eyes are full of tears, but focus now
Upon the passenger beside her, who
In her brown study she had not observed.
It's Charlie; he is holding her white hand,
And smiling gravely in her face, and now
All her affection for this dear old friend
Has given way to a new recognition.

But Freya's ghost will not be exorcised.
Wolf and Irene sit by Sumikami
Who, with her toils and grief, has gone to sleep.
Serious beyond the time of children
These twins unweeping lay on hands and swear
To catch and kill their wicked grandmother
And make their uncle pay too with his life
For Chance and for their mother's name and honor.
Only by this can their abandonment
Be rendered fitting, as a sacred debt.
And Tripitaka, as the agent, must,
Their fierce grey eyes agree, pay too.

As for Ganesh, this journey is his first
Beyond the confines of his native planet,   250
And from the time when, as a child, he'd build
Elaborate models of old-fashioned tanks
And blow them up with home-made gelignite,
He loved the crisp techniques of planned destruction;
So cometstrike cannot arrive too soon.
He watches from the port the groaning planet,
The haired portent, its wild and boreal tail
Twisted by Mars's weak magnetic field;
His grief forgot, the sole annoyance now
Is that his uncle Charlie is concerned
With Beatrice, and will not watch with him.

On Phobos a provisional headquarters
Has been set up for the Mars colonists.

Here they will watch the strike and celebrate
Both wake and fiery baptism together.
Now zero hour approaches and they gather
Before the viewscreens in the control tower.
The planet's face below is veiled with dust
That coils and spirals under layers of air
Unturbid still, so that the globe hangs there
Like a great crystal ball against the heavens.
As Kali clears the limb for the last time
They see its ragged tail turned inside out;
Now with the tidal stress and the first wisps
Of atmosphere, rendered as hard as glass   275
By relative velocity, the comet
Spalls and disintegrates, its volatiles
Like the aurora, fluorescing wildly;
Its fragments, incandescent now, leave trails
Eccentric as the tracks of particles
Within the cloud or bubble chamber; some
Skip like a slate on water and fly off;
Others burn up, and others find their mark
And in white beacons strike the planet's surface.
The head, meanwhile, has boiled into a sun
Of utterly unbearable luminance;
The screens go dark to compensate; a globe
Of radiance, a brief new hemisphere
Superimposed upon the planet's hull
Has sprung to being, as the blaze of insight
Bulges upon the cortex like a dream.
A mushroom grows within this troubled marble
(Silent up here upon the studio
Of void), and now beneath it, through the smoke
They see a white plate spread, of molten stone,
Its lip an instant's mountain ten miles high,
Which as it grows fades into cherry-red,
Crimson, maroon; then dies, to leave a ring
Within a torn ring of fantastic hills
Above a wakened core. A shock-wave swifter
Still has like a thunderclap gone out   300
Across the world; thinning toward the gross
Diameter and gathering force again
Like a sea-wave within a jetty's funnel
It closes to the point-antipodes

Of its original and bounces back,
Collapsing on return the tree of cloud
That towers over Chance's, Freya's, graves.
Now the new gases of the planetoid
Burst into flame with Mars's native air;
A firestorm rages round the globe, as blue
As hydrogen balloons set on a flare;
The funguses, which briefly ruled this world,
Burn to a fertile ash; a great cloud forms;
Last, out of skies as black as Noah's flood
Falls the first rain that Mars has ever known.

The planetside observers pass this news
In various wavery channels from their caves;
And in the room an old time Houston cheer
Goes up, as techies push away their screens
And set about the delicate procedure
Of popping and of drinking good champagne
Under extreme low gravity conditions.
And so the wake begins; for Chance's dust
Mingled with Freya's is a fallout now
Upon a soil ready at last for planting   325
With the green loveliness that is the breast
Of all the animals, not least ourselves.
The quality of mercy is not strained;
It droppeth as the gentle rain from heaven.

Now I must tell a thing that may give scandal:
The ways of men and women can be strange.
The party is possessed—as the wine flows
And old friends look into each others' faces
And see the freedom there, the undimmed fire
Of passionate intentions, and the riddle
Of the spirit's unpredictability—
With the sharp rut of wanton aphrodite.
They've been campaigning long, these pioneers;
Their bodies, scarred with their endeavors, burn
Too with the youth that unbent hope and strife
And victory can give, and with pure grief,
When tears have carried all the poisons off
And left the mind's shore clean as tidal sand.
Hilly Sharon and Marisol have quarreled

Over the use of force in planetmaking.
The quarrel turns to laughter by and by,
For Hilly is a raconteur and tells
His favorite war story on himself,
How in the Marineris swamp campaign
His suit got fouled and would not circulate   350
The body liquids, and he nearly drowned
In urine, all alone among the Eeks;
How he surrendered to them, and their faces
When he had cracked the seals of his suit;
And how he got away by playing dead.
Hilly has brown eyes and a tan upon
His cheeks, where the sun visor does not cast
Its shadow; he is small, and Marisol
Is an inch taller, with her willowy waist
And beautiful long hands and slender feet.
Sex in her stateroom in near-zero grav
Is like the hot collision of two planets;
And later, drunk, the guerrilla general
Loses his way and falls asleep, afloat
Upon the floor of Ximene's room as if
He were a half-leaked hydrogen balloon
Left over from a children's party; where
Ximene, who'd always fancied him, is pleased
To find him later, and misunderstanding
His intent, seduces him gorgeously
That night, as naked as a seal, and twice.
Ganesh has found a pretty programmer
Who has admired his work and does not mind
The shyness of the gangly teenager.
Saddest of all to tell, Charlie and Bea,   375
After they've read a story to the twins
And tucked them up in bed, and the old nurse
Sumikami's settled down to sleep,
As is her habit, tied down like a bale
Of silk—after the last drink and the last
Retelling of an old joke Chance once told,
Charlie and Bea feel in their chests the tightness,
The sweet trickle of liquid fire, the smile
So lovely that the breath must fail, of love,
Of that renewing of the world that makes
It unpredictable by any instrument

But its own course and outcome in itself.
Out of this moment then, this node of time,
There springs the origin of many stories,
Which, if we follow them, will bring that prophet
To the world whose voice may still redeem
Our moiety of it from spirit-death.
Charlie's brown hands and capable shoulders,
His muscled knees and quick teutonic grin
Pay worship to this virgin of the full
Bosom, the small shriek of her deepening laugh,
The white flesh and the mounds of bright black hair.
Sometimes the world pays up for its long waiting,
Its thwarted fall through the ages; sometimes
We come up bump on the sweet belly of things.

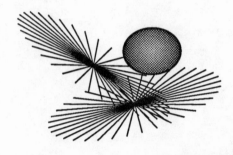

ACT III
The Mutiny of the Gladiators

Meanwhile Garrison has sought the fleshly love of Tripitaka
and has been rejected; and because of an encounter with a
Greek girl Tripitaka has realized that he is in love with
Beatrice.

Scene i
Tripitaka and Garrison

*F*or many days after the death of Chance
The warrior Tripitaka has been still;
Except when prompted by the court inquiry
Or called upon by Garrison to tell
What his instructions were, and whence, and how
His father died. It seems to Tripitaka
That he lives in a country far from home,
And the weather alters, bringing a chill
More like an autumn than the end of summer
In the Peloponnese, and days of rain.
His practice in the martial arts forgone,
That former energy has turned to dreaming;
He dreams of the failed priest his father, of
The girl who would not have him in his sickness,
Of the sweet sleep he slept when in the hands
Of Chance's doctors he was healed and tainted;
And then he dreams of Beatrice again,
And Beatrice each night comes to his side
Dressed in a white garment like a shroud,
His sabbath-bride, his symbol of election.
But sometimes Beatrice has the face of one
He knows so intimately, cannot place,
Perhaps the family image of Kwannon
That blessed the Geisha house where he was left
When Sumikami worked to earn their living.   25
At first this way of life is not unpleasant,
Though it feels as if he'd forgotten something,
Something important which should have been done,
Or it's as if an illness like consumption
Buoys up his spirit as it wastes his flesh;
But later, as his tour of duty drags,
And the comet shows in the evening sky,

As treaty terms are hammered out, and last,
The three remaining rebels leave for Taos,
A dreadful anguished languor comes on him.

Garrison hardly sleeps at all. He seeks
Out Tripitaka all the time, but gets
But little comfort there. He pays a visit
On Ruhollah, who is in high good humor
At his trial's progress, and hears his words;
The drug merchant whispers thin and fine
About the freedom that they know who act
Without the reference of myth and code;
For all such furrows in the soil of will
Must canalize the pure ichor of
Uncaused intention into tyranny.
For Garrison, whose furies have begun
To sing their woven and long song of scream,
The Chiffre, the ineffable zero,
Seems to make all at one and calm his soul.   50

The officer of Tripitaka's guard,
Meanwhile, has noticed that his finest soldier
Has something on his mind. He gives him leave
To visit Athens, tells him to relax
And find a bit of female company.
So now the warrior wanders in the town
Of Theseus and Alcibiades
And sees the hilltop where the sun lingered
On the night of the death of Socrates.
The city, like most cities of the world
These days, is oddly quiet and dim. The Church
With its injunction of humility,
Its invocation of that latent force
In men and women, to discount themselves
And be the parents' child, or curl up dead
Before the predator, or be an egg,
Has left its print on every part of life.
The old religions, golden Orthodoxy,
Crimson Catholicism, splendid Jewry
With its blacks and fires, even white Islam,
Subdue themselves to mediocracy.
And those whose wishes are so fierce that they

Refuse to take the proffer of a life
Lived in the comfort of the second-rate
Have the recourse of Penth the noble drug   75
That makes us perfect in the bonds of joy.

That year (to take up the historic mode)
Marked the inflection of our global culture
Into the Ecotheist dominance.
The Californian baroque that we
Celebrated not many months ago
Was now already waning, as the laws
Forbidding useless decoration in
Such things as housing, transportation, clothes
Soberly took effect upon the culture.
Today the fashion in the scholar caste—
A mere shadow of its former self—
Is demographics, whose statistical
Explanatory power seems absolute;
And we may use this method to describe
The changes in the cities of the world.
From eighteen fifty until twenty ten
We saw the Tertian Step, that octuple
Growth in the population of the world—
One to eight billion—and its leveling off
Shortly thereafter to a new plateau.
The sigma curve we use now to describe
The Step is perfectly symmetrical.
The curve's components are a fevered swell
Of children and starvation at the start,   100
A middle period of youth and wars,
And at the end a time of elder calm
(The young a tame reserve among the old).
And the wars, the pogroms of the century,
The killing fields, the passions of belief,
Had purged the human genotype of much
That might have made for the remarkable
In men and women. We must see our own
Van Riebecks and our Sumikamis as
Survivors of the bloody human spirit
In an age when the tired race wished to rest;
Who could not live within a finished world,
And would not buy a heaven with the drug,

Nor drug themselves with Ecotheism;
Who chose the venture and the crazy hazard:
The transformation in the fields of Mars.

But these remarks break the historian's rule
Of objectivity and balanced judgment.
It was the noblest dream of humankind
To live in peace and balance with our world;
To put away starvation and disease,
And make a decent life for all the people.
Chance and his enterprises threatened all
That we'd achieved in human happiness,
If happiness may be relief from pain,   125
Relief from the long pain of incompletion,
From any gap between the is and ought.
How sweet is the calm of uncompetition!
The balm of endless defeat, how gentle!

With Tripitaka gone, Garrison turns
A little mad. Like medicines that mock
Their patient by the briefness of their respite
From the pain, the counsel of Ruhollah
Deadens the raw place only so that ulcers
May thicken there to torture him again.
The drug merchant, meanwhile, is losing interest
In this glum gangling troubled acolyte,
And, sensing victory, makes plans to leave.
For now the World Court prosecution's case
Is fast unraveling before the logic
Of the young Ecotheist lawyers whom
Ruhollah has recruited for his cause;
The drug, they say, is purely natural;
The drug sets right what culture has made wrong;
The drug produces the external signs
That Ecotheism requires of us:
Humility, contentment, tolerance
Of others in like state, a wise acceptance
Of the world, a high threshold of boredom;
And chemists testify how dopamine   150
Receptor sites decrease in number
In the brain with long use of the drug,

And serotonin levels rise, and androgens
Diminish, and adrenalin decays.
This is the end of steroid poisoning;
Most cancer rates must fall; the brutal male
Of sperm and blood is rendered mild and good;
The woman knows no grief and cramp and rage
When the dark time of the month comes around;
The lifespan of the user is enlarged.
Some days later Ruhollah is set free.

Garrison seems an addict of the drug;
But something in him that must love his pain,
Or fear his happiness, turns him away.
His mind in any case is quite confused;
One night he goes into his mother's room,
Watches her breathing, as he's done before;
But this time he is drawn up closer still
To where he sees in veins upon her neck
Beat, undiminished, her vitality;
And as a child will gingerly enfold
A kitten with its hand, he lets his hands
Pass round her throat in loving symbiosis
So that like kneading bread or fondling
That which requires release to take its fill   175
He might thus purge his appetites in hers
And set the balance of the world aright.

But just as he's about to squeeze, she wakes;
Not in alarm, but as a dream had ended
Where it should, leaving the dreamer free
To swim up briefly to the realm of light.
Her blue eyes open like a girl's, she stares
Without comprehension into his face;
She has become quite happy now, he sees,
An innocent, a valuable statesman
For the cause of all the weak and the poor,
A symbol standing for the natural.
Instead of what he was about to do,
He therefore kisses her and lets her go;
She falls again to sleep; his spirit is
At last defeated utterly by hers.

And Tripitaka wanders through the city
Seeking he knows not what. In a café
A girl, a groupie of the Games, comes up;
She recognizes him from video.
In Athens, quite unlike those country districts
Chance chose for his last draught of life, such ease
And licence of address have gotten common;
Now it has further implications, in the style
Of a sincere religious intimacy,   200
Affected by the Ecotheists, who
Assume all persons equal in the sight
Of God, and thus all differences between
One and another to be signs of pride;
They therefore somewhat hector you with smiles,
And take your arm, ignoring the details
Of what one's choice of company might be.
So Tripitaka hides behind the show
Of military blankness of expression;
But finds to his surprise he likes the girl.
And adolescence, thank the lord, has not
Yet lost its yen to be at least outrageous;
Yanni—she calls herself—plucks up her courage
And really tries as best she can to get
This young man who would terrify her parents
To make a woman of her. Tripitaka,
Infinitely tender, must explain
The sickness for the second time to one
Whose life must not be injured by it; though
The doctors tell him any risk is slight.
But unlike Sachiko, this Yanni is
Not thus so easily put off; "You seem
To be so sad, for such a famous man,"
She says; "It's something I can do for you,
To smooth away your pain. I'll take the risk."   225
And Tripitaka's generosity
Is such that at these words he feels a shock
Of hot desire almost forgotten, so
He need not lie; she knows he is not lying
When he then tells her how he wants her, but
How it would shatter him to be the one
To soil her body with his old disease.
"But there are other ways," she says, as if

She knew of such sophistications; he
Knows he's on safe ground with her ignorance
And can invent a danger that's not there.
But in his hotel room that night alone,
Having with courtly gentleness sent home
This totally surprising seductress
Rightly convinced that she has conquered him,
He finds a certain spring of feeling flow
As if some obstacle has been removed;
And now he longs and pines with love's sour honey
For Beatrice van Riebeck, as before;
And this time strangely there is no resistance,
No stubborn censor of his thoughts and pain.
He knows now he must serve that Beatrice
As a crusader served a lady; or
Must be undone by her as justice would.
And is not chivalry the finer when   250
Quite out of date and inappropriate,
And under moral censure, it still flowers
Out of the spirit like a sport or freak
Of something ancient, guilty, beautiful?—
Something out of the priesthood of our Adam,
The antique dumbness of a beaten sword?

Garrison waits for Tripitaka's coming
As if this were the only chance that's left
To form his life into the shape of truth.
But though he watches the arrivals closely,
He somehow misses his return, and must
Be surprised next morning by his presence.
The weather has renewed the heats of summer;
The guards make it a practice every dawn
To bathe in the Alpheus where a sandbank
Dams up the current in a long blue pool.
Garrison goes there sometimes just to watch—
He loves their naked carelessness and play—
But does not join them; he is not invited.
This time there is a piebald body in
The company of bathers. Garrison's
Heart leaps, recognizing Tripitaka,
And now a strange confusion overcomes him;
Almost too shy to walk back with his friend

As Tripitaka dries off with his towel,   275
He tags along, not the assured zealot
Any more, but a boy sick with desires
He does not understand. But Tripitaka,
Renewed in spirit, and here with the brother
Of his pale beloved, not yet aware
That contradictions heavy as the world
Must now attend his actions, eagerly
Questions Garrison about the progress
Of the Taos talks, and of the plans
Of the Van Riebeck rebels afterwards.
"We have to set them free," says Garrison,
"That will be in the treaty certainly.
It means for now we've lost. But when the comet—"
He gestures at the smudge of white that glows
Low in the western sky against the dawn—
"Has safely struck on Mars, we'll try again."
Garrison speaks unthinkingly, and then
On impulse asks his friend to join him
On his secluded terrace for some breakfast.
Once there, to the surprise of Tripitaka,
Garrison starts to weep, and tells how he
Had wandered in the desert of despair,
How he had even contemplated murder
And thus how suicide seemed sweet and good
In this blind alley of the lonely world.   300
"But what about our faith?" asks Tripitaka;
"Have you forgotten what we did it for?"
Ten days before, this conversation might
Have ended otherwise, for then the younger
Was cast down with a dread not different
By much, from what his older friend feels now.
But Garrison perceives the change that's come
On Tripitaka as a sign that he
Is qualified to punish him and thus
To purge the guilt he can no longer bear.
He kneels down to his friend, and now, before
Either knows what is happening, has parted
The bathing towel and has sunk his face
In penance, adoration, and desire
Into the loins of the warrior,
With their soft flocculence of grey affliction.

Gently, as if he were a patient doctor
Lifting a flap of torn flesh from a wound,
Or like a mother with a fevered child,
Tripitaka raises the long head
Of Garrison from where it lies between
His thighs, and sets it to one side, and stands,
Turning to tie the towel back again.
He looks at Garrison and pities him;
A child whose father has molested her   325
Can sometimes feel such pity with her fear,
But Tripitaka only fears the future,
Void as it lies now of any bar or screen
To set before the knowledge of his crime.
"Oh Garrison," he says, so softly that
His friend can scarcely hear, or understand;
"I see now I have killed an innocent man.
May God have mercy on our souls." With this
He leaves the terrace; Garrison looks up,
And breathes in tremulously, feels a clump
Of fleshly sorrow rise around his heart
That must escape as a great arid sob.

And what's my purpose with these puppetries?
Psychology's a clean whore, plausible
To the sophisticated trade, and turns
A dozen tricks a day. How have my heroes
Come to this place?—where settled principle,
Coherence of intention and idea,
The cosmos balanced with the acting soul,
Imagination like a demigod
Building, from what materials a life
With all its limitations self-imposed
Or else contingent will supply, a meaning—
Where all these things are made subordinate
To the trite buttons of a threadbare motive?   350
Better the hypocrite, the moralist,
The foolish martinet, the tragic gargoyle,
Than we the suave and slimy tolerators
Of human weakness, by whose smooth excuse
The human beast divine is novelized.
And Tripitaka, who is named for one

Who kept a faith and carried through the mountains
Scriptures that have lived two thousand years,
Now feels the sullen glory of his name
Call him again to chivalry and death,
And will not let his disillusionment
With his friend Garrison divert his purpose.
He will escape all our interpretation;
He will defy verisimilitude
Bought by conformity to expectation;
He will drag us, whose notions are enmired
In cliches from the twentieth century,
"Kicking and screaming" into an ancient world.

Garrison strikes a certain contract too.
After his erstwhile friend has left, he falls
Into a great calm, like paralysis;
He recognizes what he is, a cripple,
Bound for a certain time to walk the earth;
He shall take on the robe of parricide,
Blinding himself in punishment and pride,   375
And so possess those goods for which a crime
Such as this is might be committed—freedoms
Such as shall fit a very scourge of God.

A few days later orders long expected
Arrive for Tripitaka, which will send
Him back to Flinders Dome for three more weeks
Of training for the next Olympic War.
The old dispute between Australia
And Indonesia over Irian Jaya
(The western territory of New Guinea)
Has broken out once more. The mountain tribes
Now rise again to claim their independence
From Jakarta; their cousins in Papua
Begin to send them arms; the Ecotheists,
Neutral in this conflict, see a chance
To take the world's attention from the stain
Of the humiliating treaty signed
At Taos; the Javan paramilitary
Stands at the Papuan frontier, and so
The UN has declared a state of war.
Thailand, Malaysia, and New Zealand, bound

By friendship pacts, line up with Papua
And Canberra, but still the conflict seems
Unequal by the strict Olympic code.
So Tripitaka leaves, without farewells.

*Tripitaka goes to war against the enemies of Australia in
the Olympiad; the poem follows the course of the war, and
the revolt of the warriors against the Ecotheist world
order. Tripitaka escapes with some of them and joins the
Martian forces, in an attempt to expiate the murder of his
benefactor Chance.*

Scene ii
The Olympic War

The protocols of the Olympic charter
Permit for each million of population
A state to field one soldier in the wars.
Now Tripitaka comes, in time to see
The muster of the allies: first, the Aussies,
In their lopsided hats and khaki shorts,
Eighteen men and eighteen women (marching,
Brown rangy Sheilas from the women's camp,
Including Tripitaka's friend the sergeant),
Finely equipped with microcircuitry
And lightweight life-support, and fancy optics;
Next, the Malaysians, thirty-eight of them,
Trained like the Aussies in the Brit tradition,
With chequered caps and ceremonial kris;
Then the large body of the Thais, an army
Numbering a hundred forty-one,
And boasting in their ranks two kick-boxers
Of most advanced degree, and sharpshooters
Expert in the zen arts of archery;
Then seven grinning "sheppoes" from New Zealand
With their sophisticated jamming gear;
And last, the nine dark Papuans, whose eyes
Glow like a woodfire under beetle brows,
Some of the canniest and fiercest soldiers
In the world, aficionados say.   25
They line up in parade, and silence falls;
The head count is two hundred thirty-one.
Forty miles off, the Indonesian force
Stands at attention by their simple flag
Of red and white: three hundred twenty-nine.

And now begins the toughest phase of training,
The tuning of the flesh to perfect pitch,
The melding of the forces into one,
The matching of the men and women to
The tiny powerful machines of war.
According to Olympic rules each army may
Take into battle just as much equipment,
Weapons, and supplies as it can carry,
Lighter-than-air devices banned for freight,
And nuclear weapons totally forbidden.
All other portable materiel
Being permitted, every army has
A group of weightlifters whose duty is
To carry in one trip across the mile
Of DMZ around the reservation
Those largest instruments of modern war:
The lightweight observation planes and strafers;
The tractor-bikes, recoilless guns, and radars;
The water-stills and workshops, hospitals,
And raw materials and tools to stock   50
The mobile factories that they will build.
Whole libraries exist of books and tapes
Of theory and advanced mathematics on
The parsimony, packing, scheduling,
And gaming calculus of those old wars;
Boys in those days played endless battle-games
On home computers with illegal turbos
To replicate Olympic strategies.

The battleground, ten thousand square miles
In the center of Australia, is not
A hospitable place for humankind.
Desert and scrub, the mallee and the wattle,
Gaunt-limbed ghost gum smelling of oil of camphor,
Coarse grass, stony gibber desert, dry lakes
With rims of bitter salts and sweetheart's names;
Eroded outcrops of fantastic stone;
Balancing rocks and places where the wind,
As hot as ovens, whistles in a crevice;
Sometimes a hopping mirage from a nightmare
Of the Pleistocene, a mob of 'roos;
Domes of rabbits; lorikeets, cockatoos.

Under the sun the colors burn to tan,
To dull brass albedo and brilliant grey,
Crimson and ocher of the bloodbark; sometimes
After a rain a carpet of blue lupins   75
As sweet as dawn, or cannas of vermilion
So tender that red seems the softest tint.
Always the smell of silicates and soda,
Rocks split by the heat or the night chill,
Wind over coarse grass dried out in the sun.

It's reckoned that the Indonesians hold
The military balance of advantage;
They are well trained, and will be heavily armed;
Their force is larger, and, far more important,
Trained as a single unit and equipped
With standard weapons. But the Aussies have
The home-ground savvy, and that mystery
Of territorial morale; their sensors,
Desert-trained survival expertise,
Communications, are superior;
The Papuans are fighting for their kin;
The Thais are masters of new strategies
Derived from generalship in ancient China;
New Zealand radar jamming gear is known
To be state of the art. If, then, the allies
Can weather the first Indonesian blow,
Coordinate their forces, and survive,
Time will be on their side. Such is the talk.

As is traditional, three days before
The opening ceremonies of the war,   100
The teams are brought to Adelaide to meet
The press, which, during camp, is kept at bay.
Again traditional, though not explicit,
There is one night when the Victoria
Hotel lays open all its rooms, and feasts
The young contestants, and the liquor's free.
That night the groupies from around the world
Who've followed in the fanzines and the press
The stories of their heroes, true or false,
Are given access to the warrior-victims
That they have worshipped for so long—who wear

In celebration white bands round their heads,
And who, this night, are granted any crime
They may desire before they go to war.
Across the banquet hall in a bright haze
Of human uproar, music, alcohol,
We may see Tripitaka on the dais,
Perfectly sober, legs crossed under him,
His headband bowed in deep contemplation.
Around him, and within the many rooms,
Women with naked breasts and crowns of flowers,
Boys with lit torches and with gilded bodies,
Garlanded Brahma bulls and Javan dancers,
Sequined ecdysiasts and blind dirge-singers
Bearded and ancient, their cheeks wet with tears,   125
Join in the glad communion of the dead.
Film stars and entertainers, famous faces,
Permitted here whatever licence they
And their appetites deem needful, dance
In the purple strobe-lights and the smoke
Of curious drugs; each woman is corrupted
Into the primal stereotype of woman,
So that her hormones make her swollen breasts
Drip with the child-milk; and each gun-hung male,
His shoulders and his upper arms enlarged
With white gonadic tides of rage and milt,
Feels in his limbs the steroids rot and burn;
They are like mating salmon in their plumes,
Their golden Quetzal-eyes, their jagged flesh.

Next day the troops discover in their midst
A new phenomenon—a pair of chaplains
Fresh from the Ecotheist seminary:
The brightest and the best, bursting with zeal,
Eager to win acceptance in the group.
The female's dumpy, caring, and supportive;
Full of old-time phenomenology
And very big on how we all must share
Our common feelings of inadequacy;
She wears the uniform of the thunder-thighed,
The blue stretch slacks, the blouse, the golden pin   150
With the earth-symbol—dot within a circle—
Denoting membership within the Church.

The male is a believer in free love,
An existentialist, a PhD,
Given to saying "hey;" with skinny arms,
A mustache, and that look which says that I
Am fully open to experience.
The Church, it seems, has sent the warriors
These, as reminders what they're fighting for,
And tactfully arranged for their arrival
Just at the peak of beverage fatigue.
Billy Macdonald, of the Ned Kellies,
Observes that it's an ill wind blows no good:
If their supplies run low, as often happens,
The fat one might be nice with pinto beans.

But glory calls; the morning of the war
Dawns bright and cold; the Krichauff Range, like scales
Of an ancient monster, rears over plains
Exhausted by the power of the sun.
The warriors have moved, in one traverse,
Forty-eight tons of war materiel
Across the DMZ; and that is all
They'll be allowed until the mort is blown.
Media drones buzz by above, ignored;
The techies set up radars, while the scouts   175
Advance toward the base camps in the hills;
The carriers lie gasping on the ground,
And General Kung speaks with his officers.

Three days later: first contact. A night raid
By Indonesian fighter planes against
The radars of the allies on the hills.
The mission's a success; the eyes are blinded,
Three of the five planes get away, and Kung
Is much perplexed, for by this sudden blow
He knows the enemy has spent his fuel
Reserve, and must have little left. The Aussies
Can distil from eucalyptus leaves
Some drops of bike and aviation spirit;
The enemy lacks this technology.
It must be one big strike, then. Just as Kung
Comes to this quick conclusion and prepares

His forces for the worst, there's an attack
In force, against the allied camps.

The allies have advantage of terrain:
The enemy must charge a barren slope.
But Kung has chosen to equip his force
With few firearms, and those but light ones too;
The Indonesians must take heavy losses
Storming the glacis, but it's now quite clear
The allies cannot hold the ridge. Kung sends　　　　　200
His specialists in hand-to-hand melee—
His Burmese infantry, his berserk Thais,
And Tripitaka with his kendo sword,
To hold the enemy while others move
The indispensable equipment back
To safety. Now is the old game of blood.
The sunrise shines upon the golden flesh
Of boys and girls in the bright flush of health,
Their muscles warm and ready, their swift breath
Perfectly balanced to the tasks they serve;
And all is motion, and the red blood runs
As if its springs were endless, and its beauty
As harmless as the rush of sperm or milk.
And till that moment when the mastery
Of spirit over body, joy in pain,
Bewildered by some wound that severs it,
Is broken—and the martial shape the mind
Imposes as a template on the flesh,
That fiery net invisible that holds
The feeble chemistry of life together,
Ceases to coincide with the breathed truth—
Until that time these children of the wars
Are as immortal and invulnerable.
Those who say war is horrible speak only　　　　　225
Half the truth; the other half is joy.
And Tripitaka, stripped down to the waist,
His hair tied back, his sword glittering,
Is like the motion of a running stream,
The rainbow trout within it, and the liquid
Running in the creature's arteries.
No weapon touches him. His few companions

Fall one by one, and only chance—the flash
Of a landmine going off, that clears the stage
A moment, and brings him to his senses—
Rescues him from that place of light and blood.
Out of the rearguard he alone escapes.

The Indonesians sought to end the war
By this one stroke. Indeed, the allies,
Broken into small bands and bled of troops,
Seem to be finished; but this kind of war
Is more against the sun and need and time
Than against human beings. The Indonesians
Have expended most of their supplies
And are but poorly furnished with the tools,
The water-stills, and desert expertise
That Kung relies on for his victory.
And now there is a slow guerrilla war
Waged with the bow, the stake-pit, and the knife.
The Indonesians' radios are jammed   250
And thus they cannot separate to forage;
They die of thirst, of sunstroke, and disease.
The allies live on roasted bandicoots,
The pods of wattle trees, the moist petals,
Tender stems and tubers of the lily,
And brew their water in the billabongs;
Their electronic sensors show them when
The enemy is at a disadvantage;
And then they strike, and quickly fade away.

Pictures the memory might store of this,
A little epic in itself: the smoke
Of Indonesian campfires rising from
Behind the bald head of a grassy hill
At dawn, and the smell of eucalyptus;
Dried up Lake Amadeus, like a paisley
Painted in red, grey, ochre, dazzling white,
Seen from a spotter plane whose canvas buzzes
With the light two-stroke in the afternoon;
Messenger-service on a motorbike,
Swooping and skidding over grassy dunes;
A valley all ablaze with pollen, yellow
Red and pink, the naked-stamened flowers

Of mallee, myrtle, melaleuca, gum;
A bloated body by a watercourse;
The sunflash on a flight of arrowheads;   275
A colony of furry wallabies;
A dark storm-mountain in the evening sky
Lit by the bronze sun and the silver lightning;
The yells of parrots in the ragged trees.

But Tripitaka has a troubling dream.
He sees that young girl warrior he killed
In the first dawn raid against the camp;
She was a splendid master of the sword
And might have taken him but for a stumble;
He dreams about her death, her little smile,
Her Khmer beauty, Sumikami-like;
And in this simple dream she has become
The face of Chance at Vassae when they fought;
And then the face of Beatrice; and now
He wakes to feel the thick juice of his sex
Slip from his body in a living stream.
He looks up at the shiny black night sky,
A dome of bright designs and hidden meaning
Like the great driver of a music speaker;
And all the lines of star-connections point
To the gold star that he knows is Mars
And the long veil of the falling comet.
At last he knows his soul. He must take arms
In the cause of his former enemies
And offer up his body as a penance   300
To Chance's heirs, the pioneers of Mars.

The chaplains, meanwhile, have been worth the feeding:
After each skirmish they remind the troops
Not to enjoy their triumph, nor to glory
In their skill, which is unfairly gained;
But to think only of the sacrifice
And feel the sufferings of the enemy
As if they were one's own. This last, perhaps,
Might be a thought redundant; in all wars
Soldiers in close engagement, face to face,
Have always loved their enemy, and have seen
In him or her the image of themselves;

Notwithstanding, in revenge, deceit,
And loss, a hatred cordial as any
Divorcing husband for a cheerful wife,
Junior exec for a department head,
Or pinched caseworker for a legislature.
One morning Tripitaka's own patrol
Draws the short straw and gets the company
Of "Scooter" (as the male reverend
Likes to be called). They are to circle round
The enemy's defences and report
All of advantage to the allies' plans.
At noon they take a wounded prisoner,
And having questioned her must then decide   325
How to dispose of her. If she is left,
She'll die, after some days of agony.
If she is brought along, the chances are
The inconvenience, or her cries, will lead
To their discovery as they return.
The only way is death; and Tripitaka
Draws his sword, his face as grey as dreams.
But Scooter throws his body in the way.
"Some things I won't be part of. I'll report
What happens here. I make my stand for mercy."
The soldiers know he is a commissar
Sent by the powers that be to get control
Of this, the last free ritual, however
Bloody, old, and undermined by guilt;
But it's their duty to obey him, and
They leave the brown girl begging for her death.
A few days later the fortunes of war
Bring this ground under the allies' control;
The girl is found; what she herself has not
Torn with her teeth to shreds in her last fever,
The dingos and the birds have visited.
The camp is sullen, and the word goes round
That General Kung has had enough at last;
He calls a conference of all the soldiers
And asks wherein their perfect duty lies.   350
And Tripitaka speaks for the first time:
The moment he's awaited all his life.

"Don't you think, comrades, that this world we live in
Has suddenly grown old? But we are soldiers;
We date our lives from what our lives are for:
The moment of our death. (Some of us then
Can count our ages by the days.) Or is it that
We are the eldest thing on earth, the metal
That can never tarnish, or the tree
That puts out bitter pollen every spring?
There is no place for us here any more.
These chaplains we must feed will change the rules:
The Church will settle all the quarrels now.
But I have seen at night a star of gold,
The planet of the god who rules our kind;
A world is being born, and here we are,
Fighting for what we don't believe—a star
That needs our arms and calls us to a war
Whose end's not peace but more abundant life.
Our work is to disturb the course of things,
To task the world up to its very brink,
To be the bloody spade that turns the sod,
To prove the game is honest by our deaths;
We're the account on which the world writes checks,
And where its money is its heart will be;   375
It is our duty then, say I, to take
Our swords and offer them to Mars, the new
Republic of the breath of humankind."

At this—but even now (when history
Is not a comfortable subject for
The young, for what sense can it make, what point,
When there's no hope and no direction to it?),
Yes, even now, I think, the Mutiny,
And the events it sparked, are still familiar,
And do not need rehearsal in these lines.
Recall then how the soldiers voted for it,
But for the Papuans, who, sympathetic,
Felt it their duty to continue fighting—
How in their suicide attack upon
The Indonesian camp, they died in glory—;
How then the Indonesians were "suborned"
To kiss the flag of Mars; how other groups
Of gladiators heard the call; how some

Fought through to the Woomera shuttle base;
How others, crucified for their rebellion,
Died in the flies along the desert roads;
How the new chaplains were exchanged for arms;
Of the wild struggle at the launching-pads;
How seven shuttles, burned with laser fire,
Escaped to orbit under Tripitaka.

Tripitaka after many battles against the Terran forces comes
to Mars. We learn of the cave-dwellings of the colonists;
of the progress of the terraforming; of the children Wolf
and Irene, and Chance the younger, the son of Beatrice and
Charlie; of how the children learned to fly; and of how
Tripitaka was forgiven.

Scene iii
The Coming of Tripitaka to Mars

A rush of driving rain. It could be evening
On a deserted airstrip in New Zealand,
The parking lot of a provincial high school
During vacation, in British Columbia;
A wet parade ground in the southern islands
Of pacific Chile, or the Hebrides.
Beyond the chainlink fence, though, there's a green
Too brilliant in this semidarkness: moss,
Hummocked, fantastic, with a haze of brown
Or purple flowerets, heavy with white drops
Of rain that join and pool and slowly run
Away—too slowly, somehow, and the rain
Upon the concrete dances slowly up
In languid sheets, and doesn't know where to flow.
To one side the ground falls rapidly off
And through the haze an ocean far below
Wobbles with huge and oily swells; a boom
Like the deepest bass tells of its impact.
Here the sounds, too, are strange; the falling rain
Thumps on the mosses like a sodden drum,
And now a thunderclap—for what else could
It be?—batters and trundles in the sky,
But no earthly thunder could shake your feet
And diaphragm, and drop its resonances
So down below the audible frequencies   25
To where the ear can feel and cannot hear,
As does this Jupiterian cacophany.
The sea is lit by orange radiance
In a broad track, like a hurricane dawn;
And now a brief break in the clouds shows something

The eye scarce credits, if it understands;
It seems as if the planet were cut off
Short of its due horizon, or as if
The ocean, without fuss, were pouring out
Over the sunken lip or selvage of the world;
But out beyond that edge there is a portent
Like a pillar of a cloud or fire,
Or both at once; a cone, tilted away,
As if you saw it from below, has torched
Into the swagged clouds of that nether sky
A silent blast of fire and blue-white vapor
Lit in its depths with salmon-pink and gold.

There's action at the sort of Quonset hut
That stands beside the airstrip; radars turn,
A beacon starts to flash, floodlights come on,
Making the landing field a dance of droplets.
Above there is another roll of thunder;
But this is more prolonged and purposeful,
And soon a racing shape dips through the clouds,
With blinking lights and a squat, stubby wing;   50
It banks and turns; a set of flaps come down;
It touches, bumps, and rolls out to a landing.
The airlock of the hut cracks with a sneeze,
The vapors thicken into wisps, and through them
Two human shapes appear in pressure suits.
They walk toward the shuttle with that lope
The Martian gravity invites, and as they do,
The shuttle airlock opens, and a ramp
Unfolds, down which twelve figures stumble;
They're led by their new hosts into the shelter.
Within it's bright and warm, with potted plants
Crowded in corners, as if there were no room;
And battered metal furniture, replaced,
It seems, at intervals, by chairs and closets
Made out of living plants; their shining wood
Taking the odd baroque design—of seat
And leg, and bark-hinged door—their makers wrote
Into the coded blueprint of the genes.
The first to get their suits off are the two
Who met the shuttle, Beatrice and Charlie;
The next, a newcomer, is Tripitaka.

The moment he has stepped out of the suit
Beatrice faces him. His heart forgets
To beat; her eyes are scorching in her face.   75
She strikes her enemy across the cheek,
And he, his nose running with the hoarse blood,
Drops to his knees before her, like a knight
Yielding allegiance to a chatelaine.

It's five years since the funeral of Chance,
And Don John/Tripitaka has observed
The most meticulous and purest penance,
Paid the bloodprice in work and suffering.
After the impact of the comet Kali,
The UN sought to overthrow the treaty.
The planet's government, technology,
Economy had felt the consequence
Of choosing to deny all innovation,
And its exhausted soils could not support
The aging populations of the faithful.
Increasingly it came thus to depend
On biomass imported from deep space,
From solar orbital farms that the Van Riebecks
Had hollowed out of captured asteroids.
The government had seized the earthside holdings
Of VRE as soon as war broke out,
Thus cutting off much of its revenue;
Now, since the war, the Company,
Failing to get redress for this proceeding,
Had raised its prices for the biomass.   100
The Terran government then claimed the right
To tax the garden-satellites, and when
The taxes were not paid, to confiscate them.
A navy was prepared for this purpose.
So Tripitaka and his followers
Who'd offered fealty to the Martian cause,
And been assigned, while training for space work,
To picket duty in the Lunar orbit,
Now volunteered to take the post of guard
And keep the tax-collectors from the farms.
And in those skirmishes many he'd led
To service and to glory in the stars
Died in his sight; the point-man of his squad,

A somber, faithful Thai; Billy Macdonald
Of the Kellies, who gave Don John his name;
The black-belt sergeant of the women's camp,
Whose name I don't recall, but Tripitaka
Loved her in his way, as one who held
That perfect warrior's fidelity
To what she deemed her duty, and who knew
Her own strength and honored that of others;
She was a railgun sentry and was burned
When the main fleet came through the picket line.
By now the space war had become so draining
To both economies that boarding tactics—   125
Hand-to-hand struggle in the nightmare drift
Of quarter-gravity environments—
And their expense of soldiery, paid off;
And in the fighting in the concave fields
Of Orbital Farm Five, grief-struck and thus
Incautious, Tripitaka took a wound
Deep to the belly, and one to the head
That almost did for him. To expiate
One crime, he has committed many; now
He kneels so scarred in soul as well as body
Before his dark Madonna that it seems
There can be no forgiveness in the world.

But Beatrice's blow, it seems to Charlie,
Who watches this with interest, has already
Pardoned where it most stung, and is a sign
Of Beatrice's genius of heart—
The genius he loves her for, the sense
She has of how the breath of life is kindled,
And if it be extinguished, how restored.
Queens and madonnas must be capable
Of an unconscious theater—or is it
Conscious, this unerring innocence
Of gesture, this schoolgirlish subtlety?
Chance had this knack as well, to shed his skin,
Thinks Charlie, and to start his life anew.   150

It thunders overhead, and breaks the spell.
Charlie says tactfully "Let's go downstairs."
They hang the suits up and descend the spiral

To the deep airlock of the Syrtis base.
A cavern half a mile across; lit to a haze
And dazzle by a thousand sunlike lamps
Whose merry light beats on a crowd of treetops
Of many species, standing in open groves
With grassy hummocks in between. "Now why,"
Asks Charlie, "Must our paradises all
Resemble golf-courses? Did the primordial
Anthropoids hunt with their sticks and stones
Some rabbit-warren in Gondwanaland?"
But Tripitaka stands amazed, as once
Aeneas did in Virgil's grand romance,
In Carthage, where the frescoes told of Troy;
For these walls too, irregular and cracked
As they are, bear a wandering history
Painted in brilliant oxides, cupreous
And ferrous, ocher, lampblack, limestone white:
And there he sees the first landings on Mars,
The wise coyotes of New Mexico,
Ganesh inside the guts of a computer,
Beatrice dancing, and the plains of Mars
Just as they looked before the fungoids came;　　　175
And there was painted Chance's fall at Vassae,
The comet flaming on the funeral,
And Tripitaka, too, caught in a battle
Upon the far hills of Australia.
Some of the newer images are strange
To him, especially the human birds,
Like flying babies in the painted trees.
Beatrice smiles at last. "Ah, yes, the cherubs.
They are a puzzle for our visitors.—
But here they are in living truth to prove
Our painter was still sober when he did them . . . "

And there they are indeed: three little angels,
Darting and floating in the buoyant air,
With feathery wings and that complacent look
That children quite unconsciously assume
When doing something skilled and pleasurable.
Two of them, ten years old, are clearly twins.
The boy is blond, built like a polevaulter,
And somber in his looks; the elder girl,

Her hair now darkening to golden brown,
Shocks Tripitaka's heart with a resemblance:
Beatrice as she might have been, a girl
Riding the roan mare at the family ranch.
There is the same fierce heat about the eyes.
The younger boy is truly like a cherub: 200
His hair is white gold, and he's chubbier
Than his companions; four years old perhaps,
And wobbles still a little in the air.
They swoop and perch before the visitors.
"These two you know," says Beatrice; "and this
Is their half brother and their cousin, if
You can work that out.—But I thought you knew?
Charlie and I got married long ago;
This is our bad boy Chance, who almost beat us
To the altar, if the truth be known.
Charlie gave me the strangest wedding-gift:
He let him take the old Van Riebeck name."

Despite the lightness of the conversation, tears
Lie close behind the eyes of Tripitaka,
Tears he's not known for almost twenty years.
The spirit of the strange man he has murdered,
Now, it seems to him, breathes in the mouth
Of this flushed, lovely child; and Beatrice,
Who was the argument of all his wars,
Is bound in full joy to another man;
But yet that Beatrice is enfleshed anew
In Freya's daughter, dark-eyed Irene.
This is not all. Irene has at last
Before her one of her sworn enemies:
The killer of her grandfather; to blame   225
In part for her own mother's, Freya's, death;
But still a hero in her nation's cause,
The warrior that she would wish to be;
And Tripitaka sees her trouble, and
Again he kneels, and murmurs "Pardon me,
Madam," to the child. But she turns away,
Her own confusion hidden by the gesture;
For in her hatred there is mingled something
She does not understand, and her disgust

At his deformity is tinged with sweetness.
But Wolf shakes Tripitaka by the hand,
And welcomes him, as might a prince of Mars.

And now the other strangers are presented;
Young men and women, part of the exodus
From Earth of those whose spirit called to them
For a transcendence of the edge of things;
An exodus whose myth was Tripitaka,
Who sold their goods and pasts and livelihoods
To buy plantations in a fantasy.
They walk across the dainty-flowered grass
To a low timber building by a grove;
Here they are turned over to Ganesh,
Who herds them to his lab and starts his briefing.

"You guys all know about the first few years,
From twenty-fifteen when the project started   250
To twenty-thirty-five, the comet year.
We needed pressure then, to trap the sun
And greenhouse it to melt the permafrost.
With heat the CO_2 inside the caps
Would gasify, and push the pressure up—
It all goes round in circles, just like life.
The thermal equilibrium within
The troposphere would break, and storms would dig
The dust from Hellas and the other plains,
Mid-latitude depressions mix the gunk
All the way round the sky. Dust is a greenhouse
Too, if there's not too much of it. So how
To get the heat we needed for the pressure
Needed for the heat? We used albedo.
The first bacteria just darkened up
The surface—and especially the caps—
To stop enough reradiation out
Of the planet to get the cycle going.
We helped it all along with little strikes
From comets, ringstuff—what we could lay hands on.
Planetmaking's not a precise art.
Then we got oxygen-excreting algae
And sowed them in the mulch the first bugs made
By dying of the heat they generated.

They used the carbon in the CO_2 275
To make their bodies, and just shat the ox—
If you'll excuse me, ladies—into the air.
At this stage though it didn't matter much
What kind of junk was present in the sky,
But like I said at first, the key was pressure:
We'd started with around six millibars,
Less than a hundredth of the earth's, and reached,
Twenty years later, one-eighth atmosphere.
We had a window now for liquid water
Where it was hot enough to melt but not
So low in pressure that it boiled away.
And then we sowed the molds and funguses.

"Kali was like a swift kick in the pants.
It gave us heat and water, and volcanoes;
It rained carbonic acid for six weeks;
We got our little oceans—Boreal's
The one you saw outside, it's full of weed.
The thing we needed then was nitrogen.
There was some NH_3—ammonia—
In Kali, but the real source was here:
Outgassing from the neovulcanism.
That's what you saw outside: Mount William Blake,
Flaming off Nox right now, I shouldn't wonder.
The club-ferns and the cycads are the next
We have on the agenda. You'll be out   300
On seeding crew as soon as you get settled;
It's not as easy as bacteria—
We can't afford to seed the barren ground.

"The pressure's up to half an atmosphere.
It's hot enough to sunbathe in the tropics,
But that is not a thing I would advise.
The big job now is cleaning up the air:
There's photochemicals I never heard of,
Ketones, aldehydes, carboxyls, methane.
It's like a sunny day in old L.A. . . . . "

After this lecture, Tripitaka hangs
Behind the rest to ask some questions.

He feels for this unlikely character
A kinship: as the warrior is bound
To duty and the perfectness of action,
So is the scientist committed to
Something we can't call truth exactly, but
An honor of the factual understanding;
And techné is a variant of act.
Perhaps, moreover, Tripitaka feels
Attracted to another who has known
The strangerhood of piebald parentage.
"If it would violate no confidence,"
He starts, "I would be grateful if you'd tell me
Something about the life of Charlie Lorenz."   325
"Yo. Old Uncle Charlie. Well sir, if that's
Your way of asking about Beatrice,
I could just save the time and stick to her."
At this perception Tripitaka flushes;
Is almost angry, with a new respect.
"No. Please let us speak of Charlie Lorenz."
"Okay. Charlie was born in '91,
In Halle, in what was East Germany.
Karl Friedrich Lorenz was his name I think.
He failed to graduate from Wittenberg:
The Neo-Greens, who were the ruling party,
Abolished the Ethology degree.
The Neos differed from the older Greens
As much as Nazis did from Socialists;
They thought his studies could be used to prove
Human innate superiority.
He took the line of the Good Soldier Schweik,
Played dumb with the authorities, and switched
To Ecology. If they'd known he meant
Practical ecology, they'd have stopped him."
"The Neo-Greens—didn't they come to power
When Germany was reunited, or . . . ?"
"They were the secret price of unity.
Charlie's got little jests on them: the one
About the vegetarian who was   350
A cannibal, and ate a rutabaga.
How does a Green know who his mother is?
He counts his father and divides by one.

Why don't carrots eat Fruitarians?
No flavor. Then why do they call them Greens?
—Distinguish them from vegetables. . . . Some
Were quite grim: How many Greens it takes
To put you into jail. Three: one to lock
The door, the other two to lose the key.
The big Green boss calls all the Greens together;
From now on all the rhubarb will wear pants,
To take away temptation, understand.
You had to be there, I guess you would say.
The thing that must've riled the Greens the most
Was Charlie's cloning of his own skin-tissue
Into a fetus, just to prove a point.
Was it abortion then to break the skin?
Does every shave I take murder a twin?
Well Chance found Uncle Charlie there in 'Twenty,
Still no degree, a hundred major papers
Under a dozen noms de plume; hired him
To mastermind the secret Ares project.

"Freya was just sixteen when Charlie came.
Everyone knew she was her Daddy's girl.
And that was the beginning of the trouble;   375
Rose—who is Gaea now—had realized
That she herself could never match the love
Her daughter felt for Chance and his designs.
How do I know all this? Well Charlie told me.
I guess the German thing to do—though Charlie
Doesn't always do what you expect—
Is take to wife the Herr Professor's daughter.
Freya liked Charlie because Chance liked him;
Rose saw it as a way that Chance had found
To keep his precious daughter close at hand.
But what outsiders often don't perceive—
And Rose, although she had the family strength
And guts and will, was always an outsider—
Is that Van Riebecks act on principle:
They figure that's the only game in town.
Sure, it turned out that Chance always came first
For Freya. It was Beatrice who saw
The special stuff that makes our Charlie run,

What must have made Chance pick him in the first place
—Brains being two a penny in those days.
Charlie just always gave what he could give,
And took the satisfaction of his work.
The miracle was how at Chance's wake
Charlie and Bea got lucky and got pregnant.
It was, uh, chance, I guess. The rest you know."

Tripitaka is reunited with his mother Sumikami. The life of
the colonists is described.

Scene iv
The Colony

$\mathcal{A}$s Tripitaka leaves, he notices
Under a nearby tree a little person
Dressed in a silk kimono, waiting for him.
He sees it is his mother Sumikami.
This should not be surprising, but it is.
For many years he's put her from his mind:
His father was the theme of his endeavors.
Likewise, his healing at the hands of Chance
And the others, being a debt, has lain,
With all inducements to the path of feeling,
In that part of the soul where sleep the dead.
In Greece he had slept barely thirty yards
From her whose body he had shared, yet not,
Because of ideology, come face
To face with her; now, more than he can bear,
After the shock of Beatrice's marriage,
After the bitter pang of their forgiveness,
After the strangeness of the girl Irene,
He feels that painful love, like a great tumor
Of the throat and heart, which comes to one
Who knows he has neglected the most dear.
And in that moment, as he kneels once more,
And takes her fragile body in his arms,
He knows he is the stepchild of Japan,
Of the old, tormented, filial regime   25
That turned the man into a perfect blade,
But made of him his mother's son forever.
And that in him which sought the new, the free,
The priestly deserts of Australia,
Is but an iridescence in the weave,
A watering upon a polished blade,
A wind that blows a while among the willows.

And what is human freedom after all?
At any moment that which I can do
Is only what I can, and I am bound
By those capacities inherited
From my genetic and my social past.
Am I then just a character within
A novel, chained to probability,
Verisimilitude defined as fate?
Can I do other than that thing I do?
And would that set me free in any case?
What if I could perform a random act?
What if I could subvert the text that writes me?
Ruhollah thought that was the way of grace.

But now his mind goes back to all his training;
How there was once a time when he was not
The thing he has become, one capable
Of violence perfect as a hammered sword,
So perfect that his spirit takes no pride   50
In it—a matter of indifference,
Even of disgust, to him, who has killed
So many times that he cannot remember.
That thing he is, though, he was not at all;
He was not capable of what he is.
Therefore by choice he's altered all the rules
That govern psychic probability.
Nor was the choice at random, which he sees
As simply a fine way of talking nonsense;
Nor was it yet compelled by birth or breeding,
Since neither birth nor breeding could predict
The consequences of his choice to be
A warrior (—the discipline of soul,
The possibility of forced events,
The new eligibility for crime,
The suffering of one whose flesh is sharp,
So that who touches him must be impaled,
That last indifference to his own powers)
Which might have changed his choice had he foreseen them.
The discipline itself, the martial arts,   75
Ancient as kinship, music, poetry,
Passed down from samurai to samurai,
Burned in that holy Shao-lin monastery

To a white fire of spirit's purity,
Wedded to earth and to the farmer's wisdom
On beaten Okinawan threshing floors—
That discipline itself had been the game
Which promised him the freedom of the spirit
And at last gave it when he did not want it.
Is freedom then the choice of discipline?
More; for the masters of that antique trade
Each gave to it the flower of themselves.
Each, as a poet tinkers O so del-
Icately with the living membrane
Of the tongue he loves and speaks with, each
Added *Katas*, turns of philosophy,
Little movements of the hip that might
Deliver perfect violence to that
Soft point where Brother Adversary lived,
Rituals to tune the body and the mind.
And it was these refinements, these small works
Of living art that were the way to freedom.
So freedom is the breath of the tradition.
And there's no freedom in the present moment,
But for the flash of play, irrelevant,
That turns us to a discipline of years;
Freedom is ages long, not seconds long;
Time is the medium of liberty,
And time is made by art's and love's delays,
The slow crafts of the spirit's history.   100
And now consider that great work of craft,
That terrible discipline, that fierce play,
That act of making that will change the rules:
The planoforming of the world of Mars.
This was the metaphor the warrior sought,
The scripture he will carry through the mountains:
That freedom is not found nor exercised,
Chosen nor seized, but, like this planet, *made.*

Thus service is a kind of perfect freedom.
Sumikami has taken on that art
And is the teacher and the governess
Of the Van Riebeck children. It was she
Who noticed how, at that sweet stage of childhood
When boys and girls must imitate the birds

And run with outstretched arms and makeshift wings
About the colony, their feet seemed ready
Sometimes, to leave the ground. Once Wolf had made
A pair of white wings for his sister from
A sheet of lightweight plastic foam; she tried
Them by the roaring ventilation ducts
And Sumikami watched her glide and tumble.
With quiet insistence she besought the help
Of one of Charlie's engineers, who grew
From a gull's genes planted in bamboo
The first true wings of the Diaspora.   125
In keeping with the Japanese tradition,
That still preserves the perverse difference
Between the education of the sexes,
She'd taught Irene how to dance, and Wolf
The first five steps and cuts of swordsmanship.
And this instinctive training of the body,
This second nature by which we're set free,
Together with the ease of children raised
In Martian gravity, taught them to fly.
By this time baby Chance was three years old,
The first true Martian, born on Martian soil.
Wolf and Irene loved him jealously,
The way a child will love a puppydog,
Guarding him in their arms and quarreling
Who was to hold him next. They were his teachers
In the air, and they terrified their nurse
By taking him, quite unafraid, as high
As the hot lamps set in the cavern roof.
On Mars a four-year-old weighs thirteen pounds;
These children do not need to dream of flying.

Now Tripitaka plays the colonist:
The daily toil upon the Martian surface
In a green light—the clouds are saturated
With a plumed aerial phytoplankton,
Reflect the virid glow of moss and fern   150
Back to the oceans all aheave with kelp
And eutrophied with emerald and jade—
So dark and velvet green that topside workers
Enter a world of pinkish brilliance
As strange as the pink pearl or rosy diamond

When they return to the warm lights of Base;
The long sessions with Nesh at the computers
(Now largely wetware, or organic circuits),
Which, if you've talent but no discipline,
Can gradually eat up all your time,
So perfectly is this machinery
Matched to that juice of curiosity
The brain secretes to get an itch to scratch;
The quiet dinners round the family table
Under a loggia of vine and jasmine,
Charlie at one end, Beatrice at the other,
The children sixty-five percent behaved
But making eyebrows at each other when
Parental inattention gives the chance;
The evenings when the sager citizens
Debate political economy
Towards the constitutional convention
Set for the following year, while lighter souls
Attend the little comic opera,
Or hoot at the satirical revue;
The open school where young and old can teach
And learn the elements of poetry—
Meter, the sciences, and storytelling:
Myth, dreaming, and the art of ritual
(By which humanity may purge itself
Of self-concern), and sweet philosophy,
Whose spring and dwelling place is poetry.

175

Sometimes at night Charlie will walk the lawns
Between the easy bleached wood bungalows
And let the raindrops from the sprinklers
Patter upon his head as on the roofs
And breathe in the warm grass after the shower.
Someone is practicing a polonaise
Behind a dim-lit curtain; he remembers
The pleasant suburb of Vienna where
He spent his summers with his grandparents,
And smelt the honeysuckle on the fence;
As if all that mild life of family
And home and bourgeois complication from
The previous century, the barking dog
Settling down after the stranger's passed,

The pink parabolas of lamplight cast
Across the ceiling by somebody's shades,
The soft sound of a neighbor's car reversing,
The smell of women and cigars, of cooking,   200
Polish, and upholstery, that wafted
Through an open door, the rise of voices
Talking about the Philharmonic—as
If these, and so much more, were resurrected
And poured across the windowsills of Mars.
That human suburb-place must always be,
Where children may be raised and gardens watered;
Whether in Maidenhead or Saint-Germain,
Or Tuckahoe, Lake Forest, Pasadena,
Chapultepec, Atsugi, Kuntsevo,
Or his own green dorf in the Wienerwald;
The cave of that illusion which we cast
With twined fingers by the hearth of love.
Stranger than Mars itself, thinks Charlie, but
Man muss ein Fremder sein, to know that place.

But sometimes the good dream turns to nightmare.
Charlie like all of us can feel the ague
Of being lost here in this foreign world
Whose substance is so thin the backing shows
And it would not take much to see your life
As sitting on a stone in a dank place
With nothing real to occupy your mind.
This is so hard to say. Have you not felt
The world as wearisome and artificial,
Just a few layers of tedious games between   225
An emptiness as unremarkable
As certain small bad habits of the mind
And you, the royal child your mother loved?
Have you not felt the world could be quite other
Or you could act quite otherwise, and yet
It wouldn't matter in the least; or you
Could be another person than you are,
And have that person's memories, and yet
Not be the same? And lost forever thus,
Wandering streets you cannot quite remember,
Or walking in a grand and tedious landscape
Where there is nowhere that dear place called home,

Or dearness is a feeling you may know
But not experience—lost thus, have you
Not feared sleep because it breaks the flow
Of consciousness, the only thing that's left?
Or woken from a long unpleasant dream
You can't remember, in a calm, numb panic
Unable to recall just who you are?
The endless hour of affectlessness?
The aching love and the nostalgia for
The very persons that you speak with daily
As if it were a film show of the dead,
Or worse, as if you were a ghost yourself
And visited your family unperceived   250
Or in the body of another person?
Oh, there are poets today who can put this
In perfect images of alienation
And make it almost chic to feel this way.
I speak to you in plain words thus to test
Whether you know this thing, this very evil.
I tell you there are those who from these depths,
Stripped of all powers of temperament and mood,
Can rise up like a flaming bird of courage
By their pure essence, and can bless the game,
And find that artificial universe,
That thin layer of molded plastic which
The world's revealed to be at such a time,
A garden of pathetic loveliness,
A drama that requires our tenderness.
And if that knowledge makes it worse for you
Who have not flown up from the pit as they,
So much the worse for you; and that may be
A consolation, that it can be worse;
Perhaps your anger then can keep you warm.
No other poem than this will tell you so.
If you would put away the world, and be
The ghost that you have felt yourself to be,
That, even, might be not so bad. Alone
You may fly the dark mountains of wisdom   275
Like a drugged glider in the cliffs of shadow.
Or even turn to God, but be quite sure
He doesn't buy you, though He ransom you.
He is a moody God, and oftentimes

He will have no other god before Him
And every human maker is a god.

This little cave-hole on the tortured planet
Can be a place of terror; the children have
No need to dream of flying, but they wake
Crying with fear about the roof collapsing,
Monsters and dragons bursting in above;
And Beatrice yearns after animals
Upon this world of silent growing plants;
Perhaps they miss the fleshmeat in their meals—
Such petty changes can engender turns
Of the spirit as lonely, dark, and cruel
As any struggle over principle,
Standing in tears amid the alien corn.

Only Sumikami does not feel
These hungers of the disinherited.
Her cares are for the children; her own son
She scarcely dares to think about, he is
So glorious and frightful in her sight,
So inexplicable to her that all
She knows to do is serve the family   300
Who saved him from the stroke of the disease.
She sees Irene has the light and grace
Of one who might with training be a priestess
In all the sacrificial arts of beauty.
The child's slim arm and sensitive long hand
Can seem at perfect rest upon a table
When set there for a moment in her play,
The wristbones at an angle that will take
Your breath away with simple loveliness;
Her legs are long and sabered like a dancer's;
And every trembling passage of the spirit
Shows in her face, the white brow shot with pink,
The broad cheekbones, the fine set of the lips.
But this bad girl will answer no instruction
In those arts that the Geisha-san would teach,
Dancing excepted, which she always loved.
She's clearly bored by clothes and the coiffure;
Laughs at eye-makeup when the time comes round
To try this ancient doctrine of the skin;

Breaks all her lovely fingernails, or bites them;
Deeply resents the growings on her ribs,
Regards the first bright twitch of monthly blood
As a revenge by Sumikami for
Her inattention in the female school.

Instead she wants to train to be a spy,   325
And prowl the rotting cities of the Earth,
And steal the riches of the mother planet,
Its heritage of genotypes and genes
Which, as Ganesh has told her, is the lack
That now increasingly has paralysed
The work of planoforming here on Mars.
Before the break with Earth, the colonists
Had gathered a great library of plants
In tiny cultures, stored in Phoban vaults;
But there had not been time to do the same
With all the animals that move and breathe
Within the Terran biosphere—a few
Dozen species only have been preserved,
And Earth refuses patent rights until
The Martian rebels yield their sovereignty
Back to the mother planet. And that vow
The children made when Chance and Freya turned
To fire and air within the death of Kali,
Their vow to kill their evil grandmother
And Garrison her son, is not forgotten.
Irene may not murder Tripitaka as
She wishes that she might, but now instead
She asks him to instruct her in the way
Of death, of strength in violence.

For Wolf, who was her confidant and friend,   350
Her bedmate, peer, and co-conspirator,
Has been entirely charmed by little Chance;
And since the contest for the boy's affection
Seems to be won by Wolf, she is disgusted
By those maternal feelings that had made
Her hold the child for hours in her lap
And be the boy's maidservant if he wished.
She tells herself she hates her stupid brother.
He has forgotten all their promises

And plans, and wants to play at being Daddy.
Irene knows that Wolf holds Tripitaka
Almost in awe, as if he were a god;
It would be only justice if it were
She, not her brother, that the hero chose
As his apprentice in the martial arts.

Some children seem to be a lucky gift
—To parents, to the family, to the world.
The second Chance grows up as such a child.
He is a well of sweetness and good humor,
Neat and methodical without obsession,
Ebullient but sensitive to others,
Wise beyond his years but not sententious.
Not the most graceful nor coordinated
Of all children, Chance can be quite a klutz,
But when they laugh at him he doesn't mind;　　　　375
Sometimes he'll be a very witty clown.
He loves to put on plays and rituals
That can involve at least a dozen people
Whom he will buttonhole in such a way
That it is quite impossible to refuse.
His gurgling laugh has many imitators;
He gives himself away without reserve.
He'll be a very giant when he's grown;
His big limbs shine with a warm animal life.
His goodness carries not a shadow, but
We do not feel with him as with those children
Whose innocence has marked them for some grief,
Or addicthood, or victimhood, or crime.
He is too large and flexible for that;
His shrewdness is the glory of his sweetness.
Chance is a poet, as it soon turns out;
Not of the epic or the mystic turn,
But in a mode that might remind a lover
Of such things of Herrick or of Horace
In his lighter mood, when celebrating
The Ausonian slopes in glorious September.
His only shade is, that against his will
He's been the instrument that has divided
Wolf and his sister; all his commonsense
Cannot avail against a slight foreboding.

Gaea persuades Garrison to marry Bella. A son, Flavius, is
born to them. Irene trains in the martial arts under
Tripitaka, and seduces him. Tripitaka, in shame, prepares
to do away with himself. The Martians agree to exchange
their bases and satellites for a complete collection of
Terran lifeforms, to continue the transformation of Mars.
Tripitaka, interrupted in his suicide, is chosen as the
leader of the expedition to bring back in Kalevala, as in an
ark, the life of Earth.

Scene v
The Seductions of Garrison and Tripitaka

*G*aea calls Garrison to come and see her.
The Church has sent a van to meet his plane.
The young driver's grating enthusiasm
Is silenced after the first twenty miles.
They drive through landscapes now distinctly changed
From the remembered England of his childhood:
More natural, perhaps, though farmed in places
With dull efficiency; more like, perhaps,
American midwestern countryside.
The old is much less obvious; being the sign
Of privilege, it's faded out of sight,
Ruined and overgrown and not restored,
The nation's poverty too great to spend
State money on the maintenance of things
When half the population's over sixty.
But still he feels the heavy joy of heart,
The death wish he associates with home,
As they crawl up the drive of Devereux
Avoiding potholes and wild rhododendrons.
He's been at the World Church Headquarters
Outside Geneva for the last few years,
With trips to the think tanks at Cuernavaca,
Simla, Nagasaki, and Nairobi,
And has a reputation as a comer
In Ecotheist policy and theory.   25
Despite success, he has been miserable;
Depressed, with violent dreams, and sudden urges.

All this his mother knows; she's found a way
In her true kindness and solicitude
To cheer him up, her loyal follower.
"Garrison, it's time you had a wife.
Your work is too important and too hard
To risk a breakdown, as you have been doing.
Your sexual and your parental instincts
Need to be served as well. I think I've found
Just the right person for you. Yes, she's here.
Her name is Bella, she's a real treasure.
After you've met her we will talk again:
The new proposal from the Martian rebels
About the biocultures that they want
Needs careful handling, or they will loot us
Of our heritage; and I think I see
A way to bring their schism to an end.—
But this is shop talk. Come and meet your girl."

Bella's indeed a treasure. She is mild
And pretty and affectionate, a cellist
Whose intelligence is well expressed
In music by a skilful excellence
In the melodic line and the ensemble.
She is a natural Christian: knows her limits,   50
Accepts the Parenthood of God, and lives
In the happiness of Another's will;
And Ecotheist doctrine has enriched
Her sensibility, with intuitions
Of the great poise and harmony of things,
That timeless template of reality
That brackets all vicissitudes of time:
Nature according to eternity.
The score is given by the grand Composer;
It is for us to best perform the theme.

Garrison almost weeps with kindness for her;
Few could resist that candor and that calm.
He has been places she must never go,
He thinks, and wishes to protect her from
His own accidie, his noonday demons.
He had, when Gaea had proposed her theme,
By an old reflex drawn himself within,

Ready, as one might wince, to take the blow
The spirit schools itself to now endure.
But this is different; Gaea has once more
Reached over expectations to the heart
Of the problem, and seized it by its tubes.
And Bella's studied him and loves his grief,
His crucifixion on the axis-points
Of modern history and kinship struggle;   75
Has even guessed the dreams about the soldiers,
The brotherhood that he can never share.
Her tone with him is purest commonsense,
Mixed with a gentle humor, promising
Tolerance while it shares, and strength in pain.
She could no more do other than the good
Than a sunflower can turn back from the sun.

"So, Mr. Van Riebeck, what can we do?
She'll have us married off before we know it.
We must beat her or be resolved to join her;
In either case we're doomed to be good friends."
Garrison feels hope flower in his heart,
But it all seems too easy, too arranged.
Or is it his suspicion that is false?
Perhaps he's made a habit of misgivings
And ought to take the offerings of God.
But can a gift from Gaea be from God?
What if he took it? Would not this gentle girl
Be made a hostage to his private devils?
Is not this, though, the very sacrifice
She's formed her life to make? Garrison smiles
Like sun in winter, and at length replies.
"Van Riebecks have a way of eating people,
As you perhaps have heard, Miss Morison.
To dine with us a long spoon would be wise.   100
But it is hard to contradict my mother."

What follow are the happiest days he's known;
Later that year they're married, and in autumn
They discover Bella is with child.
At Gaea's wish they move into the lodge
And in the spring a healthy boy is born;
They name him Flavius for Gaea's father.

Garrison sees the mother and the child
Asleep together by the Christmas tree;
And his heart groans, and he does not know why:
Nymph, in thy orisons be all my sins . . .

For years Tripitaka has endured
The daily pain and happiness of being
Almost in sweet domestic contact with
The pale-faced icon of his pilgrimage.
Beatrice is his friend, his good friend's wife,
His wise commander in their common work.
Many a time upon the grotesque mountains
Of the Nilosyrtis, horstblocks upraised
Between dark grabens littered with debris,
A hand upon the arm has been the saving
Of each other's life; great groves of forest,
The trees' growth boosted by a tailored gene
In the unearthly frail gravity,
Have risen from their hands, sigh in the wind.   125
Beatrice must guess something, but the thought
Disturbs her with its arbitrariness,
Its hint that something might disrupt the joy
Of sailing gently, gently, to old age—
And in the best possible company.
And Tripitaka simply has avoided
The child Irene, with her strange resemblance
Nobody seems to notice but himself.
So when Irene gravely comes to him
And in correct form kneels and bows to him
As martial arts apprentice to the sensei,
He does not know what to do, and at last,
Because his art enjoins pure certainty,
Refuses. But next day she comes again,
And next; and at last, mastered by her spirit,
He takes her as his student in the craft.
Irene is sixteen, and at this time
Is like a slender lyre of flesh and blood,
A longbow strung with sensate fire and breath.
She is the finest student he has taught.
Her stance is long and rooted, and her steps
Explode from the hips and stop like a freeze;
Her high kicks are a bright crescent of force,

Her hand-strikes fill a pattern in the air.
And now she burns with that fresh chemistry   150
A brave girl can conceive for one she follows,
And still she feels the need for a revenge
For how her teacher hurt her family;
And can that wounded rage at her betrayal
By her brother Wolf, whom she loved so long,
Be slaked and comforted by something else?

Though Sumikami missed it, her Irene
Had learned more of the art of beauty than
Her tutor gave her credit for. This art
Has been ignored in certain ages, when
An ignorant philosophy reduced
The matter to the brutal act of sex;
Yet cultivated, beauty of the flesh
May form addictions fiercer than a drug,
And human culture's fairly measured by
The force of the addictions it survives.
You, my compatriots, whom I address
Anonymously lest my words betray me,
Cannot conceive the sting of Aphrodite.
Your women are, at their best, healthy beasts;
Your men are lacking in the golden rage
That sets the flush of heaven in their limbs.
But think of Helen and the town she burned,
Of brilliant-shouldered Alcibiades,
Of Cleopatra's cloak of ibis feathers,   175
Of Krishna, the blue god, whose gopis touched
With their sweet tongues the white wrists of His Radha
Because she was His favorite in love;
Or Wang Chao-Ch'un the imperial concubine
Called Water Lily for her purity
Who died by her own hand on the frontier;
Or Philip Sidney and Penelope;
Or Raleigh and his two Elizabeths;
The long-legged courtier of Hilliard;
Or Madame Pompadour, by Fragonard;
Or Garbo, in her perfume and her pearls.
What is there more to say? Can Tripitaka,
Once her net is spread, but walk upon

Its splendid tissue to the bathing-place?
What might or may the silly lark deny
When the great sparhawk has it in her foot?
For he is yet a virgin, and her art
Is tempered to the frenzied Galahad
In him, the swan-knight of fate and despair,
The monkish warrior of Zen and death.

After she leaves him, he attains that calm
That comes when all recourses are exhausted.
The doctors, fifteen years ago, had said
That his diseases might not be contagious,
But that he would be sterile all his life.   200
He cannot offer marriage, and Irene
Has given no permission to disclose
The act which they have shared. What, then,
Can wipe away the stain of his dishonor
And make amends to her for all his crimes?
The shape of the perfection he has sought
So many years, begins now to appear.
He bathes his body, and prepares the garment
And the sword. He robes, and ties the cords
In the prescribed fashion, and sweeps the floor
Of the small wooden *dojo* he has built.
He ties his hair back, like a Lohengrin,
And sets the short blade on its lacquered stand
And kneels before it with that concentration
A sword master brings to a tournament.

At the last moment of his meditation
The door is opened quickly by Ganesh.
"Trip, there's a meeting at the wind balloon"
(Ganesh's nickname for the village hall)
"And you're the star. —So what's the ritual?"
But Tripitaka shakes his head and smiles.
Can he be purged still by deserved shame?
If not, there will be time. He rises, follows.

It's a full town meeting. Everyone's there.
Beatrice, mayor *pro tem*, nominates Charlie   225
To chair the session. "So. The word is in.
The Terran government has offered terms.

We get the tissue cultures, but we pay.
They get the moonbase, the orbital farms
And all but one of our Earth satellites.
This means we'd have no foreign currency
To pay for what we buy in Terran markets.
We would be poor, ladies and gentlemen,
And that is how our dear cousins want it."
Someone calls out: "What do you recommend?"
"If you ask me," says Charlie seriously,
"I think it is a lousy deal. For them.
They'd sell their birthright for a mess of pottage.
But let me call upon Ganesh, to say
Why we should take the offer as it stands."
"You've seen this planet flying off the handle,"
Says Ganesh, "The fire-blights, the spasm-storms,
The photochemical carcinogens,
Clogged oceans, freezes, cacofeedback loops.
Not all my fault, whatever Wai-Kwong says—"
There is a laugh at this; Wai-Kwong is Nesh's
Grouchy but brilliant lab assistant—"Some
Was the fault of our missing genotypes.
The planet's breaking out, trying to die,
Seeking conditions of stability,   250
And we can't hold it back a whole lot longer.
By now the angiosperms—the flowering plants—
Should have been started, but we have no bees.
We need the parasites that *clean* the bees.
We need some tailored krill to eat the plankton.
We need the hosts to grow the symbiotes
That make the gases that protect the rest
Of us from cosmic rays and ultraviolet.
We have a gene that makes organic freon
But no suitable beastie to plant it in.
With enough freon in the tropopause
We can sit here on Mars and toast our toes
In the best greenhouse in the solar system.
We need those cultures. And as for the cost,
I priced it out. To build a cat from scratch
Without a genome to template it on
Would cost the entire gross global product
Of the Earth for fifteen years. Kitty is cheap
If you've got blueprints. If not, even krill

Will run you into trillions pretty quick.
What Earth is offering, if they only knew it,
Is the most valuable property
In the universe. The whole shooting match.
The works. The ball, the ballbat and the park."

There are those who are yet to be convinced.   275
The seedcorn of genetic information
Lies useless if its economic food
Is totally cut off; can Mars afford
To cut the last umbilicum to Earth
So early, and to venture forth alone?
At what cost should the colonists insist
On carrying the household gods of life
Out of the dying city? And what if
The Terrans, as they have before, should cheat,
And either send a batch of useless samples
Or seize the Arkship on its voyage home?
These matters must be noted by the movers
Of the question, and considered; but at length
The vote is taken: to accept the deal.
All over Mars town meetings such as this
Are coming to the same conclusion. "Now
The question is, whom do we send, and how,"
Says Beatrice. "What we propose is this.
Kalevala must be our Ark; she is
The largest of our treeships, though she's slow
Compared to the new designs. She'll be skippered
By Commodore Vivar, whom you all know;
Hilly Sharon will lead her garrison.
The science officer will be Ganesh;
He won't accompany the outbound trip   300
But take a faster vessel and be there
To check the cultures' authenticity.
There will be five armed ships to form an escort,
And we are asking Tripitaka"—here
She turns to him, her face grave with the trust
Of all her people—"to assume command
Over the whole task force, and to bring back
The precious seed of our inheritance."
A silence. Tripitaka rises from
His chair, buries his face within his hands,

And then sits down again. Which betrayal,
Out of the many he may choose among,
Will be the least? At last he looks up, speaks.
"Yes, I shall do what you have asked of me."
Then, in an undertone that few can hear:
"And if I fail, so let my name and being
Be driven out from all your habitations."

There is no meeting now between the lovers;
Both know that something's broken that cannot
Be put together. Tripitaka walks
On that last day before his passing from it
Upon the green hills of the chosen planet.
His little flier rests on a mossy hilltop;
Southeastwards, whence he's come this calm morning,
Enormous sloping tablelands of forest   325
Broken and stepped by airy precipices
Blood-red and sheer, where faults have cleft the stone,
Fall to a glassy ocean, pink as jade,
Reflecting in its milky mirror certain
Islets yet nameless in the boreal sea.
Beyond them, from the far edge of the world
Looms up into the violet sky of Mars
A vague outline of impossible scale:
The ringwall of the Kali Crater System
Whose five concentric circles brand this world
As ours, upon its northern hemisphere.
He turns west, and the albedo changes,
The sky now purple opposite the sun,
And here the mesas of the Nilosyrtis
Rise like pink ghosts into the morning air,
Iced like a cake with groves of emerald.
Southwards the mountains rise, and rise again,
And as he slowly spins, the Gulf of Isis
Hung over by the tiny blazing sun
Comes into view once more. The light is like
A rich and brilliant twilight, or the dimmed
Warmth of a winter noon in northern Europe;
Or like the painter's shift, who may not lay
A brighter pigment than his whitest white
Upon a canvas of Arcadia   350
(Which, being so, should be a well of light);

And yet, the painter knows, even that white
Must be diminished by the glazes—by
The varnish, if the work is to endure—
And so he darkens every color to
A velvet chiaroscuro in his palette,
And softens all the details in the shade,
And saves the sharpness and the clarity
For that bright ship caught in the blaze of noon,
Beside the rocky antre in the bay,
And those arbutus leaves with backlighting
That glow like neon in the canopy;
And keeps the clot of white for that bright lozenge
Of the sky and sea where the painting's lines
Meet, at the point of vanishing, infinity.

But the man's heart will not cease its tormenting.
He must speak to Irene, but his mind
Gives him no guidance as to what to say.
His greatest eloquence would be his death;
But the imperative of that creation
All of them serve and hold to be their bond
Will not allow him to desert his post.
He knows to offer her a lover's compact,
That cosy and conspiratorial
Recourse, favored of those who hold the act   375
Of sex to be the paramount endeavor
Of the race, would be anachronism;
Would indeed sell the work that they accomplished
There on the fresh tatami mats among
Her silks and milkwhite limbs, at less than cost.
He knows the subtlety of a Van Riebeck
Vengeance, and its promise for the future,
Its impositions, its inhuman call
For what cannot be satisfied with love.
And Tripitaka is content with nothing
Less, and feels the fierce euphoria
Of playing with the masters of the game.

When he returns to base, a note is waiting
On the plain threshold of the fighting-floor.
"There is no need to speak. I saw the shirt
You wore when you were summoned to the council,

And know what it is for. *Sensei,* I thank you
For the great teaching you have given me
And bow to you upon your enterprise."
So she has made it easier for him.
He knows that this farewell will be forever.
Next day he boards the shuttle for the Fleet.
Irene shuns his embarkation, but
She watches when the ships light up their torch.
Ten days later she misses a period.

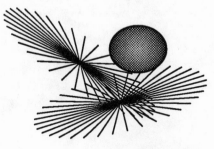

ACT IV
The Gardening of Mars

Wolf and Irene are invited to study at Oxford University.
Irene, discovering her pregnancy, decides to terminate it;
Beatrice, told of this by their doctor Vasco de Perez, and
having recently learned that she herself has become sterile,
arranges to receive the fetus secretly into her own womb.
Wolf and Irene come to Oxford; they discover the existence
of the Lima Codex.

Scene i
Wolf and Irene

*A*nd eight days after that, she and her brother
Each receive letters by the teleprinter.
Wolf's is crested with a cardinal's hat
In scarlet, and Irene's has a shield
Bearing a chevron and armorial birds.
These are their acceptances from Oxford:
Full scholarships to Christ Church and St. Anne's.
Now Oxford University, as often,
Has hung behind the times through good and ill,
And, largely independent, has ignored
Or chastised with its snobbish irony
The zealotry of Ecotheism.
It has remained a place where learning happens
Often despite the efforts of the dons.
The elders have decided that the children
Of the Mars colonists must carry back
The classic wisdoms of the human race
So that the tragedy of history,
That fertile uterus of future time,
May be continued in the generations.

Not twenty miles from Oxford, Devereux
Lies under heavy snow this winter dusk.
The chapel, dusty and unused, with smells
Of mildew, candles, and a ghost of incense,
Lost corner of the world, is mildly lit   25
By the white snow underneath the windows;
And coats of arms in crimson and in gold
Lend to the cold glow on the whitewashed arches

Warmer and dimmer tones. It's very quiet.
The pasturelands between the ancient oaks
(Neglected now, with holes and broken limbs)
Are trackless, humped, and white. The drawing-room
Must be the only warm place in the house.
The office staff are all on holiday;
Gaea has got a coke-fire in the grate
That sends up sweet fumes by the mantelpiece
Where angels carved by Grinling Gibbons play
Their viols and trumpets to an onyx herm.

"Since, Garrison, you always seem surprised
By what I do," says Gaea patiently,
"I'm going to tell you in advance what we
Are planning for the new attempt
The Martian rebels have initiated
To sack our biological inheritance.
We need and truly own the orbital farms,
And cannot act until they're in our hands.
That moment we will seize their so-called Ark,
Whatever it may cost in arms and men;
Their grotesque plans will thus at once collapse
And then the restoration can begin."   50
Garrison watches her amazed. She limps
To the sideboard, gets him a glass of sherry.
"I'm going to be retiring fairly soon.
The trouble in my veins is coming back.
I want your project to be to explain
To the core congregations what we've done."

Garrison knows it will not be worthwhile
To comment on this news. He takes it then,
But feels an ache, a hunger, curious
And yet familiar, but stronger now;
Like the withdrawal symptoms of addiction
Or like the empty place where pain should be
In one whose cancer has been numbed by drugs.
He hurries home; there, through the window, sees
His boy, arms out, running to Bella; but
For many months now that mammalian sweetness,
That lactose wholesomeness, has been to him
A bitter herb, a foul emetic purge.

The cold air is a little comfort to him;
He turns away, and gets into his car.
Mindless, without the heater on, he drives
Northeast until he penetrates the suburbs
Of the sprawled, rotting Birmingham complex;
He drives on into lights and shops and crowds
And parks the car by the old Bullring Center.   75
In Prince's Wine Bar he finds what he wants;
A Babycham laced with penth, and a youth
Called Simmy, with the shaved head, pantaloons
And pink eye-makeup of the Pringletoes.
These, being the most lost and unfortunate
Of human beings, are sacred to the Church,
For hopelessness in any form is holy;
And it is thus that Garrison atones
For loving Gaea, as he knows he must.

This has become a tale of sicknesses.
Consider, though, that in the act of increase
All creatures are most naked to decay;
Corruption riots in the spawn and milk
And branched tubules of fertility.
All of these lesions of the commonplace,
All the torn folk that die into these lines,
Are necessary to the immortal spasm
By which the new world will come into being.
Beatrice, even, has a secret flow
Of pain, a blood-abundance when the lost
Moon of earth comes to the full again;
And her devotion to the Virgin leaves
Her white, exhausted with her mensal faith;
This cannot be an ill, for could the sign
Of a perennial fecundity   100
Be anything but good? But after Chance
No other children come, and anxious Charlie
Makes her consult a doctor for her troubles.
Now whether on her many travels in
The naked radiance of outer space,
Or whether, in the weak protection of
The Martian atmosphere, crippled by lack
Of earthly seed, an errant cosmic ray
Pierced to her egg-place, or if tainted air,

Smelling of ozone, burning, or perfume,
Brewed from the alien sky and sun had seeped
Into the air she breathed, the tests display
The giant cells of deathless carcinoma
Burgeon and pair among her ovaries,
And multiply beyond hope of repair.

The operation now is safe and simple
But it leaves her sterile; it seems to her
The Virgin has forgotten or betrayed her;
And her recovery is slow and weak.
Charlie alone knows what has happened to her,
But cannot help; formerly frank and careless
Of secrets, now she hugs this to herself.
Nor is it simply sickness that has wrought
This change in her. The mortal moon she serves
Seems to be all eclipsed, her eyes which once   125
Burned in her face like brandy, now are turned
Inward, as stars that having burned their fuel,
Fall through the dark zones of their own enchantment.
For Beatrice half consciously has known
Of the devotion Tripitaka paid
To her, and, as a woman, felt it
Like an invisible and tonic vapor,
A painful and sweet edge to the turn of things;
And she's not failed to see the change in him,
The way her step-daughter has marked the place
Where she alone had stood. Her sickness then
Only confirms the cruelty of time;
And is it not, she thinks, quite just that she
Be chastised by the very principle
She worshipped—absolute presence here and
Now, surrender to the passage of the world,
Sacrifice always, in the flame of life
Of aging organisms to the young?
Is she not like the ragged nuptial salmon
Whose crimson wedding weeds become her shroud?
So when the matter of the Ark is raised,
And the debate goes to and fro, she does not lead
But watches and lets others speak for her.
But it's her choice that Tripitaka shall
Command the expedition—she'd be base   150

To rob him of that honor, for revenge;
And it will carry him away, and prove
She has no need of him; and it will take him,
Whispers the fierce Hecate in her blood,
Into a place of danger where he may,
In all honor, find his dismemberment.
But we are not held guilty for our dreams.
Our goodness is the game we choose to play.
And our success in passing to the future
Some rich enduring thing that it may spend
Is bound up with the harmony we make
Of our desires and actions, dark or known.
(But this is what the Sibyl said, years later;
We must not judge the past by dispensations
Grander, more generous in liberty
Than those the players chose to rule the game.)

Irene's pregnancy, and her acceptance
Into the University of Oxford,
Place her where many a wench has stood; her choices
Not different from a suburban girl's
Whose boyfriend knocks her up in senior year.
This bit of tissue is a miracle,
Indeed, and Tripitaka's doctors erred
Telling him, as they did, he would be sterile.
She cannot marry him, the murderer   175
Of Chance, perhaps indeed the murderer
Of Freya, whom she worships as the stars.
She cannot let him know. And yet her fate
Calls her to other than to nurse's works;
And miracle or not, a piece of skin
Scraped from a knuckle in karate practice
Has no less personal identity,
Despite its strange uniqueness, than this thing
She bears within her; but it's hers, a sign
That she can be the mother of a life.
Yet in the end prudence must still prevail;
She sees her doctor, Vasco de Perez,
And asks him to perform the operation.
Now Doctor Perez is a singular man;
The only one of the Van Riebeck doctors
Who followed them for honor of the craft

And not for profit; he it was who led
The team that healed Tripitaka; who
Diagnosed and did the surgery
On Beatrice in her late case of cancer.
Like many of Earth's best, he's come to Mars
To be among the makers of the future;
And the winged snake of his caduceus
Flies on the flag of the Martian Republic.
Many who came to Mars brought their religions,   200
Where they might not be subject to the creep
Of Ecotheism into their cracks;
Perez is Catholic, and must decide
Between Saint Aesculapius and his church.
For him the sin is not the death of that
Which will be human by and by, but rather
The desecration of an ark or symbol
Of the wild future of the Pancreator.
And so he breaks both laws, for he is wise,
And sees an old behoveliness in sin;
He tells Irene he will do her bidding,
But breaks his oath of secrecy, and speaks
To Beatrice without Irene's knowledge.
He's not so foolish as to make suggestions,
But still he knows his patient, and the blend
Of hubris and of tenderness she shares
With many of her kin. "Tell me, my friend,"
Beatrice says at once, for, unsurprised
At what has happened, she will not waste time
On more reactions, "Tell me if your craft
Or science can do this which I will ask:
To take an embryo from one woman's womb
And plant it in another's? If that other,
Even, should have no seed of her own?"
Though Perez has expected this, he feels   225
A wave of worship for a human being
Pass through him, and his answer's oddly formal:
"Lady, if you will have me do this thing,
It will be done." "Then I will have it so,"
She says, and thus their compact is concluded.

But Beatrice must speak to Charlie first.
"Will you be strong enough to bear it, Charlie?

Dear man, who's put up with our dreadful ways
For all these years, to have a sort of cuckoo
In the nest, another bad Van Riebeck?"
"You've cared for mine," says Charlie cheerfully.
"But she's my daughter. If she ever asks,
I will not lie to her about the child."
"She'll never guess. And she'll be far away.
You know we can't say anything right now:
She'd take it as a sign we disapproved . . . "
"—And have the baby, just to prove us wrong,"
Says Charlie, with a smile: "she's a Van Riebeck."
Beatrice seeks out little Chance, and takes
His furry head, as always, in her arms,
Then holds him out and looks into his face.
"How would you like a baby sister, Bear?"

It's not hard to arrange. The speck of life
Is transferred to a culture medium
Without Irene's knowledge, and next day   250
Beatrice sees her doctor normally,
But comes away more pregnant than she went.
And now a change comes over her. Last year
Even before her troubles, she had felt
The terror of a life lived consciously,
Of purposes renewed so many times
That they wear thin and seem like so much babble;
The little turns love makes upon the kink
Of feeling had well nigh fatigued its metal;
So bent, intention is unbearable,
And aches like muscles kept out at a strain,
And rots with milky acids of exhaustion.
But now a salve, a balm, flows in her limbs,
Like that sweet day in spring when first you may
Cast off the clothes of winter and go warm;
She sighs as if her calm would never cease,
And knows her life's work is to be revealed.

For paleobiology is not
A subject she can well pursue on Mars.
Her expertise has been for many years
A rich resource for others' use, but not
A living discipline of performed being.

And so, like an amphibian on land,
Kept from the waters of her ancestry,
She has felt dried and barren; to herself   275
A grotesque creature with a drive to spawn
And no moist spot or roaring beach to do it.
The very night after the fetal transplant
Beatrice dreams and dreams. She walks upon
The hills of Mars without a breathing mask,
And feels the sweet wind blowing in her hair.
With dreamlike emphasis she hears the words
"Oh there is blessing in this gentle breeze;
The earth is all before me, where to choose."
And now the place is where her father died,
In Arcady, beside the Alpheus,
And she perceives a blue so beautiful
In stream and sky that tears seep from her eyes;
A blue as brilliant as Saturn's ring,
As soft as the convolvulus that twined
About the trellises at Devereux,
As saturated as the bloom of grapes
In clusters at the ranch of San Luis Rey.
And when she wakes she knows what she must do:
She'll be the planetary gardener,
And plant Arcadia in the wilderness.

It is decided that Wolf and Irene
Will take the fast ship along with Ganesh
And thus have time to get acclimatized
Before the Michaelmas term begins at Oxford.   300
So they must hurry. The trip can't be delayed—
Ganesh needs ample time to check the cultures.
And so poor Chance must say goodbye
To three of his best friends; with Tripitaka,
Chance's hero, gone ahead already.
One morning Beatrice hears the boy's hoarse voice,
And something warns her this is not a song
Or sound-effects for his elaborate games,
And finds him weeping in his truckle-bed,
And feels the throb of tenderness that one
Who has not been a parent cannot know,
And carries him to Charlie, with his face
Hidden in shame against her soft warm breast.

"We've got a sad old baby here," she says,
And chuckles, but her eyes are full of tears.
Charlie picks up the boy and cuddles him;
Pretends to drop him, so that Chance, alarmed,
Makes angry little movements of rebellion;
Pretends again to drop him, whereupon
The boy begins to smile despite himself.
"Too spoiled," says Charlie gravely. "This poor child
Must instantly be put to useful work.
In fact I've just the thing. From now on, boy,
You are the unpaid clerk of the Commission.
You will not have a minute of your own.   325
Life will be fetch and carry, books and ink,
And speeches by opinionated men
And even more opinionated women.
It will be useful, having a small slave.
In fact I feel some orders coming on."
Chance is delighted. Charlie heads the board
Whose work is to debate the Constitution,
Prepare a draft and meld it with the work
Of other colonies around the planet
In preparation for the great convention.
Now Chance is fascinated by the process,
And hangs around the little theater
Among the trees where the debates go on.
He has already started reading Locke
And Jefferson, and asking awkward questions.
And so the servitude that now begins
Is not as burdensome as Charlie warns:
And Chance has a vocation, like his mother.

Wolf and Irene, sick with their swift passage
Through the heavens, and sluggish with the weight
Of that inertia the Earth generates,
Are put to work at once by wise Ganesh.
He sends them to the Bodleian Library
To search the catalogs for tissue cultures
That the UN researchers may have missed.   350
The core collections of the Bodleian
Were looted from Cadiz by Francis Drake:
The English took that town against the odds,
Storming ashore under the Spanish guns;

Raleigh cried out "Entramos!" and was wounded,
Young Essex threw his hat into the sea;
They say the poet John Donne was in that action.

Dizzy with the calcium therapy
Wolf finds himself caught in the scholar's trance.
He's got a terminal beside a casement
Opening on a quiet Brasenose quad
With a pale green mulberry tree in it.
There is a small anomaly that irks
The sense of neatness that he got from Charlie.
He fastens on the trail and won't let go.
He's looking for the master catalog
Referred to by an obscure private source
Which he suspects may be identical
To something elsewhere termed the Humboldt Project.
Even if incomplete, this catalog
Might organize the bibliographic mess.
He tracks the files until he finds an entry:
"Humboldt Project: see Kropotkin Index."
Of this there is no sign. He changes tactics
And starts a search in Russian History.   375
At once he gets a full biography
Of that serene and warm evangelist
Of symbiosis and commensal life.
But in the catalog there is a note:
"Kropotkin Index (Military Theory):
Access Denied To Persons Without Clearance."
Wolf grins and pats his hands together.
Now he can practice what Ganesh has taught him—
There's no security which can't be cracked;
Don't break the latch until you've checked the mat.
All machines want is to give information:
That is the meaning of the Second Law—
Just ask them nicely, they'll betray themselves.
After three hours Wolf knows he has the key.
He feeds the random prime the program gave him
Back to its guardian, and at once he's in.
Before the breakup of the Soviet empire
"Kropotkin" was a euphemism coined
To name their partially complete collection
Of data codes for living organisms.

It was a library of genes for use
In making agents of bacterial warfare
To work the downfall of Capitalism.
The U.S. version was the Humboldt Project:
Together they made up the Lima Codex.

Kalevala *comes to Earth. The poem turns to the love and
jealousy between Hillel Sharon, Ximene de Vivar, and
Marisol, leaders of the expedition under Tripitaka. The
Arkship is loaded with living tissues. Wolf and Irene
meanwhile discover the meaning of the Lima Codex: a complete
record of the genetic codes of all Earth species, which, if
brought to Mars, would make the arkship's mission
unnecessary. They seek the Codex in Peru, where it is
thought to be hidden. Gaea and the leaders of the Ecotheist
Church have no intention of honoring their agreement with
the Martians and attempt to destroy the arkship as it
returns to Mars. We observe the opening manuevers of the
battle. Wolf and Irene discover the Codex in a library in
Central Africa.*

Scene ii
The Battle for the Codex

*A*bout this time *Kalevala* arrives.
On moonless nights her spool-shape blazes clear;
Holding a low earth orbit she awaits
The lighters that will shuttle up the seed,
The tissue cultures in their strongboxes.
And now the lading process is begun:
Millions of species, mollusks, arthropods,
The many-branched tree of the vertebrates,
Divided into genus, phylum, class,
In sealed vials, thousands of inertial tons,
With life-support, are slid into their racks,
And, labeled with their Latin names and numbers,
Are nicely balanced round the barrel-hull,
A cylinder a thousand cubits broad.
Ganesh checks everything; Hilly Sharon
Unmercifully drives himself, his men
And his machines. Now Tripitaka knows
The humbling of the pure soul that must come
When enterprises needing many hands
And talents not within the captain's writ
Are set in motion; almost can forget
In sleepless hours of negotiation,

Planning, improvisation, compromise,
The shame that calls his spirit to be free.
The stresses multiply from crew to staff: 25
One day Ximene herself, the ship's commander,
Knocks at his office door and throws herself
In weariness upon his little couch.
After a while she looks up at him, smiles.
"It's quite embarrassing to ask a man
Who's never been a parent for advice
On family matters. But I need an eye
On this that's clear and free from prejudice.
The problem isn't just a private one.
You put my daughter Marisol in charge
Of the Communications Center; now I find
I just can't get my messages out of here."
There's more to this, thinks Tripitaka grimly,
And after further questions, interviews
With Marisol and with Hillel Sharon,
The whole story slowly comes together.
For many years Ximene and Marisol
Have shared their gallant desperado Hilly;
Indeed the generosity of work
In the environment of Mars in birth
Has given a glory and a sacrifice
To the renunciations that all three
Have had to make there for each other's sake.
But when Ximene and Hilly were appointed
To lead their moieties of the Martian Ark,   50
Marisol felt a pang of pride and love,
And in remembrance of the time when she
To some minds might have seemed to be a traitor
In the great matter of the comet Kali,
She volunteered to join the expedition.
Now as communications officer
She must work closely with Colonel Sharon.
His dealings with the UN and the unions,
The shuttle captains and the ground controllers,
Observers from the Ecotheist church,
And with Ganesh, who's flying up and down
With the consignments, seem to her to take
Higher priority for now than those
Routine communications a commander

In steady orbit might feel called to make.
Facilities are overloaded as
It is, with coded messages . . . The case
Is obviously a Solomonic one.
Poor Tripitaka, as the judge, is asked
To settle the possession of a man
Between two women, who as child and mother
Are rivals in the oldest love and war.
Now Tripitaka hates to lose his Chief,
Who's worked so well in loading up the ship;
But there is nothing for it. He decides   75
To transfer Hilly to another post,
Commander of the task force escort fleet,
And take the garrison command himself.
Thus judges always must chop up the baby.

                                    *

Wolf tells Irene about what he's found;
Her eyes shine and she is very silent.
At once she checks the files for herself,
Then questions Wolf on what he understands
By the phrase "data code," as it is used
Referring to the content of the Codex.
"I would suppose, some international
Convention formed to classify the genes,"
Says Wolf, who's puzzled by his sister's query
And by the fierce excitement of her manner.
"Donkey! Jackass!" she hisses, in high humor,
"Don't you see yet?" She calls up from the files
The entry under "Cloned Gene Sequencers."
Wolf takes one look and now he understands.
Fragments of DNA from chromosomes
Tagged with a dye, and graded in their length
By their phoresis through a gel, may be
Illuminated by an argon laser
And read off like a poem or narrative,
Nucleotides for letters, codons for words.
The Lima Codex is no catalog,   100
But the true book of all that breathes on earth.
It is what it refers to; played upon
A keyboard of nucleic acids, it

Will sing the very animals to life.
It was the data file Cold Warriors
Constructed their malign chimeras on;
"If it can still exist," Wolf breathes in awe,
"It must be the Old Testament of Mars."

And could this poem speak itself to being,
Then its interpretation might be such
As those so vital codes; not to be read
Upon a page nor analysed by scholars
Of the writing schools, but played out in
The actions of a ring of men and women,
Singers and sung, or danced into a drama,
Shadowed upon a wall or screen where walls
And screens may blaze into a fact as warm
As is the breath of a delivered child.
But if its codes may live, then just to read
Works alchemies upon the brain that form
From the inchoate chemistry of blood
New molecules as like to sperm as songs
Are like to chants about the holy altars;
The word's made flesh in many hidden ways.

Or is it as my enemies might say,   125
A poisonous chimera, and the snake
Whose teeth are sown in every age to be
Reaped then as strife and human misery?

Wolf and Irene book a coded call
To tell Ganesh of their discovery.
And now the hardest period of research begins:
To find the hiding place of the great codex.
When Ganesh calls they only have one clue:
A reference to the letters BBI.
Ganesh is brusque and breezy. "Hello children.
This better be important." "It's important,"
He agrees after perhaps twenty words.
"If it exists, that list is all I need.
All these specimens only ice the deal.
We've got a launch window to observe,
Though, and the codex might have been destroyed."
They tell him of their clue. "That's it!" he says.

"Biblioteca Biologica
Internacional, in Lima, Peru.
Call Giamba Vico. False identities.
Fly to Peru and see what you can find."

As student tourists, then, they walk the streets,
Bleary and sleepless, of Pizarro's city;
The pale blue air of morning, like a crystal
Tinged with the green of certain desert skies   150
Preserves and focuses the pilasters
And broken pediments of the baroque,
Their white stucco cracked by the last earthquake.
The library seems to have disappeared.
A taxi-driver, on the other hand,
Knows of the place, agrees to take them there.
The taxi climbs the monstrous barren slopes
East of the city, in the Andean foothills,
And stops beside a modernistic ruin.
Above, the cyclopean buttresses
Of condor-haunted cordilleras rear
Into an ageless sky. Below's a maze
Of not quite rectilinear avenues
In monster stones rounded like pillows but
Set so precisely each to each that one
Might not insert a knifeblade in the cracks:
The ruined city of Pachacamac.
But these ruins seem to be inhabited.
Though it is very silent, so the wind
Flutes hoarsely in the crevices, a face
As ancient as a turtle's peers and turns
Behind an unglazed window, and a shape
Covered in shapeless black, a bowler hat,
Hobbles from one door to another. Wolf
Feels a weariness of time and life;   175
The great shallow basin in the bare land
Skulled with the eyeholes of the extinct Inca
Is full of bent and speechless human beings.
Here the earth's old and poor have come to die.
Behind him is a massive sculpted house
With stooped lintels of gigantic stone,
The trapezoid forehead the builders gave
The sun kings as a sign of total rule.

To his surprise he realizes now
The architect of this was of our age,
Cunning to match this rare commission with
The art of her or his long dead godfathers,
And so perhaps speak in that quietest voice
Which rulers cannot hear unless they listen.
But like the city, glassless holes stare out
Even from this most fortresslike of piles;
The bronze doors hang from their pins, and the faces
With their sunblind eyes move within the shades.
In greenish stains, where the bronze letters stood,
Their Art Deco shapes still discernible,
Wolf and Irene read: BIBLIOTECA
BIOLOGICA INTERNACIONAL.

Wolf and Irene pass the gloomy news
To the *Kalevala*. And when the ship
Obedient to the flows of force and mass   200
That open up a passage through the heavens
Lights up its long torch, that for several minutes
Casts from the darkened Andes moving shadows,
The twins are sleeping an exhausted sleep.

                              *

Gaea meanwhile receives a visit from
The Chief Commissioner of the world church:
Bengt Andersson, with his kind white eyebrows
And his archaic ceremonial garb,
The slacks, tie, and sportcoat of a pundit
On a mid-twentieth century TV forum
Or nature series, or religious show.
The courtesies are deep upon both sides;
Garrison joins their aides about the screen.
And as they watch, the symbols representing
Orbital farms and Martian satellites
Blink from dull red to green as their crews leave
And then to blue as UN troops move in.
As soon as the last red spot is extinguished
The eyes of Gaea and the Commissioner
Meet with the frankness of unprurient power.

The nod is given, and from a hundred silos
Slides the armada they have long prepared.
These are crude ships, built for but one thing only:
To spill and burn the cargo of the Ark.
Electronic elegance and tech-   225
Nical sophistication, cybernetics,
Even if still within the arts of Earth,
Are wasted on a vessel to contend
With software that Ganesh has taught to pierce
The subtlest countermeasures, and to find
Through heterodyning frequencies the chink
Into the central pathnames of control.
These ships burn hydrazine and work by wires
And levers, and are armed with heavy guns
Firing projectiles from a cordite shell
That will explode on contact or by means
Of simple fuses burning to the charge.
At close range even crudest electronics
Can be fused out by EMP, as if
The heat of Martian genius melted wire.
The ships are lethal, armored, vulnerable,
As packed with men as eggs are packed with meat;
The strategy must be to board and fight
And take the needed losses going in.
Any conceivable success must cost
Thousands of lives, billions of Earthly treasure;
But what are lives and treasure but to spend?

*

The moment that Irene wakes, she knows
That something's wrong. They cannot just give up.
Perhaps the library was moved; perhaps   250
The Codex still exists. She wakens Wolf:
He feels the same. Discreet enquiries at
The University of San Marcos
Yield nothing useful; to pursue the matter
Would be to risk suspicion and exposure.
They go back to the ruins; in halting Spanish
Ask an old woman where the books have gone.
A blue streak of Quechua is all they get.
But now she takes Irene by the arm

And leads her to a half-blind ancient man
Whose fluent Spanish and whose fair command
Of English make him a rare scholar here.
He tells the Yanquis that he heard them say
The books were going somewhere—Africa—
Zimba or Zamba, he could not be quite sure.
Wolf pokes around and finds a broken crate
Abandoned in the dry and stinking stacks
Among a pile of periodicals.
On it he makes out an address: Centre
For Life-Science Records, Mwinilunga District,
Zambia, Central Africa. "That's it,"
Irene says in quiet triumph. "Let's get going."

*

The mass detectors of the Arkship escort,
Used to evade the larger meteors
That are encountered in the Asteroids,　　　　　　　275
Now give the first sign of the Terran sortie.
A swarm of objects shows up on the screens,
Massive but electronically dead.
The fleet's computers calculate the mix
Of laser, railgun, and evasive action
That best averts the threat, but as they do so
Some of the warheads bloom in globes of plasma;
The instruments of the *Kalevala*
Are blinded momentarily, and one
Of the missiles takes out an escort vessel.
No more surprises. Now the Terran fleet
Comes in behind its barrage; Tripitaka,
Cold and ready for them, has perceived
A boldness and simplicity of planning
That he suspects is Gaea's work, his old
Mistress and close instructress in the arts
Of treachery ennobled by its cause.
Ganesh's software net grasps out in vain,
But soon the clumsy vessels of the Earth
Are popping like ripe fruit within a tree
That little boys with catapults have chosen
To practice on with their forked dangly weapons.
And each time one of them erupts, it spews

Into the hard explosive suck of space
That pops a human head like watermelons,   300
A great grained juice of young humanity
As one might burst a colony of maggots
With a soft slide from the back of a spade.
The rebel gunners do not feel the crime,
Caught up as they must be by the huzzah
And fiery wine of mortal contestation
That renders life as trembling-precious as
The solemn alchemy of death itself;
But Tripitaka's soul receives the charge
Of debt and karma as a battery
Will mount toward the redline of its melting.
Still the Earth ships come on; he had not thought
There possibly could be so many of them.
Within their hulls it must be like the decks
Of ancient dreadnoughts or ships of the line:
A hell of noise and smoke and running men;
Babble of prayer, as it might have been
In those urine-soaked trenches of Iran
When the mad Ayatollah called his children
Of the Islamic revolution to Jihad.
And now from time to time a Terran shell
Finds its way through the lace of fire stitched down
By the Arkship's cold battle computers.
Two more of the escort ships are hit,
One of them crippled badly, as they're cast   325
In sacrifice before the holy spool
Of the *Kalevala*, the womb of life.
Over a half of the great Terran fleet
Remains, and now the range is swiftly closing.

*

As if the colors somehow are reversed,
The dawn sky blazes not with red but blue;
A sweet and painful blue that burns still deeper
Reflected in the reaches of the river.
It is the ground that's red; the whole valley
Is delicately scaled with scarlet cannas,
Turned by the morning breeze from pink to crimson;
Then a tremble, and a pink catspaw spreads.

The sparse spring rains of Africa have come
And even the umbrella-trees, the stand
Of brachistegias, the sugarbushes,
Are scarlet or vermilion with spring:
Their buds and new leaves sticky with the sap
And not yet turned to summer's tender green.
Here the most frenzied colors come with birth,
Not death and fall, as in the northern year.
Wolf and Irene reel upon the slope,
Exhausted, having jetted to Lusaka,
Changed in Solwezi to a chartered plane
And bumped by battered taxi to this place.
Giamba has sent a courier to Lusaka   350
To meet them off the plane and to provide them
With introductions and identities
From the Max Planck Institute in Seewiesen,
Together with a clearance from the church;
They are Canadian seminarians
Studying animal behavior as
It is predicted by the play of proteins
Nominated and controlled by genes.

They've ended up here at six in the morning
With rucksacks full of dirty clothes, clutching
Two paper bags containing airline snacks,
Waiting for the Institute to open,
And, strangely, happy as they'd never been
Since childhood and their first try at their wings.
For they have found again that intimacy,
Brother and sister, more than man and wife,
Womb-mates and knowers of each other's thoughts,
Insiders of whatever world they travel,
Because each knows the other is awake
And taking in with that familiar strangeness
All he might miss, as if the other were,
Personified, that easy connaissance
Of the unnoticed that we we call our home.
Sweetest of all, they are conspirators,
And in awed admiration for each other's   375
Courage, address, and perspicacity,
They find those warm grave pleasures of respect.

Built out of brick in an anonymous style,
To house material the Church would hide
Here in this lonely corner of the world,
The Institute's a compound of low buildings.
As they walk slowly through the dewy cannas,
It falls away behind a gentle rise.
A hissing roar that seems to rise and fall
Grows all about them; the Zambesi rapids.
Here in a hundred rills and torrents pours
The great clean river through a scarp of granite;
Where tiny islands, dark with somber trees,
Are covered thick with sallow orchises,
And a long wide blue-white fight of wild water
Half an inch deep scrolls up against a boulder
High as a house; and sparse grass golden-green
Blows shining on the edge of granite plains.

They eat their odd breakfast upon a rock,
Then, holding hands, like young Adam and Eve,
They climb the slopes toward the Institute.
And now it's all absurdly easy. "Yes,
Seewiesen called us. You've got rooms and carrels.
You'll find the disk recorders that you asked for."
Three hours later they have the Lima Codex.

The battle in space continues. Terran forces board
Kalevala. Hearing of the discovery of the Codex by Wolf and
Irene, Tripitaka recognizes that he must cover their escape
to Mars by staging a last stand. He sends Hillel Sharon in
a fast escort ship to ferry Ganesh Wills, whose knowledge
will be essential in decoding the Codex, to safety on Mars.
Sharon's mistresses Ximene and Marisol decide to stay behind
and die with the arkship. Tripitaka's interrupted ritual
suicide is resumed. Wolf and Irene, learning of the death
of the arkship, decide to avenge it by killing their
grandmother Gaea before they leave the Earth. We learn of
the strange love between brother and sister. They find they
can consummate neither it nor their revenge; but their mercy
serves them well, inasmuch as it is Gaea who persuades the
Ecotheist council to permit the repatriation of Martian
civilians left on Earth. Wolf and Irene thus escape with
the disks containing the Codex.

Scene iii
The Fate of Tripitaka

And now the remnants of the Terran fleet
Are grappled to the huge hull of the Ark.
Although they're locked in battle, they must share
Their atmospheres through many charred mouths.
Neither combatant can risk decompression:
The Terran infantry is not equipped
With bulky pressure-suits; the Ark-defenders
Must till all hope is gone preserve the air
That keeps their cargo, and the tree itself
That is its vessel, still alive. The sight
That meets the crippled escort might remind
One, so inured to irony, of that
Cruel moment in conception when the egg
Is seiged with feebly-beating sperms, that try
To sink their package of genetic meaning
Into the vast bulk of the Mother's womb.
Within, through sad woodlands torn and splintered
With explosions, the troops of Tripitaka
Form and reform in desperate defence.

The flagship of the escort group, the *Dove*,
Has for the past half-hour been overwhelmed
By waves of massed attackers. Hilly Sharon
Sees on his screens the toil of all he loves,
The seedpod of the Promised Land, the mother
And her daughter, both his brides, the ark   25
Of his new covenant, the Shekinah,
Rent by her enemies and violated.
He breaks off contact with the enemy,
Orders the two remaining escort ships
To burn all new besiegers of the Ark,
And docks his vessel with the mother ship.
As he does so the *Raven*, the yard-sister
To Hilly's *Dove*, is gutted by explosions.

Meanwhile the bridge of the *Kalevala*
Is calm and bright; for Tripitaka knows
The clear-eyed *Chih* of generalship, and holds
The ship's morale in his still folded hands.
No matter if he knows that presently
Defeat is to relieve him of command,
That all his enterprises come to nothing;
That the insufferable debt he owes
To the Van Riebeck clan must go unpaid;
That the true body of the live tradition,
The hearth-gods of the ancient Earth, the scriptures
It is his name and fate to carry back
Across the wastes of space to the new country
Must now be quite consumed and lost. Be calm.
As he gives orders swiftly and quietly,
Ximene beside him works her dying ship.
Both know that in attempting a relief   50
Sharon has breached his orders; Tripitaka
Passes Ximene a brief sad smile. That moment
Marisol appears upon the screen.
"Urgent. A message from the Earth. The twins
Found something called the Lima Codex. Vico
Says it's important, says Ganesh will know."
The latter, who's been working feverishly
At the master board of the ship's computer,
Pricks up his ears. "No, listen, guys, this is
The big end run—if it is what I think.

Patch me on through and let me talk to them."
In thirty seconds he has heard enough.
"Everything's changed, O.K.? New ballgame.
Mars doesn't need our cargo. It's just wetware.
Those crazy kids have aced the bunch of us.
Right now the most important thing there is
Is that small rucksack on Irene's back
With the eight high density disks in it.
That's all we need. They've got the Book of Life."
Tripitaka sees what must be done.
The Codex would take months to send, in code,
At the low baud rates of the twins' equipment.
Giamba Vico's under house arrest.
The Codex and the twins must be got out.
The only hope is that in victory,   75
Or the illusion of it, the UN
Will let them leave the planet with the rest
Of the Van Riebeck personnel. "Ganesh,"
Says Tripitaka, "Tell me the plain truth.
Who has the skill to read and use the Codex?"
"I was afraid you'd ask me that," he says.
"The answer is, nobody, not one person.
The minimum is Charlie, Bea, and me.
That means, I guess, you have to wrap me up
And send me off to Mars." For the first time
In his life, his friends see a great tear
Roll down the pitted cheek of the wise nerd.
As if it were not there, he grins and says,
"One of the perks of brains, mes camarades."

Now Hilly's boarding party, blackened with fire,
Reaches the bridge. Outside the control capsule
The battle rages still. "Mr. Sharon,"
Says Tripitaka, "You have disobeyed
My order, and I shall lodge formal charges
When this affair is over. But meanwhile,
I command you to carry Mr. Wills
And the flight staff of the *Kalevala*
To our agreed-on rendezvous on Phobos.
Their safety, chiefly Mr. Wills', is now
Your paramount responsibility."   100

Then, to them all: "We must evacuate
All but the garrison; the conflict, though,
Must be as fiercely waged as if there were
No other hope for our survival as
A viable society and world.
I, therefore, and my troops, must stand and fight."
Ximene casts one tormented glance at Hilly;
And now she speaks. "Sir, with respect I must
Point out that if the ship that I command
Does not fight too, the military goal
Of misdirection lacks a certain color.
I must insist I stay and fight my ship."
Tripitaka groans in soul but sees
How it would be impossible to refuse.
He knows already that the Terran fleet
Must be disabled here to save the *Dove*.
This may mean the annihilation of
Kalevala; he knows she knows this too.
He cannot ask her, therefore, to appoint
Subordinates to stay here in her place.
"Very well then. Proceed about your duties."
The three bridge officers now volunteer
To stay with Commodore Vivar; Sharon,
After a moment's agonized delay,
Salutes the turned back of Ximene his lover   125
And gathers those who are to fight their way
Back to the airlock and the waiting escort.

Tripitaka now prepares himself
For his last battle. In his private room
He ritually dons his battle armor
And binds about his waist the antique swords
That Nishiyama gave him at their parting,
Tying the silken cord in prescribed knots.
He breathes his spirit gently out and in,
And meditates on his unworthiness,
The gulf between his proper duty and
The acts that should have bodied out the form;
He feels too the ancient vigor flow
From the cold navel into thigh and armpit.
And if his tree should not have fruited, nor
The saintly promise of his birth be kept,

And if his mother's sacrifice be vain,
And if his first command be but a feint
To draw the enemy from greater prizes;
Yet like those breeds of peony or peach,
Or flowering cherry or the bitter plum,
Those beauties hybridized by cruel arts
To be infertile while they feed the soul,
He will now blossom into deathly spring,
The barren glory of a pointless end.   150

And how indeed are such as he employed
Upon a garden-world, a nest of birth?
What occupation for this ghost of fire?
What makes a country kitchen with a sword?
The warrior-caste, the kshatriya, the knight,
The samurai, are bloody parents for
The sweet republic of the human being.
As warrior he is a criminal.
There is a kind of perfectness in crime,
That leads the soul to a renunciation
Of all desire, all pleasure, all decay;
That seeks out pain as the one ground of truth.
But such a perfectness is worth a moment
Only, must abrogate itself into
Eternity, cleansed of the kiss of time.

Such meditations may be based on lies.
How can I say this, follower as I am
Of this strange hero of another past?
How disagree with what is true in being,
If false in fact? His seed is planted, growing
In the womb of her whose servant he
Had pledged himself to be; his tree is sprung.
Let us say this: The garden of the spirit
Only lives through infertility.
Grant that the meaning of this hero's life,   175
Is, as he knows it, only a dead end.
Grant that his seed is no more but a spot
Of albumen, a brute coincidence.
Grant this, but what would any garden be,
Without the flame, the unnatural blanch of flower
That bursts from sterile trees and seedlessness?

Time would be base and tame if only growth,
If only nature should command its flow.
Let there be immolations, sacrifice,
Corpses buried in the walls of worlds;
Let Nature bear the guilt of its extinctions:
Thus only is the spirit brought to flower.

In the evacuation, Marisol
Is hustled by her lover's troops toward
The besieged berth of the *Dove*. Halfway there
She realizes that Ximene's not with them,
And feels that panic children know when crowds
Part them from Mother. Fear turns to rage.
She struggles up to Hilly, grabs his shoulder,
Whirls him around. "How could you leave her there?
Brute. Bastard. After all the love she's given.
Go back and fetch her now, if you're a man."
Hilly looks vaguely at her, wipes the blood
Of a young Terran from about his mouth.
"You're right. They were my orders. I'd be dead   200
If I had any choice. She would not come."
"Then I'm going back. I hate you, Hilly. Always.
Don't ever think we might have said goodbye."
He tries to hold her, but she's got away;
He sees her hit and spun by a stray bullet,
Pick herself up, and stumble on. She does
Not once look back. Fresh Terran troops appear,
And he must cut his way through to the *Dove*.

                              *

Wolf and Irene have slipped quietly back
Into their Oxford digs on Beaumont Street.
They sit up late at night with the TV
Waiting for news of the great space battle
And drinking coffee black to ride the waves
Of nauseous sleepiness, the crawling flesh
Of compound jet fatigue, and grief, and rage.
The disks are in an empty plastic bowl
Which once held margarine, inside the fridge.
Irene's in a cold blue killing fury.

"The mad old bitch has got to die for this.
We swore to kill her after Grandfather.
I want to see her black blood on the floor;
I want to see her gut-fat welling out.
Everyone else is hypnotized by her,
Including you. The bitch deserves to die,   225
And nobody sees it, they all forgive,
Like little jesuses, like little birds
With the big mammasnake's stone eyes on them.
Oh Wolf, oh come on brother, we've got time.
The shuttle won't be ready for two days.
We can get out to Devereux and pop
Her damned eyes out for her, and get right back,
Nobody wiser, a good job well done,
And hop the shuttle on the Monday morning."
Like Garrison before his mother, Wolf
Shrinks at the fury of his sister's face,
And loves her for it terribly, and fears her.
"Grandfather loved her though," he says. "I've read
His letters to her. And if you or I
Believed as she does, we could do no other.
According to her guiding principles
She's good, when it can't be easy for her . . ."
"*Guiding principles*," she spits, and turns
Away, just as her grandmother might do.
"I'll do it by myself then. Don't you worry.
Set your mind at rest. You'll just wake up
And it will all be done, your conscience clear—"
"That's it," says Wolf, and feels a deadly chill
Come over him, the chill of fated action;
"Of course we must be faithful to our vow.
It's not a case of feelings or of hatred.   250
It is an act of war." For Wolf is not
His uncle Garrison, and knows the bone
That stiffens human flesh to acts of terror,
That serves our noblest daemon, as our worst.

*

Now through the stricken Ark the enemy
Pours as a flood will through a beaten city,
The levees down, exhausted volunteers
Still trying to fill the breaches, but in vain;
With their fierce general the Martian troops

Form and reform in pockets of defense;
Kalevala becomes a charnel-house
Of burnt and broken men and women; less
Would not be expected from a nation
Whose one great treasure lay exposed to sack.
The access to the bridge is held most dearly:
A clearing in the woods, a great door set
Into a hummock in the inner hull;
The woods around are full of Terran dead.
Three hours have passed now since Sharon, in tears,
Only a handful of his party left,
Has fought through to the airlock of the *Dove*,
Broken off contact with the mother vessel,
And, with the crippled escort, got away,
Pursued by half a dozen Terran cruisers;
He's blown up two of them, outrun the others,   275
And now is in the long trajectory to Mars.

General Maghreb of the Terran forces
Orders a full assault upon the bridge.
In waves the Terran youth storm through the trees;
They fall in windrows, instantly replaced
By others, with like hope of paradise.
At last it's noticed that the hostile fire
Has slackened off, and the defense is broken.
The Terran troops enter the clearing slowly
From all directions; this is what meets their eyes.
Surrounded by a heap of Martian dead,
That strange warrior who had led the charge
So many times against the Terran siege
Is kneeling, and unbuckling his armor.
Some of them aim their weapons, but are waved
To lower them by officers in command.
Now he removes his helmet, and they see
The fine dark features still defiled with grey.
Before him is a short sword on a stand.
He takes his long sword, one hand on the hilt,
The other on the blade, wrapped for protection
With a silk cloth, and snaps it effortlessly.
And now he ties his knees with a white sash,
And now he meditates a while, at ease,
And now he speaks a few words that the soldiers   300

Can barely catch and do not understand.
The ring of enemies is stunned and silent.
Now with a certain satisfaction, as of one
Who finishes a task long since begun,
He reverently lifts the shorter sword,
Sword of the spirit of a fighting-man,
And turns it carefully upon himself.
He drives a quick stab inward to the belly;
Then with both hands, the razor edge is drawn,
Fighting the tremors of the autonomic
System, which governs nausea and such
Internal, ticklish glides as this, across
The abdomen, then up toward the ribs—
A virtuoso touch—and now he falls.

What were those words he said that few could hear?
The red sun of the last day of the year;
Great and less come to one end. What they meant?
Perhaps the eyes that closed in meditation
Last saw the green bolt of an energy weapon,
And burned upon the retina in crimson
Was the soft oval of a phosphene's mask;
Perhaps the red sun is the Shinto god
Of war, the blood-nativity and aura
Of all the silken worship of Japan;
Or was it that bright disk of purest Tao,   325
Of non-attachment and the tacit Way?
Perhaps with his sun sets the sun of war,
Of all that cruelty and blind endeavor.
But if his act concludes a greater work,
That work began in an Arcadian dawn
When he incurred the debt he's now discharged;
And if there is a lesser work whose cycle
Now fully comes around to meet the greater,
It was that interrupted ritual
Of death, begun upon the fighting-floor
To celebrate the end of maidenhood.

*

Exhausted, flushed, Irene cannot sleep.
The ghastly freedom of their late decision

Has left her breathless, without rules or comfort,
Exhilarated, almost perhaps insane.
At last she creeps into her brother's room
And lies down with him in his bed, and shivers.
Slowly he wakes, perceives what he's not felt
Since childhood, the bed-flesh of his own twin.
He turns, limed in the lawlessness of sleep,
And catches her within his heavy arms.
But now a chill comes over her, the thought
Of what it is that they must do tomorrow;
She pushes from him, whispers tenderly
As if a bride upon the eve of marriage: 350
"No. Not yet. Not till the thing is done."

Ximene and Marisol upon the bridge
Have used the time that Tripitaka gave them
With his brief theater, to change the orders
Fed to the great computer at the Arkship's heart.
As the first troops arrive, they close the circuits;
Mother and daughter, closer now than ever
In their lives, clasp each other breast to breast,
Woman to woman; and the wretched lover
That they have shared is all forgiven now.
The energies that drove this ship are turned
Obediently into themselves, and so
A new sun momently is born in heaven
Too bright to look upon, that has licked clean
The battlefield of victors and of vanquished,
Fading at once to leave a field of stars.

*

The operations room at Devereux
Falls to a hush as the war-screens go dead.
Gaea's the first to break the silence. "So,
Friends and comrades, we have won. As we knew,
They had the power to undo themselves.
May we invite you, Mr. Commissioner,
To stay with us tonight and take what rest
The brief time still affords before the dawn?"
But Garrison feels a dull aching grief: 375
In that white flash he lost his only friend.

"Tomorrow evening we must meet again,"
Says Anderssen, his white eyebrows drawn down;
"We face the issue of the refugees.
Should we intern the rebels we have here
Or send them back to Mars if they desire?
Dear friend of the Church, we thank you again,
And will accept your gracious invitation.
We leave for London next morning early;
We shall expect to see you there tomorrow."

At noon next day Wolf and Irene cross
The tangled grounds of Devereux unobserved.
They peer into the windows of the place.
Almost at once they see their grandmother.
She is alone, but for the little boy,
Flavius, who runs to her with open arms,
Over and over, giving gurgling shrieks
Of happiness; she hugs his body hard
And lets him go again. Wolf and Irene
Look one another in the eyes, and both
Are full of tears. This thing cannot be done.
They know at last they never will be lovers.

That night at her son's plea Gaea agrees
To let the Martian hostages go home.
Among them are the twins, with the great Codex.

Beatrice gives birth to Hermione, later known as the Sibyl,
genetic daughter of her niece Irene and Tripitaka. In her
grief at the loss of her friends with the arkship, she falls
into a deep despondency. Chance the younger and Sumikami
nurse the child. Beatrice is comforted by a dream of the
mysteries of Cumae, and inspired by the crater landscape of
the Bay of Naples in her dream, she takes up her child again
and remembers her vocation to be the gardener of Mars.
She recruits the grieving Hillel Sharon to the work; the Codex
is opened and the first of its living contents are
regenerated. At last the air of Mars is ready to be
breathed by human lungs.

Scene iv
The Birth of the Sibyl

*I*n very complex systems resonance
Can make a music of their feedback loops;
Time, then, becomes coherent like the cells
That roll in little scrolls within the body
Of a pan of boiling water, or
A gas-giant's methane envelope; or like
The light that pulses from an argon laser.
Consider this: the very moment when
The arkship died, Beatrice screamed in pain
And drove between her thighs the crowning dark
Of one who came to sing the universe
Into its new time of most joyful gods.
And so the father dies into his daughter.
They named the child Hermione, and since
No surname seemed to serve, they made one: Mars.
In later times she would be known as Sibyl.
These lips unworthy that do speak her name.

The birth was hard and long; the elder mother
In the stretched prodigality of love
Would not rest even when she was delivered,
But took the baby to herself and sang
To it, and shared it with the worried Charlie,

And asked for the boy Chance, who came and held
The baby girl; all this while doctors worked
To stop the bleeding, and her face, a moon,   25
Waned with the shadows of her weariness.
Doctor Perez at last must fight with her,
Drive people out, give her a sedative.

And no one told her of the news, the loss
Of the *Kalevala*, the death of friends,
The fall of the first warlord of Mars.
And then when she awakes she is depleted
Both of her blood and spirit; she feels cold,
But when her other doctor, Katya Grishin,
Takes her temperature, she's got a fever.
Worse, when the cheerful day-boy brings the papers,
He's not been told to keep them from this patient;
She reads in the *Syrtis Intelligencer*
Of the last bloody moments of the war,
And how the father of her child had died.

And now the weariness of all things human
Comes on her as it came on Charlie once
When all the golden narrative seemed just
A sitting on a stone in a dark place.
And it stabs her heart, the dry homesickness,
The artificiality of this,
Their plastic life on a defiled planet;
Where is the natural place, the little valley
With the ancient stream, where Man has not
With his machines and tendencies, his eye   50
Cocked for the notice of a chance admirer,
Massaged the rich sweet land into a message?
Where is that sound of water trickling
Over the stones which lay a million years
Until the stream uncovered them again?
Where is the sound of tearing grass you hear
Across the clearing in the morning mist
Where deer, like tired dancers, catch the sun
Dim gold, upon their brown flanks wet with dew?
What is this child not her child doing here
With her, in this room under ground, where hide

The remnant of a people drunk with pride
Who at fantastic cost and stress have come
To where they are not wanted, not at home?

The weeks that follow bring a swift decline
In Beatrice's health and strength of mind.
Doctors Perez and Grishin diagnose
And quickly treat the puerperal fever, but
The deep depression cannot be controlled.
Charlie and Chance, in tears, hold her limp body,
And try to turn her distant face to theirs;
Sometimes the baby cries and she won't listen,
Caught in the trance, almost voluptuous,
Of dim, incurious, paralysed despair.
Charlie at last is almost mad with grief;   75
The boy takes up the care and nourishment
Of this his niece and sister, heats her milk
When Beatrice cannot give her the breast;
And changes her, despite his boyish loathing
Of messes smelly, mixed, and living-warm.

And meanwhile Sumikami mourns her son.
The cruellest is, she cannot have his body
That she might wind it in her arms once more
Before committing it to the great flame
Of life, whose truth burns on behind the veils
Of sweet illusion that it generates;
There is no consummation to desire,
No rending of the membrane of attachment.
She prays to the lord Buddha, but in vain;
As if she were an unrequited lover
She yearns and yearns for what she cannot name.
And the Van Riebecks, in their own distraction,
Leave her to her grief. The first, kindest thought
Is easiest; respect the suffering,
Do not intrude, do not disturb the soul
Of one who is an equal human being,
And therefore capable of her distress.
But in his insight Chance has second thoughts.
Having a thing to care for, he has borne
Better than most the grief of lonely times.   100
What can he give her that will spring the trap

The mind makes for itself, and set her free?
One day he takes his sleeping baby sister
And, though he feels the tears scald in his nose,
He lays her in his ancient nurse's arms.
"Nanna," he lies, "I can't look after her
All by myself. Mother is sick, and Dad
Must see to her. We need your help again."
And now he tells her of the baby's birth,
Breaking the promise of his secrecy;
It is her own granddaughter that she holds,
The unknown flesh-gift of her vanished son.
The boy is wise; for, from that moment on,
The nurse's care eases the care of grief.
So the sweet trap of life, baited with love,
May trap the soul's own trap, and let it go.

And then one day the weather seems to change,
As even indoors it may, and Beatrice
Remembers as an echo something strange
That Charlie said, about the Lima Codex;
She asks her doctor Katerina Grishin
If she may walk out in the open air.

Beatrice sees the mountains of the Syrtis
Under the brooding clouds of early spring,
With flecks of white snow in their crevices,   125
And drizzling rain in flaws and floating drifts.
The ocean in this light shows its own color,
A rich wine red, deep and transparent
(Though in a glass it scarcely hints of rose),
For here the ferrous oxides set the theme.
How may I tell the strangeness of this place?
Each time the poet passes on it, he
Leaves words, words, leaves, a vesture woven long
Before upon the whispering looms of Earth,
And forests with a growth as meaningless
As beard upon the body of a child
This otherness, this tedious cipherhood.
She feels the cold wind blow upon her body,
And sees it cross the fields of mutant rye,
Arranged in clumsy rectangles and squares.
She pities the uncaring ugliness

Of these poor plots set out by tired people,
Hardscrabble agriculture in the hills,
Which, she can see, cannot but breed a race
Of ignorant prejudice, strange to grace.
And yet all lands upon the earth were once
A markless wilderness, a sky-struck plain;
And in the valor of their loving labor
Our ancestors inscribed them with their names.
The riddle and the paradox of action—   150
How the unacted thing is dead and dull
Until the actor steps into the part,
Then retroactively attains a life
And freedom in the sacrifice of action
That almost make us miss the uncommitted—
Catches her quick mind, will not let it go.

Now she remembers her part as a mother,
And goes to Sumikami, takes the child
Hermione and looks into her eyes,
And settles down with her and gives her suck.
The grip and nuzzle of the nursing girl,
The soft mouth-liquor and the tug
Of trust turn up the layers of her soul;
The fine down on her body rises up;
Her hair crackles with a wave like fear,
Like tickling, like unexpected joy—
Pit of the stomach ache and pang of love
Upon the very precipice of being,
Drugged with the warm narcosis of the whole.
This is the loveliest child she's ever seen.
The hair is black and curly, and so soft;
The skin is white as cream, as ivory;
The face a little buddha's, slim and calm;
The lips composed into omniscience.
And now the sleep that Beatrice sleeps is fresh   175
And quenching, as no sleep of hers has been
For many weeks; and she's blessed with a dream.

It's like that other dream of piercing blue;
And, as the memory of one dream may
Seep through the veil into another's colors,

So this one has the catch and sob of that.
Images from her *Italienreise*:
She's with a group of people, not sure whom;
She knows them all. They have come here to Cumae
Where the dead town looks on a lonely sea;
A sacred olive grove whose silver shade
Is heartless as the dazzling grey light
That pours from every part of the blue sky;
A black she-dog haunts the acropolis;
Afternoon silence; promontories
In the distance, Misenum, sun-baked Baiae.
They pass into a cavern full of air
And light, shadowless swallows twittering.
A smell of something cooking, some burnt grain,
The cold odor of subterranean stone.
Here three caves meet: first, the Sibyl's shaft,
That passage to the ovaries of the brain.
Next, passing under it aslant and through,
The work of the heroic engineer,
Roman Cocceius, who conceived and built,　　　　　200
Driving ten thousand slaves, a ship canal
Through uncracked stone a mile into the land
Where it delivered to the Birdless Lake
The Roman fleet in times of naval war.
And last, another cave whose angle she
Cannot make orient in her mind, which seems
To cross athwart the others, and to rise
Into a depth more terrifying still,
As if a vertigo attends the sky,
As if the living stone were thin as air.
Some passion with no name: accomplishment
Perhaps?—but not quite present, round a corner—
Forces the tears between her waking lids.

She sees her way. There never was a land
But oracles and artists, or wise queens,
Or free farmers with thumbed books in their shelves,
Or potentates with some enlarging vision
(However cruel their conquests or their rule),
Must mulch its soil with myth and buried sign

If the humane and intricate would grow.
A land void of inscription, storyless,
Must suffer the departure of its youth,
The wearing out of men until their balls
Are all they know of value; desperate wives,
Who hate their lives, their paltry husbands, and   225
Their children most of all who hang on them;
And though on Earth the millions may take suck
Upon the accrued seed-juice of the past,
For generations, taking what was given
By the magnanimous and by the holy
In prodigality and pride and service;
Yet here the soil is thin and must be fattened
With gifts of tongues and visionary blood.
What may be done with this the orphaned land,
This lunar rawness, with its swamps and craters,
Its smeared landslips, and its vermilion sea?
Such, then, must be the meaning of the dream:
The *Campi Flegrei*, the fields of Hades,
Where Solfatara steams with smells of brimstone
And the gaunt bony imagined dead below
Beat on the underside of the domed ground,
And the sere grass gives way to greenish sulphur;
The doom-canted ash cone of Vesuvius,
The sad still crater-lake, Virgil's Avernus,
Dante's and Homer's regions of dim sorrow,
The great caldera of the Bay of Naples,
Whose monstrous cone blew off before the age
Of history, and left a ringwalled sea—
These were a Mars to the exploring Greeks,
Who set their cities on a seaward hill,   250
Paestum or Cumae, and who there dug caves
To house their holy women and their shrines
And sowed the place with myths and oracles.
A crater is a dish of sacrifice.
Heroes must track drowned sailors underground,
Baios, Misenus, or sad Palinurus,
And learn the bellowing gnosis of the caves.
So they may build a moment's heaven in hell,
And mark the future with the stamp of being.
And where the three caves meet within her dream,
The engineering of the scientist,

The Sibyl's riding by incipient gods,
The new dimension of this very time
She stands at on the darkling shore of Mars
Are knotted in the buckle of her vision.

As when the careful archeologist
Scratches away the tufa, ash, and glass
From some Pompeian villa, to reveal
An airy atrium, a bath and fountain,
A cryptoportico, a peristyle;
And then the crusted walls are brushed and cleaned,
Where glows a fresco, on a ground of red,
With graceful figures, priestesses and bride,
Passing through mysteries where they may share
The hot and frenzied nuptials of the god,   275
That Dionysos who drew back the veil
From Ariadne's dolorous corpse, and called
Her forth from Hades-land that she might share
The feast-time of the gods; so Beatrice
Wipes off the dust of grief from her bright vision
And knows with quickened pulse its patterned theme.

It is a matter very practical:
The gardening of crater planetscapes.
Few books record its arts and its techniques;
Yet Cicero's landscape gardeners would know,
When they laid out his grounds by Lake Lucrino,
And the patricians of the Alban Hills,
Who set their villas by the crater-lakes
Of Nemi and Albano clad in vines
And let their grottos give a prospect on
A glimmering water, framed in shady pines—
They'd be worth asking, if she might invoke
Their gentle, haughty shades for such discourse;
Yet they passed on their wisdom, as the Greeks
Did to the Romans, and the Romans to
The masters of the Renaissance; they taught
The gardeners of England how to shape
A sylvan walk to imitate the trials
Of Hercules or sharp Odysseus,
Instruct a guest-Aeneas how to choose   300
The way of piety and fortitude.

And they, in turn, taught the Americans:
The gardens of Dumbarton Oaks, and those
The DuPonts planted outside Wilmington,
Carried the same hermetic wisdom on
Across the oceans, and the garden-worlds
That glitter in a necklace round the sun
Bear the same history, the land of shades
Transformed to paradise, to fairyland,
To purify the dreaming of the tribe.
It seems that Beatrice must write the book,
Though, and reveal its secret name as Mars.

At last now the survivors of the war
Have made their rendezvous at Phobos base
And will descend to planetfall tomorrow:
Hilly and the remnants of the escort;
Ganesh, more somber now; the Martian folk
Whom Gaea has permitted to depart
To seek the desert of their promised land;
Wolf and Irene, whose fast ship caught up
With Hilly's limping squadron; and the rest.
Despite the poverty of Mars, a ritual
Has been prepared to mark the victory
And mourn and memorize the grievous loss.
On that brief hillside in the Nilosyrtis   325
Where it was Tripitaka's pleasure once
To walk and look upon the promontories
Of the young planet, they have built an ark
Of polished basalt, and inscribed the names
Of all those who have died in the Ark War.
The ark is bobbin-shaped, like that brave ship
Whose monument it is, *Kalevala.*
A copy of the Codex has been made
Which is to be entombed within the urn,
While those who came there sing the grand old hymn
That prays for those in peril on the sea.

The ritual's broken by Hillel Sharon
Who casts himself against the cold black stone
And shrieks his grief and rage for those he lost,
Ximene and Marisol, who cheated him,
Who gave their sweet love for the promised land.

But Beatrice lifts him up, and kisses him,
And speaks to him before the people there:
"You are my servant now from this time forth.
The work has been revealed. We have been called
To plant a garden in the promised land,
And you shall be the hand by which it's done."
And Hilly sees her face and worships her
As Tripitaka did once, long ago,
And dries his tears, and swears his service to her.   350
The ritual resumes, but seeing this,
Ganesh and Charlie meet each other's glance,
And the old light of sheer outrageousness
That used to cross between them in the days
They worked in *Novus Ordo*, in the mist
And crazy sunlight of St. Francis' town
Comes back to both their eyes. If Bea is hot,
If the old firm can get its mojo working,
If Hilly with his charm and energy
Is now aboard, you ain't seen nothin' yet.

And so a ritual can change a mood
And crack the blank white egg-mask of the future.
Next day the new Pandora's box is opened up,
The Codex with its boiling stew of life.
A week later the first organic forms
From the new source are cast into the sky:
Aerial zooplanktons, planned for years.
Everyone battens down and waits. This will,
If Charlie's calculations are correct,
Be something moderately spectacular.
For some days nothing happens; then the sky
Seems to turn yellowish like the vault of heaven
In old Pekin, stained with a rich dust
Of fine loess blown from the polar icecaps
Many ten thousand years ago; this dust   375
Is new and is undoubtedly alive.
Then it gets very hot, and thunderstorms,
With their mad boom and crackle here on Mars
Roil through the heavy air. And now at last
All hell breaks loose. The Hadley cells break up,
The jetstreams double, buckle, dissipate;
A worldwide hurricane sets in, and blows

As tirelessly as Jupiter's red spot;
Forests lie shattered, and the upper air
Bursts into flame as the sweet volatiles,
Those poisons to the higher forms of life,
Are oxidized and cracked, and fall as rain,
To fertilize the body of the planet.
"Hold onto your hats," Ganesh reassures
Over the landwire public service link;
"This will be over in just forty days."

And so it is. The miracle's accomplished.
The colonists, come blinking from their caves,
Trembling and sick because of their long habit,
Slowly take off their breathing masks and breathe.
How may I speak the new air of a planet?
Bitter and edged with the volcanic ash,
The clean electric taste of mountain water,
A trace of rust, of carbon, breathing trees;
Yet sweet, embarrassing, like mother's milk.

The gardening of Mars begins.

Scene v
The Garden

*B*ut now the story starts to choke and fade,
As throttled by the thinness of the breath
That passed for many years between the planets.
Just at the moment Mars began to breathe,
Its conversation and its intercourse
With mother earth was crimped into a gasp
As an umbilicus is tied before
The cutting-off that gives us two for one.
For some time Charlie's scientific colleagues
(If they were not suppressed) still kept in touch
By pirate relays on the satellites;
There was the leashed press of the Ecotheists,
The diplomatic pouch; but gradually
My direct sources narrow down to two:
Old Giamba Vico, and his bright assistant,
Who kept recordings of the firm's affairs.
Then Giamba was placed under house arrest,
And shortly after, died. From this point on
I must rely on myth, official sources,
Rumor, hearsay, later recollection;
Until the strange new word began to flow
Between the barriers and over the wall.
Since then I have obtained the garden notebook
Beatrice kept in those dark years of toil:
And this, and the darker Voice of the muse   25
Sustains me in these desert passages
That are the antechamber of the light.

It was about this time, then, that the paths,
The runnels of that probability fluid
That form the branching net or tree of Time
Began to bifurcate and twin, till Earth
And Mars had made their bleeding parturition,
And each could resonate, freed of the other,
As its own self-fated string might reconcile.

One was the live branch of the flowering Jesse;
One was the dead stick of the elder law.
And yet; can it be that freedom, for to grow
Has need of both?—that the Old Year, His jaw
So crooked, gnawing on the fertile ear
Of Spring, serves as the pruning shear, the dock
From which the golden prisoner bursts clear?
But then I the poet, who ride on his shoulder,
The old man's, I mean, into the sad shade,
Must I endure the terror of his glide,
The terror of his comfortable, mild,
Reasonable fading and decay?,
Of his forgetfulness of ever light,
Of ever bright rain raining on the field
Of joy and grief, of the obtaining act?
Better to cast myself between the shears,   50
To try to call the old night-wanderer back.

Sing, then, sweet bride-ghost, mother-mariner,
Of the garden planted in the vales of Mars;
How Beatrice bled the themes into each other
Of native waywardness and Arcady.
First, though, let us recall how it had been
Before the helmed conquistadors had come;
What lay below the gold wings of the ship
That bore the speechless astronauts to ground.

A numb plain spread with stones. A weary steppe
All bleached to tired red with ultraviolet.
Soil crusted, sere; limonite, siderite.
Hard radiation in a waste of cold.
Rocks sucked dry by the near vacuum.
Stunned with the blank math of the albedo
The eye tries to make order of it, fails.
Whatever's here once fell from someplace else.
Sometimes a crag a foot high, or a mile;
Always the sagging tables of the craters,
The precise record of a mere collision.
And yet a stunted and abortive chemistry,
A backward travesty of life, proceeds:
Parched cirrus clouds move over the ejecta;
A hoarfrost forms upon the shadow sides;   75

Dark patches colonize the regolith;
Sometimes with a thin violence a sandstorm
Briefly makes shrieks of sound between the stones;
Rasps off their waists and edges, and falls silent.
Time here is cheap. A billion years can pass
Almost without a marker; if you bought
A century of Marstime in the scrip
And currency of Earth, you'd pay an hour
Or half an hour of cashable event.
It's really a young planet then, a bald
And mild mongoloid, a poor old cretin
Worth but a handful of Earth's golden summers.

And it was beautiful. Those who first walked there
Said it was fresh as the true feel of death,
As Kyoto earthen teaware, as the Outback;
As clean as is geometry, as bones.
To spoil this archetype, this innocence,
Was to incur a guilt whose only ease
Was beauty overwhelming to the loss,
Was a millennial drunkenness of life
That might forget its crime in ecstasy.
But it was not enough to reenact
The long sensualities of mother Earth,
To take on trust the roots of history;
They must be minatory, and exact
A last accounting of the failed balance
All the intestate dowager had left.
There must be new assumptions in the matrix,   100
New ratios, dimensions and arrays;
Beatrice finds her trope in simple mass,
The crazy lightness of all things here
Set, in a poetry that brewed delight,
Against the literal dimness of the light.

After the riot, then, of Earth diseases,
After mycosis, cometfall, the plague
And infestation of the weeds, the jungles
Of a lifeforce as fresh as it was vulgar,
The time came to prune and shape the flow.
On Mars all these fall slowly, dreamily:
Waterfalls, billowy, like the clawed waves

In Hiroshige prints of sudden storms.
Snow, in soft bales or volumes, scarcely more
Than bright concatenations of a vapor.
Rain, in fine drizzles, dropping by a cliff
Stained by the rocksprings and the clinging mosses.
Rivers and streams, whose wayward pressures thrust
More, by inertia, at their banks than beds,
And so can spread in braided flats and strands
To glittery sallow-marshes, quiet fens.
Ocean waves, swashy, horned, and globular,
Like the wave-scenery of an antique play,
(Bright blue horned friezes worked to and fro,
A fat-lipped leviathan, and a ship).   125
And then on Mars all these rise swifter, easier:
Smoke, which makes mushrooms in the wildest air.
Fountains, which tower and tower, whose very fall
Is caught up once again within the column
Of their slow and weighty rise; yes, fountains
Shall be the glory of our Martian gardens.
Flames, in like fashion, scarcely dance on Mars
So much as dart into the air, like spirits
Lately penned in earth but now set free.
And the warmed thermal plumes from open fields
Of ripened grass or stubble here make clouds
As tall as chefs' hats, stovepipes full of thunder.

The poets of the Earth refine the fuel—
The hot benzene of value culture burns
To power its subtle engines of desire—
From fossil liquors buried in the stone
Through ages of creation and decay.
They can afford to toss aside the raw,
And take for granted a world cooked and rich
With ancient custom, languages numberless
As layers of autumn leaves within the forest,
Nature itself grown conscious, turned upon
Itself to make its rings so intricate,
History fertile with its own grave-mould.
And so the poets' work is little more   150
Than cracking out the spirit they inherit
In the tall silver towers of poetry
To brew those essences, those volatiles,

Those aromatic esters, metaphor,
Image, trope and fugitive allusion.
Prodigals, they burn half that they use
To purify the rest; and they make little,
Only a froth or lace of ornament.
The poets of Mars must brew the very stuff
The Earth-poets burn as waste; must mate each word
With breeder's care, and dust the yellow pollen
Over the chosen stamen; graft the stem
To coarser stock, and train the line to sprout
Productive variation years ahead.
The poets of Mars must make the myths from scratch,
Invent the tunes, the jokes, the references;
They must be athletes of the dream, masters
Of the technology of inventive sleep,
Architects of the essential shades of mood.
What they inherit from the Earth, they earn,
Through sacrifice and trouble, and they breed
More than they are bequeathed. So Beatrice,
Taking into her hands her garden tools—   175
A dream of a Campanian burial,
A trope of lightness, and a wild new world—
Begins the cultivation of the void.

This garden: let it propagate itself,
Sustain itself, an arch-oeconomy
Dynamically balanced by the pull
Of matched antagonists, controlled and led
By a fine dance of feedbacks, asymptotic,
Cyclical, damping, even catastrophic.
Let there be forest fires to purge the ridges;
Let there be herbivores to mow the parkland,
And predators to cull their gene pools clean
And viruses to kill the carnivores
That sheep may safely graze. Each form of life
Shall feed upon the wastes of its convivors;
Let there be beetles and bacteria
And moulds and saprophytes to spin the wheel
Of nitrogen, corals and shells to turn
The great ratcheted cycle of the carbons;
Each biome—grassland, forest, littoral;
Benthic, pelagic; arctic, desert, alp—

Shall keep appointed bounds and yet be free.
Let the new species bud and multiply;
Let monsters speciate and radiate
And seize the niche that they themselves create;   200
Let some be smothered or extinguished; some,
Effete, exquisite—the trumpeter swan,
The rare orchid, the monoclone cheetah—
Cling to some microclimate or kind vale,
Eking survival for a clutch of genes.

Beatrice has a wand, a metatron,
To help her in her work; a golden bough
Wherewith she will transmute and charge her world
With metamorphosis: the flowering plants.
Mars was first seeded with the gymnosperms:
Horsetails, treeferns, cycads, conifers.
Now comes the carnival of angiosperms,
The spirits of a world made up anew
In all the colors that vibrate the field
Of time's ether, giving a taste to light.
As each seedclone package comes from the shops
Of sleepless Charlie and Ganesh, she breaks
It out among her helpers; Hilly Sharon,
Her pilot, flies her among the green coombs
And verdant-headed hills and plains of Mars
To supervise the setting of the seeds.
Ganesh has multiplied the speed of growth
Tenfold, relying on the lesser weight
The plant must carry to its destiny;
And soon that glorious, pathetic fate   225
Bursts in a billion blooms across the planet
In petals bluish, pink and mauve and gold.
Now the first bees, their wise, conformist brains
Not muddled much by the new dispensation,
Blunder among the anther and the pistil.
Quivering beech-groves, the work of but a year,
Rootle and creak on hillside or in canyon,
Their white feet sunk in a sweet red mould.
From Earth we saw it through our telescopes:
Whole hemispheres turned white with fragrant daisies;
Reefs rising in long chains and rings about
Those windy coasts under a tiny sun.

On Earth the metaphors must be selected
From what is given us, what lies to hand.
Martian metaphors must be half created:
Their meaning and their medium spring to life
At the same moment, indistinguishable;
There's no pathetic fallacy on Mars,
For that world is enspirited at birth.
Nevertheless Beatrice makes the choice
To start her strange concerto with the theme
That was the first to clothe her aspiration:
Arcadia. She takes the cratered south
And sets it, in the warmer latitudes,
With aromatic herbs and oleanders,   250
Wild grapes, sages, and bougainvilleas
That riot up the sheltered inner slopes
Of craters named Copernicus and Galle,
Slipher, Hipparchus, Kuiper, Ross, and Green,
Lampland, Le Verrier, Helmholtz and Liu Hsin.
Sometimes a still lake fills the shallow cup,
And sometimes craterlets with their own lakes
Form wooded islands in the greater wells.
A gentian sulks among the pungent grasses.
The windy crater-lips are set with pines
Whose broad crowns never cease to shift and sigh.
Goats graze the hillsides, and the tall falcon
Quarters the depthless acres of the sky.

And in the temperate zones the theme is softer,
Warbl'd upon an oaten flute in autumn,
What time the grey-fly winds her sultry horn
(And ruddy Phoebus gins to welke in west);
The woodland shadows creep across the vale
And Earth, the evening star, gleams on the stream.
Here the deciduous, the bountiful
Of sacrificial leaves, that scorch
In fevers at the year's chilly ending
And drop their heavy garment like the flesh
Of saints or martyrs, here the sycamore,
The oak, the arched elm and the poplar   275
Tower about the glades, the noblest trees,
And blossom in the spring gigantically,
Reckoning bloom by tons, by the ten thousands.

And on the hillsides the wild rose in fall,
The crocus and the daffodil, that flower
From their giant Martian corms and bulbs
Twice, even thrice in this eternal spring.

The variations of Arcadia
Branch out like palm-sprays from the parent stem:
The classical, heroic, and grotesque,
The meditative and the modernist.
Beatrice plants the fossae, those straight trenches
In the surface, whose high walls arrow down
In curved perspective to the close horizon,
With formal cedars and with lakes and lawns:
Tempe, Mareotis, Alba, Elysium.
Above the fosse hovers a purple sky
Filled with a wind that does not blow below.
Canals, in honor of the ancient fiction,
Are dug along the axis of the rift.
The dark tobacco-smell of sunwarmed box
Dazes the wanderer in these parterres;
A fountain clatters at a vanishing point.
All is in classical humane proportion.
And the Islamic gardens of the Taj   300
And those Khmer quadrangles of tropic flowers,
Those stone arcades of tantric statuary
Are pressed for metaphor and simile.

She saves the heroic mode for certain places
Where Mars, like a young actor full of talent,
Offers a tragic gift, wild and untrained:
The Valles Marineris, and the craters
Of the Tharsis Ridge, three grand calderas;
Olympus Mons upon its pedestal
Of basalt and obsidian, ten miles high;
Certain new seacoasts, whose amazing cliffs
Jar the mind's eye with desperate fantasies;
The polar caps, with their gigantic wastes,
Scalloped crevasses, and blind nunataks.
Here she leaves much alone; and her esthetic
Follows the puritan iconoclasm
Of the American parks and wildernesses.
Sometimes she has a giant or a horse

Etched on a hillside like a Nazca god
Or neolithic Wessex henge-maker;
Sometimes Promethean disfigurements,
The huge machines of planoforming, or
The technologies of the robot mines,
Can give the crowning shiver to a valley
Cragged with the terror of the shadow of death.   325
But much is left to chance and to the weather.

Ganesh's biotech is everywhere,
Balanced by Charlie's crisp ecology.
Beatrice likes the powdery mushroom-groves,
Their dusky fins, smooth caps and flanged white shafts,
That smell of spores and collapse heavily
If you but set a shoulder to the trunk.
She plants them by the moist grots and caves
And varies them with scarlet agarics,
Boletes and chanterelles. For the grotesque
She has besides the swampland with its mangroves,
Bottle- and screw-pines, and the littorals;
And then there are the subterranean lakes,
Still as the face of death, and black as ink,
Where bellowing magma-reservoirs once spewed
Their white slags reddening into the air.
Sometimes her sculptors, tired heavy men
And sweaty grinning girls with laser chisels
Will leave a trunked Ganesha by a cave
Or a tall totem in a forest grove,
Or a silenus ithyphallic where
A spring breaks through the mosses of a cliff.
The very giantism of the trees
Released from Earthly gravity, can give
The comic scale to landscapes of the sun.   350
The human towns are built of living trees,
That grow their creaking vaults and sinewy beams;
They smell of sunlight, bark, and crystal resins
Like Adirondack lodges years ago.
(The public buildings though are made of stone,
Handsome, porous, ranging in tone from fawn
And golden to dark brown and maroon;
Their classical facades and fitted ashlars
Meet for the canons of the new republic.)

And there are landscapes made for meditation
Where mists blow between crags scarcely less airy
Than the vapors they divide; where the pines
Bonsai'ed to knotted dwarfs, yet fledged with pins,
Make groups so subtly asymmetrical
The mind's made docile to a still amazement
And its each stroke of thought's as natural
As leaves a bamboo brushstroke leaves behind.
The white strings of the waterfalls make chords
As hoarse and endless as the breath of time,
And halfway up the mountain there's a hut
Where a small scholar feeds his poem with wine.

And then there are the rhapsodies in blue,
The landscapes of the jazz age, the new world.
The Martian airports, with their lettering
Of flanged silver like the Emerald City   375
Look out from lounges, where you sip a cocktail,
On sunlit hills with round trees in their clefts.
You take a streamlined monorail as neat
As was the California Zephyr in its prime
Through a dramatic evening scene of cloud
And silver-shine suspension bridge to towns
Whose transit stations and whose trocaderos
Are lit and pink with parabolic neon.
Seaside resorts are smart with small hotels,
Striped canopies, and staircases and pools
In a Miami Art Deco pastiche,
With bronze door-lintels like the Empire State,
And ocean-scenes of palms and pink flamingos
And blues as frail and pale as frosted glass,
Dimmed lamps and the sound of saxophones.
At night, sidereal archipelagoes,
Lunules electriques, cieux ultramarins.
On ne regrette les anciens parapets.

Each of these gardens now awaits its story;
Its genius loci clasps its fetal hands.
Since all material is but arrangement
Each new arrangement's new material.
Feel now the great Swan's wing Beatrice weaves
To clothe the arms of Mars; the pelt of life
That makes a purpose from a purple dress.

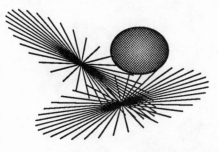

ACT V
The Words of the Sibyl

*The poem now turns to the childhood of the Sibyl. The Sibyl
is the first source of the revelation special and proper to
Mars, as the sayings of Isaiah, Jesus, Buddha, Mohamed, Lao
Tse and the others were revelations proper to the Earth.
Irene, learning that she herself is the mother of the Sibyl,
attempts in rage against her stepmother Beatrice to destroy
herself. The Sibyl restores her miraculously to life. The
poem now records the Sibyl's words about gods, time, and the
origin of things.*

Scene i
The Sibyl's Awakening

*I*f my words are unworthy, let them die,
Let them be burnt and the voice too that speaks them.
What should the voice care, if it had been given
The casket and the stones, and the precious moment
When they may be spoken, and then misread them,
Interpreted a shallow or obscured thing?
Even to touch the ghost of such a chance
Is blessing, paradise beyond all curses.
Even the fake partakes of such a fullness,
Given the nature of the original,
That it could scarcely be content with any
Ordinary proof or genuine.
If this should be the threshold of the god,
Who is the world at last come to awareness
Of itself, of its superlation of
Itself, its sweet incipience forever
Now to step into its natural home,
And yet its always being on the verge
Of what adventure will betide soever;
If that god should be sister to mankind,
Most dear sister, Urania, Sophia,
Sister of Christ, Radha among her gopis,
The long promised and veiled Shekinah,
The bride of Life come from her long mourning,
Her long incomprehension of herself,   25
Into the torches of the marriage chamber;
If this were such a threshold, who would not

Gladly and joyfully be turned away,
The doors locked on him, cast into the darkness,
Having once had his hand upon the latch,
Having but smelt the spirit of the feast?

How might one know the touch of such a truth?
Surely at least by its surprises. This
Is the book of Hermione the Sibyl,
Who was as we have seen a pretty child,
And who'd expect the pretty to be so
Heart-cordial to the body of the world?
Now in her eighties, but still full of grace,
The geisha Sumikami nursed the child;
And what the mother would not take of her,
The art of beauty, now the daughter learned.
They say she would walk barefoot in the snow
As Heian ladies did, to kill the skin
And leave the feet as soft as herons' down;
Her flesh was white as milk; her lips, her teats,
And certain other parts, were red as blood.
She early learned to dance and then to sing;
Her voice, they say, was of all voices ever
In the world, the loveliest: it held
Shell within shell, all timbres that have rung   50
The tympan of the air since time began:
The purity of the simple crystalline,
Aeolian tremors of the questing wind,
The fluted overtones of calling birds,
The sweet hoarse naivety of the beasts,
The noble close intent of human speech,
Frank shy intelligence of consciousness,
And something still angelic, like an eye
Winged, with wet lashes, come to comfort us.
That voice would make you tremble into love,
And yet you could not touch it, hug it to you,
As you might a body; as you would desire.
This beauty was not vainness, but a gift,
As one might, with a flush, and look away,
Give to another a great armful of flowers,
Smelling so fresh that you were faint with grief.
That beauty was a living fairy tale,

A stroke of precious and unearned luck.
They say Hermione as a little child
Would play amid the strange white loom of fibers,
The chrysalis of optic filaments
That linked the great computers of the planet;
And then Ganesh taught her the interfaces
Whereby the cybernetic impulse might
Innerve the penetralia of the brain;   75
And as organic wetware came on line,
Evolved by software planted with a drive
To pattern and intelligence, she drew
Draughts of fresh knowledge from this clear spring;
And when she tired she slept and dreamed the world
And woke to love from everyone about her.
She was a learned lady then, a bluestocking;
Imagine her discourse at eight years old
Of Pseudo-Dionysius and Berenice,
Of Mithras and of Hermes Trismegistos,
Of Tiamat and of the Empress Wu,
Of the Lao-Tsu Goddess, whose river-body
Is the world, and of the wise Shamankas,
Of the sea-born Saint Mary of Egypt,
And of Yao Chi the turquoise courtesan;
Or of before the fortieth negative power
Of the first second of the universe
When none of the four forces yet had branched
To paint the screen of physicality;
Or of the limbic passages of dream
Whereby the structure of the brain is formed;
Or of the disciplines of dance and breath
Whereby the soul may penetrate the flesh;
Or of the divinations and the *sortes*,
The yarrow-stems, the singing of the signs.
Her mistresses were those medieval ladies   100
Who carried the long secret of the Sibyls
On into times when it might spring again:
The scholar-queen of the *Heptameron*,
Christine de Pisan, Marie de Champagne,
Margery Kemp and mystical Julian,
Elizabeth the Duchess of Urbino,
Who taught the Cardinal the scale of love.

At twelve she had a dozen aching lovers,
And yet all chaste, as pure as is the snow;
This was a thing intact, inviolate
As is the chiefest casket of your soul,
That without which all motive falls to nothing,
That which you treasure up even to death;
Not a virginity of inexperience,
But that great shiver of the total spirit,
Faced, in the flower of reflexivity,
With the dark predicate of everything,
The absence of itself that is the place
Where its effective gifts must now be given.
Chance was the one who could interpret this;
He was her knight, her servant, and her scribe.
This book would be impossible if he
Were not the breath of wholesome cooking-smoke
That shows the sunbeam from the open door: 125
The Hemmings and the Condell of the poet,
As Aaron to the harelip friend of God,
The faithful Plato to his Socrates,
The loving John and Mark of the Messiah.

The first story of her theodicy
(As I shall try to pluck it through the veil
That parts our past from that new-minted world)
Concerns poor Chance, who must have come to know
Her strange conception and her borrowed birth
—How she was both his sister and his niece.
It was the year Irene lost the election,
And Chance had been her campaign manager.
Her brother Wolf had nicely won his precinct,
And, as one version has it, Chance had come
To comfort her in her defeat and envy.
His artless chatter with his wounded boss
Turned to his favorite, Hermione,
And how her ancestry made her an Eve,
The reunited blood of all the races.—
It was not like him: somehow he let slip
The truth that Freya was her grandmother.
(And yet events proved Chance the wiser here
Than anyone might guess, even his mother.)

Irene's ear for detail did not err.
What Chance could not have known was how   150
Close to despair she must have been already.
Her mother, Freya's, death, still unavenged;
The suicide of Tripitaka who
Was still her only lover in the world;
Her long estrangement from her brother Wolf
(For what had passed between them might not be
Harmlessly taken up nor yet forgotten)—
All these were heavy on her, and the story
That she forced from Chance ratified them.
Her sweet stepmother had then in one blow
Deprived her of her act of sacrifice,
Deceived her as one might a foolish child,
And stolen from her what she did not then
Hold valuable, but was beyond all price.
Irene gave out little sign of what
She now intended. In the afternoon
As was her custom, she put on her wings
To fly the coasts about the Nilosyrtis;
She must have thought herself alone when she
Plunged from ten thousand feet into the cliffs;
A party of schoolchildren saw her fall
And she was brought back broken to the city.
But when Hermione saw what had happened
She made them part about the bloody litter
And came and laid her head upon the head   175
Of this dead woman who had come to claim her.
Breath came then to her Voice. "Mother, come back.
I have forgiven you already. Come."
And now Irene sighed and moved her eyes
And so in time was healed of all her wounds.

What is the truth of stories such as this?
I tell it as it were a tale of motives,
Of a psychology half guessed, half given.
Better perhaps to have said such as this:
"Upon the twelfth Earth year of her indwelling
A woman dead or near to death was brought,
And by her words the Sibyl made her whole."

So she began to speak. At first it was
A closing of the eyes, a little shudder,
A smile of sweetest rapture in her face
And but a few words, undecipherable.
Sometimes the words were nonsense: "Coasts of form,"
Or "Going up," or "See the violet green,
The edges, sugarloaves, the continents;"
Or she would stare for hours into a flower,
Or in the face of a beloved person,
Charlie perhaps, or Chance, or her Ganesh,
And they for her sake bore the scrutiny
As one endures a kitten's choice to purr
And claw you in its little rage of love.   200
But she would say "How lovely, lovely, lovely,"
And the bright tears of joy would fill her eyes.
And soon she came to tell of small events
That would befall tomorrow or the next day.
A china bowl painted with peonies
That had belonged to Gaea back on Earth
Was much beloved of Beatrice, and once
Hermione removed it carefully
From where it stood upon its wooden shelf.
Next day the bad cat Mittens, trying to catch
A sunbeam, scrabbling, fell where it had been.
(This story came from Chance's fiancée,
Rosie Molloy, who told it to their grandchild
Many years later, who then told it me.)

Chance says of her that when she closed her eyes
And breathed like that, she rose above the world
—Not just above the planet, but above
The very palings of the universe—
And saw its borders burn with green and gold
And saw it whole, all creatures great and small
Each nested within each, like Chinese boxes,
And as a climber in a coastal range
Can see the richly colored bogs and channels
Of the lowlands that run off to the ocean,
She saw the many lands of various futures,   225
Divided by the cultivated fields

Of what is past and done, laid out to view.
"God fell into the world," the Sibyl said,
"And this our home is but Her dreaming body."
"Why did She fall?" Chance asked when he heard this.
"To dream," said she, as if it were a game.
"Why did She want to dream?" asked Chance. "Is God,"
She asked, "free or not free? first answer this."
"Free." "When you dream, can you control the dream?"
"No." "Are you free in dreams, then?" "No again."
"But if you did not dream, would you be free?"
"I do not see how this can be, but no."
"Then to be free you must first learn to dream,
And dreaming is for us not to be free.
And we must be God's dreams, and set Her free."
"Then we must be the prison of our God?"
Said Chance. "Yes. And the prison's name is Being."
"But newborn babies do not dream, they say."
"A newborn baby is a fuzzy god.
It dreams that it might be, and might be free."
"How many gods are there?" Chance asked at last.
"As many as dreams," replied Hermione.

"How may there be both many gods, and one?"
"The one that fell," she said, "since time had not
Begun then, could not die; that god remains   250
A ghost beyond the living walls of nature.
The fallen one became the universe,
The lord of light, radiant stupidness,
And slept the drunken sleep of quantum physics,
Then woke enough to dream the dreams of matter;
And each dependency of engaged being,
Each organism patterned by its past
And governed by the shaping of its whole,
Being a dream, possesses its own god,
Its hidden kami, or its genius;
And every living being has its spirit,
And every resonance of shape or function,
Thunder or ocean, fire or flowering spring,
Love as an Aphrodite, war as Mars;
Helios, Vishnu, Quetzal, Izanagi,

Enlil, Kavula, Gainji, Viracocha,
Each is a nisus in the play of time.
The artifacts that we have shaped to serve
Our purposes, our weapons and our tools,
Our edifices, engines, arts and hearths,
Our quick computers with their eager minds,
Are gods, too, dreams of the fallen one.
And every human spirit is a god,
The divine baby promised in the gospel,
Until it falls into the world of death,   275
Of love, of act and of awakening.
For there is yet the Falling God, and She
Is the rainbow that floats upon the falls;
She is the resonance of all the dreams;
She it is now who speaks this with my tongue
And breathes the meaning of awakening:
That the awakened is the dance of dreams,
The marriage-feast of all the petty gods."

But these are always my words, and not hers.
I fear, I fear, what reader there may be
Will find only an eccentricity
Of thought, a flailing at an ancient gnosis
Now discredited, or else a sermon
By certain folk in other circumstances,
Strangers with an unnatural emphasis.
Or else the words seem wicked, blasphemous,
The exploiters' bald persistence in their crime;
Or if the revelation of the Sibyl be
Taken for what it is—the further gift
And new creation of the womb of time—
Then any screen that stands between her speech
And those she came to heal, is desecration.
But what I have is shreds and paraphrases,
Imperfect memories at second hand,
And I must patch them to some kind of story   300
To make them mean what I divine they mean.
And now the very languages of Mars
And Earth are parting swiftly, so the verbs
Of hope for that world are, for this, despair;
And what would be abstract where life is known
Down to the last detail, would be, for those

Whose world is yet creating, concreteness
As fresh as water splashed upon your face
Some shining morning on Pavonis Mons.

And that was where she made her shrine at last:
The Peacock Mountain, where a giant cleft
Pierces the towering hexagons of basalt
And forms an airy cavern a mile high;
And in the inner recess of the crack
They built her simple cells of fine cut stone.
A subterranean river foamed and rose
Here, in a torrent white as milk; and smoke
Went up from cedar fires upon the hearths
Tended by maidens of the Sibyl's fane.
The great computers of the Library
And those few ancient books that they had brought
Out of the Terran burning had been housed
Deep in the caves below; deepest of all
A subterranean ocean like a glass
Reflected darkness into darkness, but   325
Would blaze with crimson fire when shown a flame.

"Time, for the ancients," once the Sibyl said,
In that sweet trance that lit her face like snow,
"Was as a circle turned back on itself,
So that the years came back, and brought with them
The same bright freight of faces, beasts and stones,
The same colors seen by different eyes,
Same eyes, different colors, same colors.
They heard the hurdy-gurdy of the time
Bring round the caroltide, the rosy hymn,
And all souls knocked together in the bag,
The cosy gossip-hut of history.
Lo *fortuna velut luna vol-*
Vit et revolvitur. But the moderns
Sprang a lonely tangent from the wheel,
And time lay out behind and on ahead,
And we were shackled to a fatal rail
That ran beyond the sight of family,
Beyond the memory of home, beyond
The last sweet old tune singing in our head.
All there was left was the swift wail of passage,

Hiss of the wheel against the vanishing steel.
The ancients never could escape the past;
The moderns murdered it and then they grieved
Because their present was become a ghost.   350
What shall we know of time, then? That the past
Is all that has lived on into the present;
Nothing is lost that was, the tense of past
Cannot endure the verb to be, and what
Is once is ever. The live and only past's
The inside of the present, its unpacking
And its contents; as the water is
Of the new-spreading stream upon the desert,
Or as the sap is of the blossoming tree,
Or as the seed that swells the lover's gift,
Or as the milk that oozes from the bud.
Time is a tree whose roots are also branches,
Whose forked twigs form a globe of growingness.
The lace they make, by their outreaching flow
Of choices made or taken, branched where act
Collapses the wave-function to event,
And by the spaces that were paths not taken,
Will constitute the very shape of being.

"The ancients and the moderns knew the future
As like a line laid out before our feet
That we must tread lest the frail calendar
Be unfulfilled and chaos come again.
But I say to you that there is no future
But that one which we make, and we are all,
Photons and stones and grass and beasts and folk,   375
Making it up, dreaming it as we go.
Take it, my beloveds, my brothers, sisters:
Freeness, the dark coal of void in God's hand,
Wherewith She blinds Herself that She may see,
The potion that She drinks, of real dreams."
"Tell me," said Chance, "Who drive the eyed wheel
Of my spirit, Tell me what were the dreams,
First, and in order, of the dreaming god?"
"First was the dream of possibility.
All chances that are first, that need no other
For their articulation, must so be
As not to thwart each other; those that did

Died before birth and never came to light.
The mightier probabilities were those
That sang in harmony together. Next
Followed the dream of nextness, what could be
Given what is. How to find room for all
The schedule-trees in all directions that
Stochastic play may find? Three open ways,
The air of space, breathed out; but algebra
Forbade another. Next, six inner ways
Coiled themselves into every point of space.
Still, there was pain, the gravid ache of math
Knowing its logic's death and stretched limit.
So time was born then in a burst of light."

Afraid that the teachings of the Sibyl may be a tedious
mystery to some of his audience, the poet in a more familiar
style describes how Charlie and Ganesh populate the new
world with animals. The occasion is taken to explore the
workings of evolution and ecology, and such subjects as
swans, flying, wings, the avian city, avian economics and
avian ethics.

Scene ii
Evolution and the City

*A*h, very well. I have seen your poor eyes
Droop and wander, stray to your wristwatches.
And I too feel the air come thin, and gasp
In the bright environments of the mountain.
Let us return, for a short space of time,
To the warm villages down in the foothills,
Dinner and bedtime, cockcrow and afternoon.
I interrupt the discourse of the Sibyl!—
And I cry for our unworthiness, our weakness.
Still we shall go back to the holy mountain.
It is a promise, understood between us.

But till we are prepared to reascend
The cliffs, let us go to and fro and see
How Charlie and Ganesh have broached the Ark
And let forth all the curious animals.
Most family-like to us, the vertebrates:
Elephas bearing his head's gondola,
Bufo the toad, who bloats his moony toot,
The bustly cassowary, with slim toes,
The teleosts, their scaled eyes set in bone,
The shad, the arched tunny, and the perch;
The pangolin, with her smart streamlining,
The salamander, who must work each foot
Out of a different idea; the shrew,
As swift and vicious as a village sneak,   25
The gentle cow, her eyes rimmed with *kohl*,
The heron, like a purple thundercloud
Seen across marshland in the setting sun;

Pissing against the odorous stump, the dog;
The hummingbird who throws his huge helix
About the jacarandas and who leaves
A flash of green buzzing into your eyes;
The valved and wallowing baleen, her flukes
Awash with bitter curds of cream, her breath
Thumping like furnace from the pouched blowhole;
The jackdaw in a mob of clever jackdaws,
As exercised as Guelphs or Ghibellines;
The crosseyed skate, who sidled for too long,
The gorgeous flowing camouflaged jaguar,
The pig with his shrewd eyes, the staring owl,
The lemur retinal, the manatee,
And *Mus* the mouse and *Pan* the chimpanzee.
But Charlie and Ganesh had more in mind
Than filling out the plenum of a zoo;
They were composing a community,
A new branch of natural history.

Consider the creation of the swan.
Whether we picture it in space or time
It owes its being to a hierarchy
Of other organisms. We must learn   50
To find the beauty in this web of lives,
This seething texture of dependency.
Inside the lungflesh of the leopard frog
That the swan preys on in certain habitats
There lives a nematode which is in turn
Parasitized by zygomycota.
The frogs prey on the ephemoptera
Which feed as larvae on the fungal growth
Of fecal matter from the waterbirds.
Mites populate the feathers of the swan;
Its colon swarms with microsymbiotes.
Follow the swan's genes back, and there are branches
Where grebes and petrels, storks and pelicans
Fork outward from the stem, then distant kin,
The swifts and passerines; and further back
The archeopteryxes, and their roots
Which also fed the undreaming monotremes,
The platypus, the anteaters, and so
—Turning a moment to climb up the stem—

Marsupials, the mammals, and ourselves.
And further down the chordates split again
To tunicates and dim cephalochords;
And now the great branch of the arthropods,
The insects, spiders, and crustacea;
And the mollusca, with their pearly shells   75
(And such strange creatures as the echiura
Whose tiny male lives as a parasite
Inside the female's kidney; she is called
The *fat innkeeper* and is used for bait;
One of Ganesh's favorite animals,
The bat ray, pops her from her hole as you
Might clear a toilet with a rubber plunger);
Then down the stem again, where rotifers
And mesozoans branch away; and then
The radiates and formless parazoa:
The sponges in their blind communities.
And down again, to the stromatolites
Which lived two billion years without change;
And then to mineral colonies and clays.

Sometimes the way down is the way up.
If we could take this path a little further
We'd find those silicates and carbonates
To be compacted ash of burnt-out stars;
The nuclei themselves cooked up inside
The crushing fusion of their white-white cores;
Their particles the frozen motes of light
That burst in nightmare from the primal atom.
And we would know that moment as the fall
Of the Uranian Goddess to Her dream.
But if we took this way then we might err,   100
Believing that the arche of the joy
Of all creation as it sings itself
Is found by a retracing of the path
The world took in its long ecstatic fall;
"To thy high requiem become a sod."
Pass through that point where down is changed to up;
And as the sounding whale breaks for the surface,
And as the vaulter sprints behind his pole,
And as the poet must not yet look back
Lest the beloved be reclaimed forever,

And as the swan's wings whoop above the water,
Gold feet spurning the lower element,
Let us turn back toward the holy mountain.

First we must learn to fly. But who will teach us?
Recall the story of the willow-pattern:
A Mandarin engaged the poet Chang
To teach his daughter, beautiful Hong Shee.
Though he was young and poor, they fell in love.
The father in a rage locked up his daughter,
But she escaped out of a secret gate
Where Chang was waiting, and they fled toward
The little bridge engraved beneath the glaze;
But they were seen, and men with guns pursued;
And Chang was shot and Hong Shee drowned herself.
But the gods changed them to a pair of swallows   125
And they still dance the lakes and willow-waters.
Wolf and Irene, who learned that planet's skies,
Will be our flying-teachers so that we
May be as swallows in the air of time.

It was the children first, of course, who took
The sky, their natural inheritance.
This large land mammal always yearned to fly,
As if the wrong circuitry had got wired
Into a biped quite unsuited to it:
Large boned and dense, "bad power-weight ratio,"
Ganesh liked to point out; and yet nature
(Being fantastical in her conceits,
Not above cruelty, even, if the joke
Seems worth it; or is it incompetence,
Which governs, after all, ninety percent
Of what goes on anywhere?)—yet nature
Makes us dream of being mighty birds,
Coasting the buttresses of mountain chains,
Lifting away upon a breeze of power,
Escaping monsters, terrors, to the air.

Wolf stands upon a windy hill, his goggles
Pushed up on his head, his grey eyes distant,
A sky-dauphin, like Saint-Exupery:
Let's listen to him lecture to his students.

"Your muscles were evolved to bear your body   150
Against the leaden gravity of Earth.
By now the exercises you have done
Have given you that strength again. On Earth
You could all jump a meter in the air.
Here some of you can leap to twice your height.
Now watch Irene. She weighs forty pounds.
See: she can long-jump over thirteen meters
And her hang-time's what? Two point eight? Thank you.
That's enough time, you'll see, to take two strokes,
And get a glide you find you can sustain.
You can all press an easy eighty pounds,
Enough to beat the drop rate and the drag.
Then you can get your feet into the stirrups
And make your flying height. A hundred meters
Keeps you out of trouble, and you still
Have depth perception while you feel you need it.
Landing is tough, I know. For those of you
Who really can't, we've got the brained wings
Which do it for you, 'drop the flaps,' we say.
That means extend and cup the primaries,
Open the secondaries, and stall out
Just as you hit the ground. If you're afraid,
We'll start you on the old folk's muscled wings,
And we can even strap a gasbag on,
Though that's against the spirit of the game."   175

If you have ears to hear. The metaphor,
This feathered glory I ask you to put on,
Is not intangible, light though it is.
Consider how recursive is its order:
First, the full wing itself, white as an angel;
Then the wing's wings, which are its fletch of feathers,
Each with a tuft of warm and gentle down;
But then the feathers too are feathered with
The crispy barbs that clothe the inpithed quill
To form the rigid vane; and these have barbules,
Which again bear hooklets, set to catch
Any chance split and heal it without seam.
(The Sibyl likened wings to our felt time:
She said that underneath the surface structure
We knew the time of animals and plants,

The time of stones and atoms, and of fire.
So many pens are woven to a pinion,
The prince's pennon bears his sister's swan.
Oh fly with it, fly with it, fly with it!)

Wind sifting by, divided by your blade;
Wingtips trailing a curl of turbulence;
Your fingers rule the carpus, metacarpus;
Your masked face feels a burr of parching speed;
A long glide down the aeroclinal wedge
Into the sudden buoyancy and fetor   200
That rises from the sweetness of a meadow;
The swift-approaching wavetop of a ridge;
The gasp and fall away into the chasm
That succeeds, the flicking turn along
The cliffwall till the updraft catches you;
The spiral up into the towering sky
As fields and trees diminish like a lens;
The silence as you leave the world of bells,
Cries, stamp and snort of animals, the rush
And burble of the streams, the sigh of trees;
The sunny blisses of the middle air,
The dizziness of summer afternoons,
The suck and dumbness of the ear's drawn drum,
The choice of detail from a hemisphere
Of world, all given sharply to the view
Like a crisp plateful of delicious viands,
Like a soft carpet stitched with tiny needles;
The many-colored coat of mortal dwelling.
How do we get down? We should have a kite-string,
We should have a fishing-line, a reel,
A spool to reel us in, a puppeteer,
A yoke, an apron-string, and we have none!
Ah joy and terror, now we truly know
The meaning and the function of a roof:
It is a lid to keep the sweetness in!   225

Thus lesson number one, the school of joy.
Without it nothing that was made was made.
Now lesson number two, that certain virtues
Are indescribable by definition,
And unintelligible, thus inimitable

In the individual. Socrates
Said that we must construct an airy city
If we would so articulate the good
As to make justice worth the defining.
I quote now from the *Politics* of Chance
The Younger, that book written to preserve
The arguments that led up to the framing
Of the Martian constitution—part
Federalist Papers, part de Tocqueville.
Imagine then a city made for birds.

First, this cloudcuckooland is made not found.
To make is might and may; mate, machy, maid;
Matrix and mastery, mother and man.
There is no break between "begot" and "made"
For to beget with knowledge is to make
And to make lovingly is to beget.
This but rehearses what the Sibyl says.
Consider next the meaning of a wall.
To us a barrier, but to a bird
A place to perch and preen its shining wings,   250
A place to talk and scold, and build its nest.
No property on Mars can be fenced off,
And no one be fenced out. So what is mine
Must be so by consent, not penning in;
Or else a fifth wall must be set above
That starves my property of the rich sun,
The power of growth, the lever of the future.
The energy it costs to lock things up
Is more than that consumed by their remaking.
Thus property, possession, change their meaning.
They are the sign of neighborhood and trust,
The gratitude of the community;
And money is the counter of that bond.
Further, the valuable changes weight:
Value embodied in material
Cannot be anchored easily, and flies;
Therefore the value's essence, that's its form,
The information and its competence,
The inner riches of an education,
The gift or training of the storyteller,
The layered discipline of expert thought,

The training of the athlete or the mystic,
The power of constant love and memory,
Become the prize, the precious, and the price.

Consider then a new oeconomy　　　　　　　　　　　　275
Of spirit and the making of the spirit.
It is a floating world, where wealth is what
Accrues about the things we give away.
Theft is expensive here, a taking on
Of labor and abstraction, as one might
Burden a well-cut jacket with small change.
They travel light who fly; the millionaire
Carries no money and no credit cards.
Here power is given only to creators,
Who try at once to palm it off on someone;
As in a healthy university
The dons maneuver to avoid the chair.
And that collecting impulse in our genes,
That banker's genius that dams the current,
Setting aside a head of capital,
Finds satisfaction only in its potlatch,
Translating matter into obligation
As turbines turn the fluid's fall to light.
Luck's lightness here can counter merit's weight;
Justice burns in the oxygen of mercy
To drive the engines of the free republic.

At first the lightness of the flow of value
Demanded mere originality
In Brownian motion, barren innovation.
Mars had its brief, silly postmodernism.　　　　　　　　300
Then as the Sibyl spoke the cosmos blazed
With its mysterious, bounded clarity,
Its mutual, guessed, but still intelligible
Working out of its own destiny,
Its evolution as its gods awake
To dream the higher dream of consciousness.
And as the artists worked they found the genres
Rooted in the grey loam of the brain,
Where flows of value knot to branch and bole,
And differance can make a difference,
And flowering risks a nest egg of tradition;

They found the arts that made the cavemen human
And strained our chromosomes to genius:
The epic melody and sacrifice,
The mask, the rite, the fresco and the song,
The interactive game and the debate,
The drama of the one and chosen act.
So when the dancer turns within her fiction
Of the air, though here her weight is less,
Her mass and angular momentum
Speak the same language, standard, copious,
As any of her sisters of the earth.
And when her arms go out, and the spin
Slows to the stopped gift of a white embrace,
Her audience feels that ancient shock of love   325
And grief, as the brain-liquors hit the heart,
Which moved our ancestors when they saw her
Against the firecast shadows of the cave.

Walls are as weak for persons as for things.
For Aristophanes the avian city
Was orgiastic as the land of dreams.
The cuckoo's cuckoldry, the barnfowl's incest
(As Chanticleer with Pertelote his sister),
The fuckflight of sweet Marvell's coupled tercels,
Made every place a lover's rendezvous
And every time the date of assignation.
And for a brief time so it was. This planet
In its virgin loveliness would offer
The choice scenario for scenes of flesh:
The place where one might, under open sky,
Undo a whiteness or a swarthiness
Marked by the stigmata of generation
To the peeled eyeball-sense of your parched lover;
And a soft foot, cradled in bright green mosses,
Might tug a thigh against a loosening belly.
The learned Aristophanes could fear
The bold invasion of the mother's bed,
Every man his own blind Oedipus,
The town buried in its cloacal swan.

But in a garden where no fruit's forbidden,   350
Fruit swiftly grows insipid to the taste,
Unless some richer savor, saltier
Or tarter, comes to invest the core.
The self of promiscuity is watery,
The flesh indisciplined can know no pleasure;
The greatest joy is to see your own children
Grow in the house you share with your beloved;
The meat of immortality is this:
Progeny, influence, and fertile death.
Who mates with many lovers mates with one
Only, the image of your own desire;
Who mates with one mates with a thousand beings,
All the geography of another world,
And then the changes in that world brought forth
By your inhabiting of it, your own
Being inhabited by another world.
The only journey is in faithfulness;
The unfaithful never can escape from home.

What Martian opportunity selected for
Was inner constancy and truthfulness:
The free bond of the noble citizen
Knowing the work of joy and free to fall.
Like greylag geese, like the trumpeter swan,
The Martians made new rituals of love,
Ships of enacted practice that might carry   375
The tempered soul through the cold wastes of time.
The children saw their parents as their heroes
But in their time took up the fired quest;
And learned to laugh at their own child-desires
And learned to make a gift that might well match
The huge gift their parents gave to them.

Such was the education the young lovers
Rosie Molloy and Chance, who hand in hand
Wandered the vales of this Arcadia,
Or soared about the shining precipices
Of Olympus Mons, such was the teaching

They must have found out somehow for themselves.
(A practical joker, Molly had the Sight,
And Chance could never get enough of her.
They married, had a dozen red-haired children,
And ran an artist's colony for years
In a big growing house cloned from an oak.)

One last lesson from the city of birds.
Despite the fractal modelling of weather
Within Ganesh's subtle cores of logic,
The Martian storms are violent, unexpected.
Death in the air is but a part of life,
For who'd forgo the ecstasy of flying?
And so this city makes old Death a guest
And does not fear him when his dark cloak blows.

We are shown the Sibyl's home in a mountain cave, and hear
her words on the tree of life, the tree of knowledge, and
the creation of the world; and on incest, marriage, the
sexes, death, immortality, and evil.

Scene iii
The Tree of Life

I cannot give the names, but there are those
Who knowing of my work have aided me
In secret, letting me use the uplink
Scrambled in tightbeam to evade detection;
And thus I had the chance to interview
Some who had heard from parent or grandparent
Personal histories about the Sibyl.
The Martian language has diverged from ours
And I must labor to make out the sense;
It has a wildness in the vowel sounds,
A bold and archetypal stress of meaning,
A diacritic tremor in its syntax
Reminiscent of the ancient Greek.
But I would always ask, What was it like
To have a private audience with the Sibyl?
And the accounts differed so strangely, I
Found I was dreaming her in my own fashion,
Given no single image to tie down.

The pilgrim, having labored up the slopes,
Prepared in spirit and bathed in the pools
Of effervescent water from the springs,
And having made his gift to the priestesses,
Would come into a pleasant chamber in
The rock, with a great window open on
The plains and distant estuaries of Mars.   25
A scent of cedar smoke, and something else,
Some light narcotic like the smell of wine
That floats about an altar, or like incense,
But more astringent, cleaner, filled the place,
Together with the distant sound and odor
Of icy waters pouring through their caves.
Sometimes she would be waiting; sometimes one

Of her dear comfortable friends was there,
Ganesh, or Charlie with his pipe, or else
Her two mothers, Irene and Beatrice,
Who spoiled her like an unexpected child,
Or Wolf, who teased her, or her favorite, Chance;
Sometimes she would come in alone and speak,
Briefly and terribly, her eyes distant,
So that you knew you must, on peril of
Some mischance of the soul, consider well
The oracle she spoke, and carefully
Do the clear good and avoid the evil.
Sometimes she was your closest counsellor,
Like the best and most understanding friend
You ever had; or a conspirator,
Laughing with you about the big surprise.
Sometimes—if this can be believed—she was
An old cartoon character, Betty Boop,
With curls, a pretty figure, and a squeak;   50
And only something strange about the eyes,
The milky pallor, and the fearful grace,
Would tell you, you must heed all that she said.

"The tree of life," she said, "Is always branching.
Its three-way joint, fixed past and open futures,
Is all it needs to make a universe.
If we pry close enough to pierce the grain
Of space and time, the edge of the most small,
Out of that ground of emptiness there shoot,
Like forked buds, positive and negative,
The credit and the debit particles
Whereby the balance of the world is drawn;
And from the primal superforce there springs
First gravitation, then the strong and weak,
And last, our sweet electromagnetism.
The radiant energy of the beginning
That sought at first simply escape, would branch
A new species of itself, that which spun
And tied its probabilities together
And said again in one place what it said
Before: this was the birth of bonded matter.
Inside the stars it grew into the forms
Of elemental heavy nuclei,

And one great branch of matter cooled and set
Until its elements became a language   75
And a printing-press to publish what
We read as the compounded, polymered
Or ringed or dancing forms of chemistry.
But matter groaned beneath the tyranny
Of causal laws and that long wearing out
Of order to decay by which it paid
To get a place and an identity.
The god, whose dream it was, yearned to be free,
And freedom is the inverse of decay.
That which is free is not exempt from law,
But in obeying makes itself new laws,
So that its future state is more determined
By what itself enacted than by what
The world's old laws demand that it enact.
Thus certain chemistries and turbulences
Govern themselves, dict their own future state
More sharply than whatever calculator
Might be conceived to do so, and more swiftly.
That which is free has more space to survive,
And populates more branches of the tree;
And time itself was branching higher tenses
Wherein the richer systems might be free.
The richest chemistry of all was life,
The branch of branches, and the tree of trees.
And each new branch was wiser than the last   100
And could consult its own past history
With more reflexion than its ancestors,
As Fibonacci numbers grow, containing
All their past generations in themselves.
(Their golden ratio delights the sense
Of humankind in pattern or in tone.)
And so the tree of life became transformed
To the tree of knowledge; that change was sealed
By the self-shaping of the human race.
We are the bees by which the living world
Will fertilize itself across the voids;
We are the eye by which the pyramid,
The Yggdrasil of time, may know itself."
It happened at that time Ganesh was present,
And it was he who asked the hardest questions.

"Sweetheart," (sometimes this was what he called her)
"Isn't the tree of knowledge opposite
In shape, habit of growth, and operation
To the tree of life? Logic, for instance;
It doesn't grow new stems or twigs or branches,
But fits together old ones in a fork:
Major premise, minor premise, conclusion,
Or the transistor's input, gate, and output.
If you mean "knowledge" in the Bible sense,
It's still a fusion, not a fissioning: 125
Momma and Poppa join to make a baby.
How does the tree of life reverse itself?"
"Yes," said the Sibyl softly, "My dear toad,
That is exactly how it comes about.
How wise of you. The little crotch or lambda
Of which the world is made, only at first
Opened toward the future. Now it points
Both to the future and the redeemed past,
Or plays the caret to insert a gloss.
You ask the Sphinx's test, whose answerer,
The three-legged one, was he whose feet were nailed
Together on the mountain, that he might
Not know himself to be the riddle's answer.
Time is its own reversing, and its cross;
The life of knowledge is the life of life,
The branches are the rooting of the roots . . . "
We know the look on old Ganesh's face;
The ecstasy of the intelligence,
The urge to know and question, the excitement
Of being where the mental action is.
All prophets of the past, all the messiahs,
Wise women, Zen seers, Huichol spirit-dons,
Even the kindliest Hasid, would take
The opportunity to put him down,
To cut the gawky stalks of human reason.   150
But Ganesh knew that he could trust his friend,
And questioned her again: "So you are saying:
To know the world is how to make it grow?"
And she, so gentle: "Dear old toad, you know it.
You bring the world to life with your own gismos.
The elder law would curse you for your knowledge;
But I say to you, you are of the blessed."

Ganesh, though, wouldn't be put off by this.
"If when we know, we know our ancestors;
If knowing is a kind of generation;
Doesn't that make it incest when we know?"
"To see, with Ham, the nakedness of Noah,"
Murmured the Sibyl in her prophecy:
"That in the ancient law was to be cursed
And be an unclean Canaanite, a slave.
But every marriage is incestuous:
We are all sprung from Eve. Even to tell
The story of the curse is to be cursed.
We must all serve each other then, and be
Clean baptized in the fluids of corruption.
The kingdom of heaven is like a seed,
A yeast, a ferment; and if God is love,
Consider how impure a thing is love:
How much akin to ours is the warm skin
Of wife and husband; how our love makes out   175
The brotherhood and sisterhood we share,
And those dear members, how we generate,
Are strangely matched analogies, the hers
And his; and how your lover's selfhood is
The naked mouthskin of your own enfleshment.
I am the Sibyl, and my father's mother
Was a whore; her mother was a whore.
Disciple, you have taught me not to bless;
The better blessing is the oldest curse."

But Chance was also there, with his son Liam;
And he now asked if it was her intention
To set aside the ancient laws of incest.
"Let there be new laws," said the Sibyl then;
"Not to forbid the marriage of the kin,
But to command the choice of fertile strangers.
How may we know the strangeness of ourselves
Without encountering the very other?
The sin of incest is not in pollution
But in the choice of safety over risk.
It is the sin of the promiscuous,
Who shapes each lover in the image of
His own inviolate sterility.
Love is a venture into foreign ground,

A hazard of the precious germs of life,
A finding of your sister where you might   200
Not have expected it, at the world's end;
And only thus is the world bound together.
There have been many teachings of the love
Of neighbors, and the love of man for man,
Of sisterhood, of parent and of child,
But there has never been till now a teaching
About the love of woman for a man,
The love of man for woman; such a love
Was only dignified as sign or image
Of marriages more mystical and holy.
But now I say to you all other unions
Are but a symbol of the marriages
That men and women make between themselves.
Let there be few of them, lest they be common.
Let them be judged as justly as the world
May judge them in its most envious censure;
And for the rest, let there be only mercy."

"If then it is the difference," said Chance,
"That makes the lovers perfect in their love,
What is the difference of men and women?"
At this the Sibyl smiled and looked at him
Under an eyebrow, but he held his peace,
And presently she answered soberly.

"The selfhood of a living being," she said,
"Is in its origin and essence female.   225
What makes the difference between the thought
Of a cold stone and a warm animal—
Even between a wisp of ash, of oil, of gas,
And the green plant or germ that feeds upon it—
Is that the life is she, is feminine,
Conserves intact her selfskin membrane, keeps
A clean environment within her walls,
Feeds, senses, knows herself after what fashion
The depth of her inheritance dictates,
Learns and creates her organs or her tools,
And buds and nurtures copies of herself.
And now began the great experiment:
A second mood of being was posited,

Whose composition risked the species-life.
It was a distillate of femaleness,
With one more chromosome, an almost cancerous
Effundence of those hormone chemistries
That make the female sharply what she is:
This was the origin of the male gender.
If female is the mark distinguishing
The living organism from the dead,
The organismic from the mechanistic,
Then male is the fierce mask the female makes
To test and to adventure what she is,
A tragic and extreme exaggeration,   250
A taxing of her metabolic limits,
Always in danger of returning to
The automatic, the impersonal,
As if the armor might become the man.
So maleness is the test of errant genes,
The sickly flowering of femaleness,
The burning through of sex into the monster
That may once in a thousand years give birth
To one so beautiful she is the mother
Of a whole race of new living beings.

"And with the male came death. For till that moment
Each species was immortal or extinct,
And every parent was her progeny,
And every sister was a twin so close
That each one was the same identity.
Maleness entailed the individual life,
The alienate, the novel point of view,
The unique package of reshuffled genes.
But now this clumsy hazard of the male
(Sowing dissention in the sisterhood,
Making the self no longer mean the same),
Required a leveller of generations,
A scythe to reap the entwined wheat and tares,
That the next season only the good seed
Should be implanted in the field of time.   275
And so our death is written in our cells,
Its black letters spell our consciousness.
It was with this lethal inoculate
That the wise female injected herself;

And thus the goddess woke to dream more deeply
And know herself through the inflaming venom,
The snake-secreted madness of the male."

"Then death," said Chance, "has got a special meaning.
Of what advantage is it that we die?"
"Yes," said Ganesh, "I've always thought it crazy
The more evolved an organism is,
The more unquestionably it will die.
We die more definitely than a rat,
Who's got his species-life to fall back on;
A rat more than an ant, who's just a cell
In the nest, and an ant more than a virus.
And rocks and such don't even die, they just
Like wear away; and protons last as close
To forever as you get, except photons
Which don't wear out at all. So what's the story?"
The Sibyl smiled. "As bad as it can be.
Consider this: if humans are more mortal
Than the animals, and if our death
Is that which marks us as the more divine,
The gods must be more mortal than ourselves.   300
Death is the best survival strategy.
Survival is continuance in time;
And if we want the immortality
Of photons, we already, surely, have it—
Light is the stuff of which our flesh is made,
And of itself it cannot ever die.
It is our souls that die, that go to sleep
Each night, and are reconstituted in
The altered matter of our morning bodies,
That pass away as every present moment
Gives way and life and breathing to the next.
A dying soul in an immortal body:
This is the truth we see if we would cling
To immortality in the old law.

"Now we are ready for another law.
All creatures are creators of the time
They have their being in, and if that being
Permits no space for others (as a hadron

Excludes its sisters from its place and tone)
Then in that space it shares no limit, and
May well be called immortal in its time.
Such are the basest entities, immortal.
The higher beings are more sensitive
And share the complex times they generate,
And with respect to after and before   325
Are bounded by the surfaces they share
With one another, knowing and being known.
Their boundaries are thus their deaths, and thus
The sacrifice of love they make to share
Their universe with other sentient things.
For since reality is concrete only
As all of its participants are sensed
And registered by each, and each by all,
Death is our gift of being to the world.

"If immortality is in that gift,
Survival in a law above the law,
A living in the conversation of
The world, beyond the meaning of your death,
Such that the minds of others bear your mind,
And you embody spirits from the past—
It will require the gift of all you are,
And stands or falls by each of us, for each
Is to himself a very universe.
The kingdom of heaven is indeed at hand,
Not *there*, or *after*, but at hand, as one
Might take a pencil from a tabletop.
That kingdom is indeed a mustardseed,
That kingdom is a leaven in the world.
The time of that familiar place is always
Out at a right-angle from the old time;   350
It is what joins all old times back together.
Oh my dear friends, all Paradise is here,
It's here in this room, as close as childhood,
Close as the death we die all the more swiftly
The closer that we share each other's souls."

Now all this time Irene had been there,
The Sibyl's mother, but had kept her silence.

But now she raised her head and looked upon
Her daughter, whose own being she had willed,
Once, to have cancelled, to have rendered void,
And murmured softly (we could hardly hear):
"Sibyl, in none of what you say to us
Is anything of wickedness. But how
Are we, who live in the grip of the world,
To take the malice in ourselves and others?
You've said that evil is the shade of good,
A shadow cast by some mere privateness
That makes privation of the light and being.
But is there not an evil, active, clever,
Seeking out ways to do another harm?
Aren't there demons in the human soul
That seek the innocent and would destroy them,
That smear and tire the noble and the great?
You give us lovely good philosophies:
What can you say to us about the evil?"   375
A tear stood in the Sibyl's eye; the stone chamber
Seemed to darken as if all might be lost.
"Ah yes, these things are still to come to pass,"
She muttered, almost to herself. "So be it."

But then the Sibyl smiled, began again.
"My dearest friends. Any philosophy
That makes a place for evil is in love
With it a little, and permits its franchise.
Might not the matter be misplaced?—evil
No subject for philosophy at all,
Not even a true noun or adjective;
Only a preposition to denote
What you should fight even unto your death?
—And if it is not that, then it's not evil
And therefore should not overmuch concern us:
A nothing that receives its shape and being
Just from its names, from the opinion of it.
Were it not better to prepare yourself
As, so they say, my father did, in strength
And skill of soldierhood, so when it comes
You slay it if you can and obtain merit

(And if it is not that, then it's not evil)?
Why should it be more complicated in
Itself, interesting, sophisticated?
Why should we give it house-room in our souls?"

*Perhaps as a demonstration of the truth of the Sibyl's last
strange sayings about the nature of evil, the poet
interrupts her words for the last time to give a swift and
impatient account of the fates of Gaea and Garrison.*

*Thus, after a long sickness Gaea dies. Garrison, in
deference to what he falsely believes to be her last wishes,
sends Flavius his son to murder the Sibyl. Flavius comes to
Mars in the guise of a pilgrim, but in the presence of the
Sibyl he hesitates to use his weapon. Irene in an attempt
to disarm him is herself killed; the Sibyl is wounded. But
she pardons the assassin, and he returns to Earth. Finding
his mother distracted to madness by neglect, Flavius slays
his father Garrison in the arms of a lover.*

*But for a few brief references in Act V, scene v this is the
last we see of Beatrice, Charlie, and Ganesh. Their work
and destiny are unfinished: they are woven into the future
construction of the planet Mars. Likewise, the poet does
not tell this in the poem, but in 2068, shortly after the
assault upon the Sibyl's life, the old nurse Sumikami passes
away at the age of a hundred years, leaving the room of the
poem and the world as unobtrusively as she entered it.*

Scene iv
The Passing of Gaea

*T*urn then once more to the dark vale of shadows,
To this Earth with its manacles of mass.
But when I speak of it after such fashion,
My heart twists within me, with loyalty,
With love for all this planet once has been
And still may be, and, in that part of nature
Which never did condemn itself, is now.
Lately I walked the streets of old Manhattan
In the bright fall weather of Indian summer;
Under my overcoat the bulky wad
Of an early draft of this manuscript
Intended for a place beneath the floorboards
Of an old friend's apartment; my arthritis

Gives me a limp that usefully disguises
The awkwardness of errands such as these.
It's not my purpose to discuss myself—
An epic poet ought to be a drudge
In service of his brilliant agonists—
But it was just that kind of autumn day
That makes you love your life on any terms,
With the big planes and maples of the Village
Casting a shade of orange on the sidewalk
Brighter, it seems, than the navy blue sky;
And though the air is cold, a summery breath
Will swim up from the warmed fronts of the brownstones   25
Sharp with the brewed smell of fallen leaves.
So I must tell the history of Gaea
And her son, and her son's son Flavius,
That the tale be completed, and my work over.
We shall return once more to *Mons Pavonis*,
To the Peacock Mountain on that planet
So very far away, that living dream,
To hear the Sibyl speak of the divine beauty;
But stay now for a while upon the Earth.

When Gaea heard about the Lima Codex,
And how her victory was snatched away,
She wept, and Garrison, who was nearby,
Came and perceived what he had never seen
In twenty years, his mother's flowing tears;
And she looked up and saw him, and her heart,
In rage at her detection by her son,
Seemed to turn inside out, and like a fish,
Beat with a quiver and a spasm on
The inside of its bowl; a pain so huge
It was grotesque, it would be funny
It was so out of all proportion, struck
At breast and arm, and felled her to the floor.

But Gaea's constitution was as strong
As the burned stump that puts forth year by year
A clutch of virid leaves in frosty spring;   50
And though the artery that serves the heart
Was knotted with the plaques of decayed passion,
And all the muscle of its forward face

Was scars and spongy lesions, she survived.
Garrison now became her nurse; he sought
By this to mitigate his guilt for her.
In doing so he must ignore his wife:
He treated her as if she were not there,
And scarcely recognized his little son.
And Bella in her loyalty grew thin
And sickly pale, neglectful of her music,
Scattered, distracted in her manner; even
Eccentric, so that little Flavius
Sometimes could not predict what she might do.
The boy, though, in the fineness of his spirit,
That idealism that must seek a hero,
Only admired his father all the more,
Falsely believing that his empty silence
Betokened expectations stern and noble,
Tacit acknowledgement of manly duty.

Now Gaea's doctors thought she would soon die,
But she would live another twenty years.
We can adjust to certain times of strain
If we believe they soon will have an ending;
But Gaea would not die, she plain refused   75
To give the colonists that satisfaction.
And Garrison must feed her, change her bed,
Take her for little walks about the grounds,
Listen to her increasingly fantastic
Plans for the redemption of the Earth
From the great insult we had offered her;
And as the years went by, her kidneys failed,
And she lived every moment of her life
In a great bedroom crammed with furniture,
Steeped in the childhood urine smell, where once
She and her Chance had wrestled in their love.
And Garrison became inured to it,
And could see nothing strange in what he did;
But on occasion he would disappear,
Leaving her in the care of a hired nurse,
To find relief in certain degradations.
And Bella bore it all, would not complain;
And Flavius grew up without a father
But worshipping the absence as an ikon.

There came a day, springtime at Devereux,
When Gaea felt a new force in her body,
And sat up in her bed, a wattled creature,
Now fat to monstrousness, but beautiful
No less about the eyes and lips; she stood,
Swaying and sighing, on enfeebled legs.   100
Garrison moaned about her, begged her humbly
Back to her bed, not knowing which was worse,
To force her or to let her have her way.
She did not understand the thing that drove her;
It was a joy, a strength that she remembered
From her long past political juvescence;
Seeking a meaning for her mood, as always,
Rose the impetuous, she chose to make
Her gesture as a mission to her son.
"Garrison, stop that noise and listen to me.
I want a promise from you, then I'll go
Quietly back to bed, as good as gold.
There is a prophet or a leader now
Upon the planet of the naturekillers.
Some say it is a witch, descended from
Your own guilty stock and ancestors.
I shall die soon of grief, that they have wrought
The great pollution despite all I've done;
I want you to avenge me, or if you
Are too afraid and old and weak to do so,
To send your son about my business.
Kill her, or else my death is on your head."
What could he do? He made his wretched promise,
And she, after a stagger to the window,
That she might see the flowering crabapple,   125
Sadly unpruned but pink with buttery sweetness,
Went docile back to bed and was tucked in
As if she were a naughty little girl.

A few hours after this, poor Garrison,
Who thought this was another of her scares,
Threatening death while she greenly endured,
Departed on a little quiet excursion.
But while he was away, a miracle
Seemed to envelop Gaea's dying body.
That joy within her grew, and now at last

She understood its true and inner meaning.
It was not, as she'd thought, her ancient courage,
To fight against the demons of her cause,
But something strangely opposite, the gift
Of a forgiveness, even of a love
For all her enemies, a creamlike calm
That smelt of apple-blossom and blue sky.
And now at last she felt the cruel grip
Of life relax itself upon her body,
And sent for Garrison, that at the last
She might rescind the terrible commission
She laid on him; but he could not be found.
Still, in a state of blessedness and peace,
As true salvation as one might desire,
One night, attended only by her nurse,   150
Just as the apple scent gave way to may,
To flowering hawthorn, Gaea passed away.

When Garrison returned and she was dead,
He went a little mad. He calculated
What he was doing when she died, imagined
Her despair and final loneliness,
Knew that his only chance for peace was gone,
But set himself the sterner to obey
Her last behest to him, of her revenge.
Flavius was called from university,
And stood, tall and red-headed in a coat,
At graveside in the weed-grown cemetery,
While many hundred of the core elite
Within the Ecotheist faith, who marched
With Gaea in the glory days of change
And triumph in the quiet revolution,
Heard the Commissioner himself pronounce
The words of burial, farewell, and welcome
For the dead back to her namesake's home.

To understand what followed, we must know
How Flavius constructed his life story
Out of what pieces time had given him.
As Ecotheism matured, it lost
The gaunt and strange excesses of its youth,

The flights of a Ruhollah or a Cade　　　　　　175
(That popular fanatic who advised
Sterilization for the human species),
And Penth became quite as respectable
As English tea, and about as exciting.
But now the Church took on the force of time,
And Flavius felt for it as Frenchmen might
Hearing the Marseillaise, or British workers
Feel for the Red Flag, or Americans
For yellow ribbons, hot dogs, fourth July.
His father was the hero of his myth,
A grim and distant bearer of the faith,
The paradigm of moral probity.

And thus when Garrison proposed his plan
Later upon the day of funeral,
Flavius felt the dull glow of election,
A dedication to that chosen torment
Which spins the paltry story of a man
Into a thread so tight it cannot break,
Into a garment that will stand when he
Who wears it has outstayed the dying flesh.
"I cannot go; I am too old, I would
Be recognized, I would stand out among
The young illegal emigrants; but you
Might plausibly find out a skyslave runner
And get a ship to Mars. It was her wish,　　　　　200
And I must lay it on you as a duty."
"Father, I understand. This is what you
Prepared me for, what I was waiting for
Through all these years. It is as well that you
Never were close to me, nor I to you;
It would have been unbearable if we
Had lived as ordinary people do,
Who are not called to overriding duties.
But I'm afraid for Mother. She's not strong.
Promise you will support her when I'm gone."
This was the kind of person that he was.

It would be tale enough for many poems
To tell how Flavius could penetrate

The underground of Martian sympathizers
And find the right connection for a ship
That, creaking, shuttled emigrants above
The atmosphere into a low earth orbit;
How he must fake the sale of all his goods
In payment for the new life in the stars;
How the great treeship docked against the shuttle;
How border guards were tipped off to avoid
That sector, how a leaky pressure seal
And viral blight had almost killed them all;
Of planetfall, and of his pilgrimage
Across the twilit and alive new world   225
To where the Peacock Mountain soared away
Into a pinkish sky. But we are near
The end of our long journey, and must hurry.

At last the pilgrim came into the presence
Of that lady it was his oath to kill.
Chance was there with her, and his other cousins
Wolf and Irene; one who knew the cast
And motion of the elder Chance might trace
The family resemblance in them all.
At once the Sibyl knew who this man was,
With his red hair and Garrison's long face.
Her mouth turned down with love and pity then,
And she spoke quickly, softly, to forestall
Her friends lest they be moved to shield her from him.
"So you have come. Your name is Flavius,
And you are kin to us, and you are welcome.
We do not offer any violence,
But ask that you stay with us for a while,
Converse with us, come to know what we are,
And then decide what it is you must do.
How would it be if we might speak awhile
About the beautiful, of what it is
And how it serves the making of the world . . . ?"
Now Flavius had a weapon in his coat,
A handgun, cunningly disguised to look   250
And function as a little voice-recorder.
And as she spoke, almost against his will
He drew it forth and held it out toward her.
He could not take his eyes from her; her voice

Would seem to him the loveliest that there was,
And she was what all other things were for,
All other persons' being strove to be.
What he would then have done we do not know.

For now Irene knew why he had come,
And saw him point a weapon at her daughter.
At once her training in the martial arts
(The dark gift of her master Tripitaka,
The Sibyl's father, murderer of Chance)
Caught up her body in its steel pavane,
And in a flying turn she spun herself
Against the wavering aim of the assassin.
It was his slowness in the Martian field,
Not yet acclimatized to the strange lightness,
That stumbled her, or he would be disarmed
And no harm done, so many tears the less.
He did not know he'd let the weapon fire.
The crash was black and heavy in the room.
There was blood everywhere; Irene on
Her knees, sinking toward the floor; the Sibyl
With a great stain of red across her side,   275
Soaking the clean white garment that she wore.
A single shot had wounded both of them:
Irene in the throat, and fatally;
The Sibyl by the weaker ricochet.
But now in blinded fury Wolf had flung
Himself upon the miserable man
Who, as it were a snake, had dropped his gun;
The Sibyl shrieked to rob him his revenge,
And Chance, who'd caught her, swaying, laid her down,
And tore Wolf's fingers from the killer's throat.

The Sibyl's wound was bloody but not deep;
She led the mourners at the funeral
Of that unhappy lady whom she owed
Two lives, and who in turn had owed her two.
Wolf's madness did not pass for many weeks,
But in the end the Sibyl healed his soul.
Flavius got more mercy than he wished:
The Sibyl would not have him harmed, and Chance
Argued before the court that he had been

As if a soldier of a state at war,
And that it was not certain at that moment
If his intent had truly been to kill.
It was decided he should be sent back
To Earth, to make what covenant he might
With his unhappy spirit; it was clear   300
That now he worshipped what he would have murdered,
And, for himself, wished nothing but his death.
Thus justice can be kind and mercy cruel.

For did the Sibyl know what he would find
When, after three years' exile, he returned
To Earth and sought his home and family?
And if she did, what may that mean for us,
Who must—for who is wiser than the Sibyl?—
Be therefore privy to the inner work
Of history, when history has meaning?
Did she thus choose this way to twitch aside
The curtain on the great dream of the God?
Is, then, the deepest meaning of the world
Not just or merciful, but beautiful?

So Flavius arrived at Devereux
At dusk on an exhausted autumn day,
The frost upon the long and rotted grass,
A red horizon between barren trees.
This is the last time we shall look upon
This place, so let us bid a fit farewell.
He found the windows lit, the offices
Of the world church bright with activity,
But no sign of his father or his mother.
The lodge was empty, and it smelt of stone.
Upon inquiry Flavius discovered   325
That, sick of Devereux, which still reminded
Him of Gaea and the past, Garrison
Had moved with Bella to New Mexico
And opened up the ranch at San Luis Rey.
Not wishing to announce himself before
He could explain in full what he had done,
And ask his father how his duty to him
Could so conflict with what he felt was right,
He did not contact anyone, and spent

The last night of his enormous journey
In a drab, clean hotel just west of Reading.
And in the evening of an endless day
Caught in the limbo of a single hour
As time-zones reeled away beneath the wings
(Except for two hours in the terminal
At DFW, dozing upon
A row of seating greased with ancient sweat;
Waking at times to see the afternoon
Of Texas wane across the deep blue sky
Feathered with white cloud through the tinted glass),
He drove a rented car through falling sleet
Up the strange valley of the Rio Grande.
Sometimes the ice-fog cleared, the low sun glared;
In the last light the mesas were gigantic,
Each with an altar-cloth of soiled snow;   350
Soon it grew dark; an Ecotheist preacher
Was all there was upon the radio.

Though no one heard his knock, the ranch was lit,
Uncurtained, with a blare of TV sound.
He tried the unlocked door and entered in.
The noise was coming from a backdoor room.
He pushed on through and this is what he saw.
A heavy Indian nurse, dazed out with Penth,
But kindly-looking, sprawled before a screen.
His mother sat up at a kitchen table,
Rocking herself from side to side as if
A mechanism with a battery
Governed a motion slowing gradually
Until its last reaction should be spent.
Flavius knew at once that she was mad.
He could not watch, and left the room unnoticed.
The living rooms were uninhabited,
The lights left on, and in some disarray;
No fires burned in the great hearths, but warmth
Poured dryly from the heating vents. A sound
From the old master bedroom caught his ear.
He turned the doorknob, opened up the door.
Two bodies swarmed upon the bed, one brown,
The other white. He thought at first that they
Were man and woman but a sort of count,   375

Of what was what, made it quite clear that both
Were males, and now he recognized his father,
And saw the other was an Indian boy.
As they became aware of him, and broke,
And stood, attempting with the sheets to hide
The knowledge of his eyes, he reached across
And took a shotgun from the rack above,
And, with a kind of dull surprise, took aim,
And fired both barrels at his father's body.

Would it be different if we had known
That in these last few months with young Ortiz
Garrison for the first time in his life
Had found the happiness that had escaped him?
That if his son had not returned, his lover,
Tiring of this adventure, would betray him?
Is death the worst can happen to a man?
What if we knew that Flavius's trial
Resulted in a brief and lightened sentence;
That with his care and love through many years
Bella got back her wits sufficiently
To play the cello as she used to do
Sitting beside the window in the scent
Of springtime in the lodge at Devereux?
That in the end Flavius would return
To Mars and die in service of the Sibyl?

We return to the words of the Sibyl: how truth and goodness
are but offshoots of beauty; of the nature of beauty, its
reality, its mystical experience, its neurochemistry, its
persuasiveness, its reflectiveness, its divinity, its
presence in history. A hymn to beauty follows. The author,
unable to finish the poem, is blessed by a vision of roses
which brings home to him the meaning of the Sibyl's
teaching; and he is thus enabled to pass his conception on
to another poet in the distant past.

Scene v
The Roses

*B*ut then the story would renew itself,
As time does always, as after a sleep
The healthy body yawns, looks round, begins
To think about a bite for breakfast; as
The lover's ardor at a nape or ankle
Will, after trance, suffuse the world once more
With warm and lovely colors, delicate.
But we must strike out at an angle from
The self-renewing flow of mortal things
That for a moment we may see their meaning
And set an end to this one course of time;
For endings are the pruning of the branch
That makes it bud, that makes the mystic flower.

"How do we know the truth," the Sibyl said,
"Between two explanations, or a thousand,
Each with an equal claim to evidence,
Each with an equal logical coherence?
It is the beauty of that one which marks it
So that the scientist-philosopher
Is in no doubt where our allegiance lies.
And if we would extract the seed, the essence
Of the truth, we must know the ways of beauty.
For beauty is the oneness of the tree
Of life with and within the tree of knowledge,
Its oversapience that makes it spring   25
To further budding as it mates itself;

And if that branchingness is all that is,
Then beauty is the secret name of being.
Consider how the plants and animals
Blaze to their loveliest expressiveness,
The flower, the paroxysm of their song,
The ritual dance, the flash of scale or feather,
Just at the moment when they pass their being
Over to the following generation;
Thus beauty is continuance of time.
But sex does not produce a printed copy;
The being that is reproduced is neither
Copy nor monster, and the space between
Is what we mean by beauty, beautiful.
Survival thus is nothing but transcendence.

"How may we know the good? Old Socrates
Who was my friend when I was Diotima,
Took his last drink because he asked a question:
Is an act good because the gods have willed it
Or do the gods will it because it's good?
If good is but the power of the gods
We need no word for it and no concern
To find it out; it is what we can do
Because we're not restrained from doing it.
How then do the good gods know what's good?   50
What was that light elusive Gautama
Preached of, behind the netveil of the eye?
That gentlest of friends, whose feet I bathed
With tears and myrrh, said that the good was Love,
And he in turn bathed his disciples' feet.
What is it that we love, what draws our love?
Why do they paint my Krishna's body blue?
The heart and inner seed of love is beauty.
When all commandments have been laid away,
Being but parables to clothe the soul
Into her thalamus, her marriage-chamber;
When every strict accounting of her acts
Be rendered, stricken from the reckoning;
When every 'why' is answered;—there is left
But the one law, to love the beautiful.

"So truth and goodness are the first two leaves
That branch from the archaic stem of beauty;
Or better yet, the father and the mother
Are truth and goodness, but the heavenly child,
That makes them what they are, and why they are,
Is the divine fruitfulness of beauty.
The two great revelations of the Earth
Were truth and goodness; now we hold the third,
The cornerstone rejected by the builders,
The thing we need another world to know,   75
The loveliness that is the seed of love.
As being is the outer form of truth,
And loving is the outer form of goodness,
Creating is the outer form of beauty.

"Those who would be disposed to set it light
Say beauty's in the eye of the beholder.
But all the universe is eyes, and 'I's,
And all that is is what those eyes behold.
Sensation is the densest form of being,
Perception is the concretest sensation,
Esthesis is the sharpest of perception.
The stone records the presence of a tree
By mass and by electromagnetism:
That is the tree's whole being for the stone.
The deer can know the tree by shape and color—
What to the stone would be ghosts invisible.
The boy who sees the tree as beautiful
Knows it so much more clearly than the deer
As does the deer more clearly than the stone.
The power his species wields to make such judgments,
Ratified by its mastery of Mars,
Enfranchises the vision of the boy.
Ten billion years the universe has labored
To see itself through our confirming eyes;
That gaze must sum its being as beautiful.   100

"And what the mystics felt was nothing less
Than that totality, that radiance
Which is the god herself awakening

To dream herself to being in ourselves.
Whatever is the whole, the eye that sees it
Is ecstatic, and must find its proper place
Outside the boundary of all it sees;
And in its step back from the living edge
Of all that is, it grows another limb
Upon the many-branched frontier of being.
The dendrites of the great tree of the brain,
Whose cortex is that single milkwhite rose,
The living metaphor of the whole world,
Glow into music as the vision stirs,
And their soft nodes distil a heady fragrance
That bells the skull a lanternful of light;
And the sweet bees of the cell vesicles
Carry the pollen to the pistilled axon;
And molecules of pattern never known
Record the pregnant kiss of mothering.
The liquor of that consummation drenches
The forked and blossomed panicles of nerves,
And forms a mighty image in the eyes
And words of the illuminated seers,
The holy shamans and the inflamed saints.   125
That image is the trace or touch of God:
When they would represent it, it appears
As a mandala or the beating waves
Of a repeated chant; each circle is
The new boundary of included time,
The new high water mark of consciousness.
Sometimes they sing it as an inner light;
For as the brute time-beater of the brain
Is mastered by the sun, an inner sun
Governs this new testament of time.

"I have taught how the world is acted through,
Performed by fiat of its symbiotes.
What brings them to their vote, their congregation?
What is the medium of their Amen,
Affirmed participation in the game?
What could it be but beauty—harmony
Promising further, darker melodies,
Promising struggles to resolve the chord?
What is it but the ache of a suspense,

Before the covenanted union comes,
The drawing out of time from the bent bow,
That makes a doorframe for Arcadia?—
Beauty is thus the knitting-in of time,
That weaves a pattern from the wayward threads.

"Beauty's the meaning of the divine dream,   150
Its principle, the personality
And mood of the great dreamer of the world.
If you would know her mind, then study beauty.
When we have gone out to the edge of things,
Questioned the very axioms of being,
Taken the world itself as that computer
Which stores all knowledge and predicts the future,
And asked the fatal question of the sphinx
Whose answer is the answerer itself—
What are you? What is your own end and future?—
Then we have entered in the house of beauty.
This can't be proved. But here the world must crack,
Must grow another layer of itself,
Even to contemplate the question's meaning.
Beauty is what we can affirm outside
All axioms, all rules of yes and no.
It is itself the leap of self-inclusion,
The dark glow of an affirmation deeper
Than any mandated by axiom;
The urge itself of axiomization
To make a pattern that can grow a mind.
Beauty is the beginning of the worlds,
The evolution of the life of being,
The melt that crystallizes into meaning.

"That crystal is the hierarchy of being,   175
Whose meaning is its very history.
But as a perfect scale must still be broken
To make a melody and spin a time,
As spring must take the frozen forms and melt them,
And laughter must succeed to tragedy,
So every harmony and every structure
Are but the raw materials of beauty.
Although no message can be sent or taken
Without a medium whose shape is clear,

A perfect carrier-wave conveys no message,
And time without a difference must cease.
That which was once the union of the meaning
With its embodiment in act and form
Becomes the medium itself of a new gospel:
Hierarchy broken for a richer hierarchy.
That fierce subsumption, as a fire or feast,
That transubstantiation of the old,
Is beautiful, and is the tragedy
And the metabolism of the world.
When that which is, is that which ought to be,
The mountains of the world are beaten flat,
And nothing moves, having no place to go.
This is a true paradox, that that which is
Ought not indeed be that which ought to be.

"Then ought we simply to accept the flow,   200
Make no demand for a consistency
That must be shattered by the rush of time?
This is the last temptation, to be quiet,
Be wise, seek not to know the whole;
To play the little games time offers us,
A life just of sensations, not of thoughts.
But then there should be nothing great to die,
We should deprive the world of tragedy,
And everybody would be tourists, passing
Through countrysides whose villages are empty,
Void of committed dwellers in this life;
The gamblers would have cashed in all their chips,
Put on their hats and headed for the exits,
Gods with no mortals to play the game of Troy.
Time grows by means of the attempts to halt it,
And freedom is the crash of an achieved will
Into the fulfilment of its denial.
Beauty is violence, incipience,
And transience, the lovelier for what
Is sacrificed in that rich wastefulness.
Beauty is breathtaking and cruel,
And would be evil were it not worth all
We sacrifice so that we might endure it.
There is no afterlife; eternity
Is an intenser form of time that strikes   225

Out at right-angles from an entire life
And knows as many tenses more, and moods,
As we do than the immemorial beasts.
Time must be dammed to make this current flow;
Light blazes from the point of the resistance.

"Chance my great-grandfather hurled all his being
Against the tendency of history;
My father Tripitaka, in the faith
That time could be denied, did murder him;
He in his own time slew himself that we
Should get a life he served but could not share;
Great-grandmother Gaea lived a life that I
Declare as excellent, as sacrificed
To freedom as our own conquistadors.
Charlie would kill a world to give it birth;
Ganesh could tickle dead things into life.
Wolf and Irene never found their love,
Yet were transformed by loss to singing birds;
Beatrice made a garden from the death
Of her own inner garden with its seeds.
My brother Chance might have been president
Of this republic; he served me instead.
All knew that life is hungry as a flame:
Even that man who lately sought my life
Was faithful to a thing that defied time.   250

"The world-dream of the god is history,
Whose inner meaning is the joy of dying,
The flash of light on wheat, on clouds, on eye,
That dies the moment that it has its being.
Why should we in our fear of tragedy
Reserve our gift to beauty lest it die?
The grief of suffering is the melody
The goddess sought to be enfranchised by.
The holiest unworldliness is this:
To love the world and die upon its kiss.
Truth is a dab of scent a girl put on
You catch upon a lit spring afternoon.
Truth is a ripple on piano keys,
Wind in the leaves, moonlight on fruit trees.
Our cunning sells our birthright for a song—

Eternity so brief and life so long.
Give all you have to history, because
All paradise is here and always was."

And this would be the ending of the story
Had I disposed material more fitly
To the first chosen and constraining form:
So law may force on us unchosen freedoms.
To tell the truth, I had run out of things
To say; as the task neared its conclusion
(Which was to be a summons to my world   275
To take up once again the glory road)
I fell into despair, which was the deeper
The more I praised the destiny of Mars.
What was there left for my own ruined planet?
I could compose no more, and the long weeks
Of sodden fall went by, and I was dazed
And sleepy like a sickly child, and dreamed
Profusely, strange weary meaningless dreams.
The last weekend of Fall it was my turn
To get the writers' co-op car to drive.
I was in luck. It was a lovely day,
Almost like spring, smelling of earth and sea.
I drove up the Taconic to the lakes:
Some of the suburbs are inhabited,
And the old black folk had put on a display
Of Christmas decorations, shiny red
And green, and angels and a plaster creche.
Though in the broad daylight it was tawdry,
It moved me; in a kind of aching joy
I drove on into the deep countryside
And stopped beside a tangled entryway
Where a thick wild scent had attracted me.
So picking briers from my hair and clothes
I walked along what must have been a drive,
And the cold fragrance grew as I limped on.   300
It was a great old mansion—built, perhaps,
To be the homestead of a stockbroker—
And it was heaped and overgrown with roses,
Sprays, drifts, mountains of crimson blossoms,
Bursting through windows and half-opened doors,
Climbing the chimneys and the buckled eaves.

Some hardy strain, most likely, with its roots
Deep in a septic tank, southern exposure.
The savage perfume almost knocked me out;
But what was strangest was to know these flowers
As if they never had been cultivated,
As if they never bore the name of roses,
As if they were the most natural of plants,
As if their scent were like the bark or mould
Of any woodland passing into winter.
How lovely was the wild scent of this flower!
Were not all human things as natural,
Was not all history as sweet as this?

When I returned I read the Sibyl's words
And saw at once another meaning in them.
She had been thinking of us after all,
Even the lost ones in our land of shadows:
There was a path that such as we might follow.
I had believed I must be miserable
In my ill health, and clogged with enemies,   325
Discouraged by the State so very gently
The hero juices never learned to flow:
I have no testament to make of prison camps,
Gaunt intellectuals with fiery eyes,
Or deaths beneath the clubs of the police,
So that resistance to this kindly pressure
Seems the ungratefulness of a spoiled child.
(When it is less important I will tell
The game of cat and mouse and quiet betrayal:
But paranoia, even justified,
Is not as interesting to the reader
As to the author—and quite rightly so:
It is a sickness the authorities
Use to contain the struggles of the prey.)

But now I saw I always had been happy.
I had my task, my manuscript; so what
Could they do to me that they had not done,
Stealing the copies, making sure my friends
Did not get their promotions or their raises,
Letting me always know I was observed?
What was dispiriting was being so near

The end of all those labors, and the moment
When I must think upon my death in this
To me so foreign and so false a land.
And all the time, the Sibyl seemed to say,   350
As I transcribed but did not hear her words,
I had been serving history; I was
The worn stone in its stream that turns its course,
That multiplied by many, makes the mountain
That causes it to flow at all. Freedom
And freedom's soul, the all-creating beauty,
Attended me, and made my labors rich.
If modest talents and a faulty ear
So flawed the work that it would never stand
Beside the giants of the Earth's wild past,
Yet this might be the best, because the only
Epic of protest in our darkening glide;
And so the opportunity of hope
Never is absent while time yet endures.

But what was I to do now it was over?
Polish, revise of course. There have been those
Who've worn away a mighty oeuvre that way,
And should be quite content to start again.
But that would surely be, considering
The heroes of my tale, who never let
Revision dally in the way of action,
A counter-imitative kind of fallacy,
Hypocrisy before the gates of being.

No. For the roses, their solstitial blood
Casting a haze of incense on the thickets   375
Naked of all but a few rattling leaves,
Trailing their veil, fragrant, invisible,
Across the hillsides, now reminded me
Of that bright cave distant by so much space,
By such an unimaginable cold,
Where a girl—Sibyl, pretty in her curls,
Preached how the universe was yet so young,
How all this was a prologue to the play.
This manuscript will perish when I die
Or when the earnest guardians of our good
Find it and give it to the cleansing flames;

But there may be another poet, perhaps
No better gifted than myself, who will,
By that communication poets know,
Speak it again in quite another form.
Perhaps he has already, or she has—
For why should not the conversation pass
Both ways across the anterooms of time?—
Perhaps the time I live in fades so fast
Because its sap has gone to feed a future
Turned by the least new budding to a way
I cannot dream. Is there a kind of music
In the long story of these men and women
Whose ending may transfigure its beginning,
Bury the teller in the telling? Listen.